TALKING TOGETHER

TALKING
TOGETHER

Public Deliberation and Political Participation in America

LAWRENCE R. JACOBS,

FAY LOMAX COOK, AND

MICHAEL X. DELLI CARPINI

THE UNIVERSITY OF CHICAGO PRESS • CHICAGO AND LONDON

Lawrence R. Jacobs is the Mondale Chair and director of the Center for the Study of Politics and Governance at the Humphrey Institute of Public Affairs and professor of political science at the University of Minnesota.

Fay Lomax Cook is professor of human development and social policy and director of the Institute for Policy Research at Northwestern University.

Michael X. Delli Carpini is professor of communication and dean of the Annenberg School for Communication at the University of Pennsylvania.

The University of Chicago Press, Chicago 60637
The University of Chicago Press, Ltd., London
© 2009 by The University of Chicago
All rights reserved. Published 2009
Printed in the United States of America
18 17 16 15 14 13 12 11 10 09   1 2 3 4 5

ISBN-13: 978-0-226-38986-8 (cloth)
ISBN-13: 978-0-226-38987-5 (paper)
ISBN-10: 0-226-38986-3 (cloth)
ISBN-10: 0-226-38987-1 (paper)

Library of Congress Cataloging-in-Publication Data

Jacobs, Lawrence R.
    Talking together : public deliberation and political participation in America / Lawrence R. Jacobs, Fay Lomax Cook, and Michael X. Delli Carpini.
        p. cm.
    Includes bibliographical references and index.
    ISBN-13: 978-0-226-38986-8 (cloth : alk. paper)
    ISBN-13: 978-0-226-38987-5 (pbk. : alk. paper)
    ISBN-10: 0-226-38986-3 (cloth : alk. paper)
    ISBN-10: 0-226-38987-1 (pbk. : alk. paper) 1. Deliberative democracy—United States. 2. Political participation—United States. I. Cook, Fay Lomax. II. Delli Carpini, Michael X., 1953– III. Title.
    JK1764 .J33 2009
    320.973—dc22

                                            2008051324

This book is dedicated to the facilitators and deliberators in our lives—Benjamin Page, Sidney Verba, our students past and present, and our children, Emma Jacobs, Bella Jacobs, and David Lomax Cook.

"People live in a community by virtue of the things they have in common; and communication is the way in which they come to possess things in common."
—John Dewey, *Democracy and Education*

CONTENTS

ACKNOWLEDGMENTS

Talking Together is a collaboration in all senses of the term. It started more than a decade ago as conversations over shared concerns and extended to a survey of organizations convening public deliberations. At some point (perhaps over lunch or dinner), it dawned on us that our shared interests were leading us to a book. During this journey, we have been very fortunate to benefit from suggestions, questions, and challenges. A veritable army of research assistants have made this possible, and we are delighted to acknowledge the contributions of Dan Bergan, Lynn Prince Cooke, Dukhong Kim, Eric Ostermeier, Sasha Soreff, and Dan Stevens. We would especially like to thank Melanie Burns for the length and depth of her contributions. Jason Barabas was a wonderful collaborator in the research that appears in chapter 6 and assisted with some of the early research.

Our research was aided by the work of three survey organizations. The survey of Phoenix residents, which forms the core of the analyses in chapter 6 of Americans discussing Social Security, was conducted by National Opinion Research Center (NORC). We appreciate the assistance of NORC's senior survey director, Sally Murphy, and its survey director, Kymn Kochanek. The Survey and Evaluation Research Laboratory of Virginia Commonwealth University implemented the survey of deliberative organizations analyzed in chapter 7; we benefited from the contributions of its staff. We are particularly thankful for the time and care invested by the University of Connecticut's Center for Survey Research and Analysis and, especially, its director, Sam Best.

We are grateful for the support of several organizations that made our work possible. Pew Charitable Trusts funded two of our surveys and provided a stimulating work environment for one of us (Michael X. Delli Carpini). We would also like to express our gratitude for our home institutions, which have encouraged and supported our research in a variety of ways: the Institute for Policy Research and the School of Education and Social Policy at Northwestern University for Fay Cook; the Hubert

H. Humphrey Institute of Public Affairs at the University of Minnesota for Lawrence Jacobs; and Barnard College, Columbia University, and the Annenberg School for Communication at the University of Pennsylvania for Michael X. Delli Carpini.

We are also grateful for the valuable feedback from our colleagues and their mix of encouragement and gentle skepticism on some issues. In particular, we would like to heartily acknowledge the written feedback and collegial conversations of the following colleagues: Harry Boyte, James Druckman, Christopher Karpowitz, Joanne Miller, Benjamin I. Page, Robert R. Shapiro, Kay Lehman Schlozman, Katherine Cramer Walsh, and two anonymous reviewers. Our editor at the University of Chicago Press, John Tryneski, nurtured the project during its long gestation and offered critical advice along the way.

We are delighted to pay tribute to what has become a community of labor and learning. Thank you to all of our collaborators for a project that you fostered; for its interpretations and analyses, however, we are fully responsible.

ONE

The Discursive Turn
Citizens Talking Together

Americans pride themselves on their devotion to democracy. They cheer America's standing as a leader in extending broad civil and political rights to its citizens. They laud the nation's struggles to remove the barriers of gender and race in exercising the right to vote. Americans' pride is further supported by the country's pioneering role in inventing the machinery to mobilize masses of voters—the political party. The country's Bill of Rights establishes the bedrock for a vibrant and democratic society by guaranteeing freedom of speech, association, and assembly.

Many presidents have drawn on Americans' pride in their democracy. President George W. Bush tapped Americans' devotion to democracy in defining the theme of his foreign policy during his second inaugural address on January 20, 2005: "It is the policy of the United States to seek and support the growth of democratic movements and institutions in every nation and culture, with the ultimate goal of ending tyranny in our world." But even as President Bush directed U.S. foreign policy to promote democracy, Americans continued their long debate over the viability of democracy at home. In part, the scrutiny of American democracy was stirred by the contested 2000 elections and by subsequent debates over who has the right to vote and how ballots are counted.

The political firestorm over the 2000 elections was part of a broader and sustained debate about the participation and engagement of citizens in American democracy. Americans, we are warned, are retreating from the public arena. Although voter turnout increased in the 2008 and 2004 presidential contests, only about half of eligible voters turned out in previous elections, and only about 40% voted in the mid-term elections in 2006—consistent with the average since 1974. The general trend over the past four decades has involved declining turnout, especially among the young (CIRCLE 2002; Gans 2002; cf. McDonald and Popkin 2001). In addition to low or decreasing turnout, fewer Americans have reported that government officials are responsive to them and that they have confidence and trust in candidates, parties, and the core institutions of government and civil society (Teixeira 1992; Patterson 2002; Erikson and Tedin 2001; Zukin et al. 2006). A number of observers of American public life conclude that low or declining participation in the electoral process reflects a broader civic disengagement that is rooted in the erosion of community networks and the decline in "social capital" (Putnam 2000; Rahn and Transue 1998). These alarms have often drowned out dissenting research that finds little consistent evidence of declining civic and political engagement (Delli Carpini and Keeter 1996; Smith 1989; Abramson 1983; Skocpol 2003; Skocpol and Fiorina 2000; Ladd 2000.).

Fears concerning the erosion of citizenship merged with trepidation at the performance of representative government. "We have arrived at a paradoxical historical moment," Iris Young argues, "when nearly everyone favors democracy, but apparently few believe that democratic government can *do* anything" (2000, 4; emphasis in original). The hand-wringing over disappointing voter turnout and public distrust and frustration with the current political process reflect a deep and enduring suspicion among political observers that democracy may expect too much of citizens. The public may, it is suggested, lack the interest, commitment, energy, and capacity to make democracy work in an effective manner that serves the country's permanent interests. Some research suggests that a distracted and turned-off citizenry is ready to rely on "stealth" government that gets the job done without bothering them (Hibbing and Theiss-Morse 2002).

These are not new concerns. The Federalist Papers, composed in the late eighteenth century in support of the ratification of the U.S. Constitution, explicitly justified its reliance on the "scheme of representation" because ordinary citizens were too often guided by passion, intolerance, and ignorance. The limitations of citizens could be partially offset, they argued, by representatives who would "refine and enlarge the[ir] . . . views . . . [and] best discern the true interest of their country" (Federalist Paper #10). The proposition that everyday citizens were capable of this more refined and enlarged deliberation remained unpersuasive, perhaps even beyond what was conceivable.

In the centuries since the ratification of the U.S. Constitution, numerous thinkers and commentators have echoed these doubts about citizens (Held 1987). Joseph Schumpeter (1976), for instance, warned that citizens were distant and largely uninformed about the affairs of government, leaving them vulnerable to manipulation by those with an "axe to grind." He concluded that the role of citizens should be limited to choosing the deciders of government policy, leading him to define democracy narrowly as a "method" by which voters choose among competing candidates to whom they then defer. Giovanni Sartori (1987) worried that "quantitative rule" was trumping "quality rule," diminishing the necessary role of political elites in securing the national interests.

America, then, is of two minds when it comes to the capabilities of citizens and therefore the feasibility of democracy—one optimistic, and the other skeptical. This book breaks free of this schizophrenia. Instead, it offers a realistic analysis of public deliberation in practice, a form of citizen participation that defies one-sided conclusions.

Our analysis is based on one of the first comprehensive studies of a critical component of democratic citizenship: the process of citizens talking, discussing, and deliberating with each other on public issues that affect the communities in which they live—from one-on-one conversations to e-mail exchanges to more formal meetings. We refer to the diverse ways in which citizens talk about community issues as "discursive participation." This form of political participation is distinct from (though it interacts with) other forms of political participation that require action, such as voting. The organizational infrastructure, normative values, and practices of different forms of discursive participation generate collective resources and benefits—what we call "discursive capital." These collective capacities for discursive participation are related to the broader concept of social capital (Putnam 2000) but are characterized by certain unique features related to the form, extent, and impacts of discursive participation. Mapping the individual and collective nature of discursive participation is a central purpose of this book.

We reach two conclusions. The first supports, in part, the optimistic view of citizens. Discursive participation is more common than assumed, encompasses the most taxing forms of citizen engagement—face-to-face deliberation—and does not appear to suffer from the most significant limitations that critics have flagged (though limitations are clearly present). Many Americans are engaged in debates over competing social values (for example, the right to choose regarding reproductive options versus the right to life), conflicts over government taxation and spending, and the clash of values and interests witnessed, for instance, in the heated forums over the war in Iraq.

Discursive participation might be dismissed or downgraded because it is "just talk" and lacks the kind of institutional guarantees found in electoral and legislative politics. We resist such sweeping conclusions and the "either/or" choice between discursive and institutionalized politics that this criticism implies.

Citizen discourse and deliberation form a tangible and, indeed, necessary feature of a healthy democratic citizenry in three respects. First, joining together with other citizens is rewarding in itself. Expressing views on matters of public concern and engaging in disputes with others lead to the potentially satisfying experience of learning about opposing views, responding to the social urge to understand and communicate with neighbors, and moving from purely private preoccupations to the formation of judgments related to pressing issues of common concern. Second, discursive capital is essential for a thinking and watchful citizenry. Third, public discourse and deliberation can motivate engagement with the electoral and legislative processes. Public talking contributes to the formation of public opinion, to the identification of the interests and values that citizens have "at stake" in the political process, and it helps motivate citizens to pursue them.

This book's first conclusion, then, is that citizens engage in more extensive and meaningful public talking than previously suspected. Our findings challenge the enduring tendency to attribute the ills of democracy to a lazy and withdrawn citizenry, breaking from a long tradition that has belittled and dismissed the competence of citizens and from more recent critiques of public deliberation as elitist, exclusionary, and politically insignificant.

Where our first conclusion is optimistic, the second is sobering: discursive politics in contemporary America falls short of the hopes and optimism of deliberative theorists. We find that public deliberation does not reach the high expectations of its proponents with regard to universal, representative, and rational communication and outcomes that generate agreement and politically efficacious citizens.

We are motivated and guided by enduring debates about democracy and citizen deliberation, but the focus of our analysis is on discourse and deliberation in practice. Whether, how, and to what effect citizens discuss matters of community concern in public is the focus of this book. We examine discursive participation along a series of continuums and search for tendencies that defy sweeping glorifications or dismissals of citizen deliberation.

The next section reviews two traditions that have questioned citizens and their public deliberation as the bulwark of democracy. The following sections emphasize the need for conducting actual research on public talking and suggest that the contemporary debate over citizen deliberation helps to conceptualize a series of dimensions along which we can study public talking.

The Theoretical Debate over Deliberative Democracy

The competence of citizens has been the subject of a long-running debate concerning democracy. Critics of democracy highlight the failings of ordinary people; they oppose what they portray as mere "quantity rule" (Sartori 1987) and recommend limiting the role of citizens to selecting their representatives (e.g., Schumpeter 1950). By contrast, advocates of robust democracy emphasize the competency of citizens and the benefits of popular sovereignty and public influence on government (e.g., Dahl 1989).

The debate over democracy rests, in large part, on the *process by which citizens form opinions*. Healthy democracy requires "extended learning" (Sirianni and Friedland 2001, 20), "conversations and discussions" that "carefully examine a problem and a range of solutions through an open, inclusive exchange" (Gastil 2008, xi–xii), and "citizens reasoning and persuading one another about the values or course of action that they should pursue together" (Fung 2004, 17). A critical test, then, for whether citizens play an active role in decision making is not only whether government institutions "aggregate[e] [their preferences], but also the nature of the processes through which [their preferences] are *formed*" (Smith and Wales 2000, 52; emphasis in original). For voting and other forms of citizen input to be robust and trusted by elites, critics of contemporary democracy have insisted on evaluating the "processes of opinion and will-formation that precede voting" (Chambers 2003, 310). The debate over the process of opinion formation forms the foundation for discussions of deliberation and is the subject of the next section.

TRADITIONAL CRITICISMS OF THE PROCESSES CITIZENS USE TO FORM OPINIONS

The processes that citizens use to form their preferences have been subjected to three long-standing criticisms.

Emotion and Passion

First, ordinary individuals have been faulted for relying on emotion and "passion" (as the Federalist Papers put it) in place of a thoughtful and considered process of weighing evidence. Federalist Paper 49 warned that without a temperate, representative form of government the "passions . . . not the *reason* of the public would sit in judgment" (Cooke 1961, 343; emphasis in original). Indeed, the system of representation that defines the American constitutional order was established as a bulwark against the flawed process by which citizens reached decisions.

Schumpeter rested his case for limiting the role of citizens on their tendency to "dro[p] down to a lower level of mental performance" that relied on an "affective" process that was "infantile," "primitive," and prone to "irrational prejudice and impulse" (1976, 62). Against the backdrop of Nazi Germany, Schumpeter warned that ordinary citizens are "terribly easy to work up into a psychological crowd and into a state of frenzy in which attempt at rational argument only spurs the animal spirits" (257).

George Kennan, a principal architect of American foreign affairs after the Second World War, was equally alarmed at the "erratic and subjective nature of public reaction." He warned that the public's short-term process for reaching judgments is "easily led astray into areas of emotionalism and subjectivity which make it a poor and inadequate guide for national action" (1951, 93).

Short-Sighted and Empirically Clueless

The second persistent criticism of citizens is that they form views about public affairs through a simplistic process that is myopic and detached from empirical reality. Schumpeter charged that citizens "lack a direct and unmistakable link" with the reality of national and international affairs (1976, 261). In a similar vein, commentators on American foreign policy have criticized the public for reaching views based on the "simple moralistic and legalistic terms of absolute good and absolute evil" and on a hunger for "quick results" that "sacrifice tomorrow's real benefit" (Morgenthau 1973, 153; see also Kennan 1951; Rosenau 1961; Almond 1960). Walter Lippmann concluded that this flawed process meant that the "masses cannot be counted upon to apprehend regularly and promptly the reality of things" (1955, 24–25).

In contrast to the public's flawed approach, Schumpeter argued that government officials possess direct and accurate knowledge of the complex challenges facing modern societies. America's prominent foreign policy advisers agreed that government officials possess the "knowledge. . . . experience and seasoned judgment" (Lippmann 1955, 25) as well as the capacity to "tak[e] the long view" and accept "small losses for great [future] advantage" (Morgenthau 1973, 153; see also Lippmann 1955; Kennan 1951; Rosenau 1961; Almond 1960).

A Puppet Citizenry

The third criticism is that the public's reliance on emotion and ill-informed, short-term moralism leaves it vulnerable to manipulation. "The weaker the logical element in the processes of the public mind," Schumpeter argues, "the greater are the opportunities for groups with an axe to grind . . . to fashion and, within very wide limits, even to create the will of the people" (1976, 263). Similar fears by the framers of the U.S. Constitution led them to put the power to select presidents in the hands of an Electoral College. The assumption of the Constitution's framers was that the Electoral College would consist of learned and accomplished citizens who would use their independent judgment to select the next president. Indeed, contemporary analysts warn that modern presidents go public in an effort to shape public opinion to support their desired policies and strong-arm Congress to following their lead, circumventing the constitutional system of checks and balances (Lowi 1985; Tulis 1987; Jacobs and Shapiro 2000; Kernell 2007).

Deliberation and the Rescuing of Citizens

Debates about the content of citizen preferences, the processes by which citizens form attitudes, and the opportunities for citizens to affect government decision making have stimulated intense and rising interest in deliberation among theorists of American democracy. Far from offering a salvation for citizens, however, the growing attention to deliberation has been met with stiff criticism. In the next sections, we review the rise of citizen deliberation as a core component of democratic theory and then discuss the recent criticisms of it.

Starting in earnest in the 1980s, disaffection with the existing system of representation spurred interest in citizen deliberation as a promising approach to rejuvenating American democracy (Bessette 1980). The American system of governance is little more—according to the deliberationist account—than a cash register, aggregating the demands of individuals and groups that succeed in projecting the loudest, clearest, and most consistent messages through voting, lobbying by pressure groups, and other forms of political activities.

Deliberationists drew on several decades of research to assail the bedrock assumptions of what Theodore Lowi (1979) described as "interest group liberalism"—in which the preferences of individuals are fixed and predetermined, citizens are largely motivated by self-interest (instead of the broader notion of the common good), and the function of politics is to aggregate the demands of the organized and vocal. Lowi argued that semi-autonomous relationships among the leading lobbying groups, members of Congress, and executive branch agencies controlled a substantial part of decision making in Washington. Government has, in effect, ceded authority to pressure groups that use it to advance their narrow private interests. The result is "socialism for the organized" and a decline in the legitimacy of government as accountable and devoted to pursuing the public interest.

Schattschneider (1960), McConnell (1966), and even pluralism's early promoters (Lindblom 1977; Dahl 1989 and 1985) concluded that America's
system of representation was beholden to special interests; attention to
the "public interest" was little more than an accidental by-product of a
process of accommodating the best organized and most vocal.

Citizens, such writers argue, are relegated to pleading for "their share,"
passively choosing between binary choices or deferring to experts. The
prevailing "decision processes," Archon Fung observes, "attempt to aggregate individual opinions or preferences in a single choice . . . through
voting, majority rule, and other adversarial processes . . . [or to establish
processes] in which power is delegated to authoritative experts" (2004,
17). The neutering of citizens prompts Frank Bryan's sweeping conclusion
that "nearly all representative structures that provide the frame of governance for the 'democracies' of the world are substitutes for democracy,
not approximations of democracy" (2004, 3–4). Moreover, deliberationists
identify a systematic bias in this form of representation, charging that
the "lack of presence or 'voice' of the politically marginalized, such as
women and ethnic minorities, in political decision making means that
their interests and perspectives are systematically excluded or at least not
adequately addressed" (Smith and Wales 2000, 51).

Deliberationists offer a positive and hopeful avenue for reviving democracy: they argue that informed, well-reasoned, and independent
thinking by citizens who engage in public talk could replace rule by semi-
autonomous elites and an aggregative approach to representation—an
alternative that promises to improve democratic accountability and legitimacy. "The supposition," Lynn Sanders succinctly explains, is that "deliberation enhances democracy" (1997, 347).

The high hopes that public talk would revive civic life and popular
sovereignty in government policy prompted John Dryzek to observe that
the "essence of democracy itself is now widely taken to be deliberation,
as opposed to voting [and] interest aggregation" (2000, 1). The aim, Cass
Sunstein similarly observes, is to "design political institutions that promote
discussion and debate among the citizenry . . . [in place of] systems that
promote law making as 'deals' or bargains among self-interested private
groups" (1988, 1548). Indeed, many advocates are ready to declare success:
Carmen Sirianni and Lewis Friedland detect a "broader civic renewal
movement [that] has begun to emerge" (2001, 8). Matt Leighninger an-
nounces the arrival of a "'shadow' political process . . . that is participatory and democratic but not official" that has replaced the less meaningful
"past attempts by public officials to gather input" to stay in compliance
with federal laws requiring "maximum feasible participation" by citizens

(2006, 14). No fewer than seven edited volumes have been published within the past decade to celebrate, foster, and investigate what is seen as the deliberative turn (Rosenberg 2007; Gastil and Levine 2005; Aaken, List, and Luetge 2004; Fishkin and Laslett 2003; Macedo 1999; Elster 1998; and Bohman and Rehg 1997).

Citizen deliberation was expected to improve the legitimacy and accountability of the American political system. In place of consent derived from elections and interest-group bargaining, deliberationists promised "accountability" or "reciprocity"—a public process of "reason-giving" that would elevate public understanding and encourage government officials to explain their actions in ways that citizens would be more likely to accept as legitimate (Gutmann and Thompson 2004). Public discussion, explanation, and, especially, justification of government policy would expand the information available to citizens and incorporate them in the making of policy (Fishkin 1995). The emergence of a more reasoning citizenry was expected to coincide with a new hunger and realism among policymakers for "shared governance" that would mollify constituents who distrusted government and were informed and enraged about complex and enduring challenges that resisted traditional approaches to governance (Bryan 2004; Leighninger 2006; Sirianni and Friedland 2001; Fung 2004). The payoffs were extensive—from better-informed and wiser citizens to greater government responsiveness to citizens and better policy decisions.

The proponents of deliberation, then, frontally challenged the persistent doubters of citizens as informed and active participants in civic and political life by proposing a process that would transform individuals into enlightened citizens and restore democratic policymaking. Public deliberation, its advocates promised, would establish a *process* to anchor the views of citizens in informed and rational persuasion—it would create "debate and discussion aimed at producing reasonable, well-informed opinion in which participants are willing to revise preferences" (Chambers 2003, 310) and "democratic control [that] is substantive rather than symbolic, and engaged by competent citizens" (Dryzek 2000, 1). The "authenticity" of democracy would be restored by facilitating the development of citizens and opening up government to broader participation and influence, giving citizens a say in and an understanding of policy (Chambers 1996; Gutmann and Thompson 1996).

The Five Conditions of Deliberation

Democratic deliberationists spelled out five conditions under which public talk would invigorate citizens, restore the legitimacy of political decisions, and establish authentic democracy: universalism, inclusivity, rationality, agreement, and political efficacy.

UNIVERSALISM. The first condition is that participation in democratic deliberation is expected to become universal, thereby breaking the hold of elites and special interests. The "inclusion of everyone affected by a decision . . . [and] equal opportunities to participate in deliberation" are essential components of deliberation (Bohman 1996). Restoring democracy through public talking requires that "all citizens entitled to participate in the process of political dialogue [be present]" (Smith and Wales 2000, 53). Dryzek similarly notes that deliberationists expect "all individuals subject to a collective decision to engage in authentic deliberation about that decision" (2000, v).

INCLUSIVITY. The second condition is that democratic deliberation must include the range and diversity of citizen voices. Even if citizens are physically present at public deliberations, it is vital to ensure that a full range of voices and interests are heard, respected, and incorporated. Focusing on "who actually participates" shifts the focus from the character of the attendees to "the character of the actual participation" (Fung 2004, 29, 4). The underlying premise is that individuals with higher social and economic status will dominate unless the forums are appropriately structured for inclusive deliberation.

Breaking with the selective and skewed voices of citizens in interest-group liberalism, deliberation theory promised that the voices of "free and equal individuals" would all have an opportunity to be heard (Smith and Wales 2000). "Inclusivity relates to . . . voice"; all citizens have an "equal right to be heard"—to "introduce and question claims [and] to express and challenge needs, values and interests" (Smith and Wales 2000, 53; see also Benhabib 1996). Creating opportunities for all citizens to give voice to their concerns is essential for establishing a public forum that includes different viewpoints and makes it possible for citizens to identify alternative perspectives and actively engage with them (Gutmann and Thompson 1996; Button and Mattson 1999).

"The democratic element in deliberative democracy should turn," Amy Gutmann and Dennis Thompson argue, "on how fully inclusive the process is" and on the use of "an expansive definition of who is included in the process of deliberation" (2004, 9). Inclusion, they suggest, is "the primary criterion of the extent to which deliberation is democratic" (10). Young similarly insists that "all members of the given polity should have effectively equal influence over debate and decision making" reflecting the "diverse opinions of all the members of the society," especially the "particular perspectives of relatively marginalized or disadvantaged social groups" (2000, 6–8). Pittsburgh's establishment of a Police Civilian Review Board illustrates public discussion across racial and economic "structural difference": white, middle-class people who at first saw no urgency in the Review Board changed their minds after reading about and hearing the experiences of African Americans and others (Young 2000, 3). Fung points to Chicago's policymaking processes for policing and public education to illustrate the potential for crossing discursive boundaries when "facilitated and structured deliberation" replaces the normally exclusive process in which the "voices of minority, less educated, diffident, or culturally subordinate participants are often drowned out by those who are wealthy, confident, accustomed to management, or otherwise privileged" (2004, 5, 29).

Where universalism opened the doors for all citizens to walk into the arenas of public life, the principle of "inclusivity" took the next step of establishing a positive expectation that the *voices* of diverse citizenry would, in practice, be heard. This was expected to contrast with the bias in electoral politics that makes participation in voting, contributing, and other activities uneven because of economic, educational, and status inequalities.

RATIONALITY. The third condition of democratic deliberation is that public talk about politics must rely on reason—offering evidence, advancing claims grounded in logic and facts, and listening and responding to counterarguments (Benhabib 1996, 69; Gutmann and Thompson 2004, 12–21; Cohen 1998, 186). Democratic deliberation was expected to produce "free and open exchanges of information and reasons sufficient to acquire an understanding of both the issue in question and the opinions of others" (Bohman 1996, 16).

The "*reason-giving* requirement," according to Gutmann and Thompson, is "the first and most important characteristic [of deliberative democracy]." This requirement applies to both ordinary citizens and government officials: citizens and decision makers are "responsible for giving mutually accessible and acceptable reasons" (2004, 3, 59, and 62). Democratic deliberation expects "citizens or their accountable representatives [to] give [reasons] to one another in an ongoing process of mutual justification" (3, 126).

Requiring citizens and officials to offer reasons and to respond to challenges was expected to "eliminate false empirical beliefs, morally repugnant preferences that no one is willing to advance in the public arena, and narrowly self-regarding preferences" (Smith and Wales 2000, 53). Using this reason-based process of deliberation, citizens would become "more public-spirited, more tolerant, more knowledgeable, more attentive to the interests of others, and more probing of their own interests" (Warren 1992, 8). It would also, as Joshua Cohen explains, "tie the exercise of power to conditions of public reasoning" (1998, 186).

Placing the process of reasoning at the center of democratic life was expected to improve the *quality* of citizens' deliberation by expanding their information and understanding and by encouraging skills in communication and listening. This process of broad public education represents a continuation of John Dewey's (1954) vision of democracy as the formation and sustenance of a community in which information is ample and widely shared and citizens come to appreciate and act upon the interests and values they share with their neighbors.

AGREEMENT. The fourth condition is that vigorous citizen deliberation should generate agreement (Chambers 1996; Smith and Wales 2000; Benhabib 1992a; Gutmann and Thompson 1996). Deliberationists suggest that a process that involves universal participation, inclusivity, and reason-based argument spurs ongoing reflection among citizens about the values, assumptions, and terms on which arguments rest. This constant reflection by citizens shines public light on disagreements and latent or submerged conflicts, which in turn encourages mutual recognition and broadens understanding of and respect for competing views (Forester 1999, 62–64). "See[ing] the world as it appears from perspectives different from ours" generates an appreciation of joint gains and a "common shared perspective" (Benhabib 1985, 348–49).

Deliberationists, then, expect citizens to overcome conflicts and arrive at agreements on practical solutions as they learn, search for new options, and remake themselves through the process of publicly discussing arguments and supporting them with reasons (Forester 1999, 185, 196). The convergence of citizens stems, in part, from adopting a public-spirited perspective that makes citizens aware of their similarities and pulls them together to achieve the "common good." Finding "common ground" through the expression of different points of view is a far cry from the approach of interest-group liberalism, which invites the pursuit of narrow self-interest and attempts to discredit the positions of opposing interests (Susskind and Ozawa 1984, 14).

Although deliberative theorists argue that agreement will result from public talking based on reasoned dialogue, they acknowledge that disagreements will remain. Deliberation offers, however, at least two advantages for handling lingering disagreements. First, the process of "reason giving" and public "justifications" helps citizens "economiz[e]" or "minimize their differences with their opponents." This frees "citizens and their representatives [to] continue to work together to find common ground" (Gutmann and Thompson 2004, 7). Second, although immediate agreement may not be possible, the commitment of democratic deliberation to the "pursuit of principles of mutual respect" facilitates "justifiable agreement in the future and . . . promote[s] mutual respect when no agreement is possible" by helping dissidents be "more easily reconciled to the outcomes" (Gutmann and Thompson 2004, 20, 36, 93–4; see also Fung 2004, 17). Civic dialogues about race, for instance, may pull whites back from unity but may generate greater respect across difference, which in turn may stimulate listening, negotiation, and, at times, the discovery of common ground (Walsh 2007).

POLITICAL EFFICACY. The fifth condition is that democratic deliberation ought to have significant effects on politics and government policy that are manifested in related and interactive ways. Democratic deliberation improves the confidence of citizens in their own efficacy by helping them see the relevance of government and politics to their private lives and by increasing their political knowledge, leading them to participate in voting, volunteer for elections, attend rallies, write letters to officials, and engage in other forms of political participation (Gastil and Dillard 1999a; Kim, Wyatt, and Katz 1999; Knoke 1990; McLeod, Scheufele, and Moy 1999; Walsh 2004). This represents a feedback effect of a particular form of politics (democratic deliberation) and government policy (responsive and legitimate) on the capacity of citizens to identify their interests and appreciate their political influence (Mettler and Soss 2004; Pierson 1993; Campbell 2003).

The political significance of deliberation, its promoters contend, supplements electoral politics. "Talk-centric democratic theory," Simone Chambers explains, "focuses on the communicative processes of opinion and will-formation that precede voting" (2003, 310). Deliberationists suggest that an authentic process of public talk invigorates and educates citizens and promotes a healthy evolution in what they demand and expect of their elected representatives. By stimulating citizen participation in more informed and substantive public debate, democratic deliberation is expected to improve the quality and responsiveness of government (Gutmann and Thompson 1996; Chambers 1996).

Politics, democratic deliberationists insist, involves not only battles between opposition candidates for office and for government policy but also the "contestation of discourses in civil society" (Dryzek 2000, 5). Indeed, some deliberationists place more faith in fostering discourse in civil society than in enlivening representative democracy, which they criticize as myopic in its preoccupation with direct political or legislative results and as narrowly instrumental in treating the preferences of voters as fixed. Democratic deliberation, they suggest, sets the boundaries of policy discussion by shaping the "shared means of making sense of the world embedded in language . . . [as well as] assumptions, judgments, contentions, dispositions, and capabilities" (18). "Discourse," with its "shared terms of reference" is fundamental to forming coherent narratives or accounts that set the expectations to which political representatives must respond. Martin Luther King's protests and speeches in the 1950s and 1960s contributed to the formation of a discourse about race relations that prefigured a shift in policy. This emphasis on the political significance of discourse in civil society redefines politics as a process of collective and public communication for expressing and reconciling deep moral differences and reconnecting individuals to what they share rather than an instrumental means for achieving the fixed goals of isolated and anonymous individuals (Habermas 1989; Gutmann and Thompson 1996).

Although some deliberationists locate the primary value of public talk in its targeted impact on citizens and warn against too much emphasis on policy impact as merely "instrumental" (Ryfe 2002; Button and Ryfe 2005), others stress the significance of affecting government policy for shaping the direction of authoritative power and encouraging future citizen engagement (Levine, Fung, and Gastil 2005; Fung 2004; Gastil 2000; Young 2000). Frank Bryan concludes from New England town meetings that "real democracy . . . occurs only when all eligible citizens . . . are legislators . . . [who] make the laws that govern the action of everyone within in their geographic boundaries" (2004, 3–4). The results are engaged voters and wise and effective policies.

In short, public talking—according to the broad community of deliberation theorists—exerts significant political influence by empowering citizens, invigorating and educating voters, and shaping the terms of debate and discourse in civil society about what is considered viable government policy. "Deliberating is not just another activity on the list," Gutmann and Thompson argue, because it "provides the means by which the justifiability of the other activities can be determined" (Gutmann and Thompson 2004, 56).

The Reaction against Citizen Deliberation by Democratic Theorists

As some contemporary democratic theorists heralded citizen deliberation as a cure for the ills of representative government or even as an alternative to it, others have questioned the nature, scope, and purpose of public deliberation within American society. One astute observer argued that "deliberation should not necessarily and automatically appeal to democratic theorists" (Sanders 1997, 348). In particular, the five conditions necessary for democratic deliberation have each been challenged, leading to concern that deliberation as a form of democracy is unrealizable and/or undesirable. Specifically, deliberation has been faulted as elitist, exclusionary, manipulative, divisive, oppressive, and politically insignificant.

Elitism

Far from offering hope for widening political participation, critics charge that public talking in general and political deliberation more specifically are infrequent and skewed to individuals with higher levels of incomes and education. "In a world of severe inequalities," John Forester insists, "strategies that treat all parties 'equally' end up ironically reproducing the very inequalities with which they began" (1999, 8–9). Although some citizens may be blocked from participation, "many citizens do not wish for, and indeed might react negatively toward, efforts to engage them more directly in political decision making through deliberation" (Price et al. 2003, 5; see also Denver, Hands, and Jones 1995). The process of self-selection precludes universal participation in public deliberation, a tendency found in other forms of political activity (e.g., Lazarsfeld, Berelson, and Gaudet 1944; Berelson, Lazarsfeld, and McPhee 1954; Huckfeldt and Sprague 1995). The reality, some analysts charge, is that many Americans have little interest in politics and would prefer not to be involved, deferring to government by stealth (Hibbing and Theiss-Morse 2002).

The result of the bias in political voice and participation is that deliberation becomes another enclave of elitism or "gated democracy"—reserved for the same group of affluent and better educated Americans who vote more frequently, disproportionately use financial contributions to lure candidates to their favorite positions, and are already well-endowed with social capital.

Exclusion

Second, critics charge that even if citizens are physically present at public deliberations, many of them are likely to find their voices and interests discounted or excluded because of entrenched inequalities in information and expertise, skill in public speaking and persuasion, and other resources that systematically advantage certain participants in deliberative forums (Fraser 1997; Williams 2000; Sanders 1997; Dryzek 2000, chap. 3). Deliberationists are faulted for a naive view of citizens as "devoid of race, class, and gender and all the benefits and liabilities associated by Americans with these features" (Sanders 1997, 353).

The views of critics are at odds with the confidence of some deliberationists that even with biases the "disadvantaged groups usually . . . find [effective] representatives from within their own ranks" and that deliberation—when compared to the alternative—remains superior (Gutmann and Thompson 2004, 10, 49–50). Critics charge that the structural forces rooted in race, ethnicity, and income unavoidably condition the capacity of disadvantaged groups to participate effectively in deliberation; the result is that decisions based on public talking may actually materially hurt marginalized groups, widen their sense of dissatisfaction with politics, and further erode the legitimacy of the governing process in their eyes (Young 1996). As Lynn Sanders cautions, "the current state of American politics is sufficiently exclusive, sufficiently afflicted by patterns of dominance, so that evenhanded group deliberations are unlikely . . . [and] seem likely to replicate the hierarchies" (1997, 371).

Coercive and Manipulative Communication

Third, deliberationists have been criticized as excessively preoccupied with reason as the method of communication in deliberative activities (Honig 1996, 258, 272–73; Mouffe 1996, 254). Critics argue that anchoring deliberation in reason imposes a set of stringent demands on citizens regarding the acquisition and processing of information that is unrealistic for most individuals and invites or perhaps requires a dependence on experts that discourages the direct engagement promised by deliberationists. As one analysis of deliberative forums observes, the expectation of reasoned argumentation "shifts the possibilities of an open-ended, lateral dialogue into a stilted, one-directional exchange that . . . fosters deference and passivity" and "prioritize[s] supposedly neutral bits of knowledge" at the expense of the values and opinions of marginalized groups and individuals. For example, Native Americans attending a Portland citizen forum on water pollution complained because it deployed technical language and administrative detail that served to delegitimize and marginalize their values and opinions (Button and Mattson 1999, 629, 628).

Deliberationists have also been challenged for reducing all "valid" communication to that based on reason. Insisting that deliberation "should be rational, moderate, and not selfish implicitly excludes public talk that is impassioned, extreme, and the product of particular interests" (Sanders 1997, 370). A more expansive notion of public talking would include "unruly and contentious communication from the margins" (Dryzek 2000, vi, 4–6).

Lurking behind much of the criticism of deliberation is the suspicion that "status and hierarchy shape patterns of talking and listening" and that the rationalistic approach "discredit[s] on seemingly democratic grounds the views of those who are less likely to present their arguments in ways that we recognize as characteristically deliberative" (Sanders 1997, 349). Convinced that reason-giving is an artifact of economic and socio-cultural conditions, the critics of deliberation warn that an insistence on rationalistic deliberation will systematically disadvantage marginalized groups and obscure the interests and views of the dominant groups behind claims about pursuing the "common good" (Sanders 1997, 370; Williams 2000, 125; Benhabib 1992b and 2002; Fraser 1992, 130).

In addition to challenging the appropriateness of reason as a basis for public deliberation, critics have also questioned whether deliberationists are posing an unrealistic and utopian standard. These critics point to evidence that public talk is often derailed by negative or simple arguments and by the exploitation of emotional appeals that are anchored in stereotypes and attacks that play on personal suspicion and resentment (Sullivan, Piereson, and Marcus 1989; Cappella and Jamieson 1997; Mansbridge 1983).

Divisive and Oppressive

Fourth, the emphasis of deliberationists on structured public talking as a tool for creating agreement has been disparaged on two somewhat distinct grounds. Some critics warn that the airing of diverse and conflicting perspectives in public forums may well *intensify disagreements*, sharpen conflict and competition, and polarize citizens (Mansbridge 1996; Sunstein 2002; Mutz 2006). The public airing of conflicting viewpoints can reinforce existing social divisions and fuel self-serving rationalizations that perpetuate divisions between "them" and "us" (Sulkin and Simon 2001; Walsh 2004). A study of meetings in racially integrated and racially segregated towns found, for example, that agreement was reached in the latter because its forum accepted and legitimized opposition to integration (Mendelberg and Oleske 2000).

Others take issue with the claim that public talk leads to agreement in a somewhat different way, arguing that public talk may produce what appears to be agreement but only after stifling genuine disagreements and differences (Young 1996, 126, 133; Sanders 1997). Conflict is inevitable in a society in which resources, status, and privileges are unequally distributed (Mouffe 1996; Honig 1996). The effort to produce agreement "encourages suppression of . . . conflict" and encourages "false unanimity" (Mansbridge 1983, 276–77). A study of citizen forums found, for instance, that participation intent on the "pursuit of consensus and unity tended to push aside conflict, which meant the loss of voices and the sidelining of confrontation" as participants "suppress[ed] the conflict orientation believing that finding 'common ground' was more important" (Button and Mattson 1999, 620, 619; see also Smith and Wales 2000, 159). "Calling for compromise," Sanders notes, "may be perilously close to suppressing the challenging perspectives of marginalized groups [in contexts of unequal power and status]" (1997, 362).

Insignificant Effect on the Political Process

The fifth criticism of deliberationists is that public talk is politically insignificant as a way to expand the influence of broad publics and marginalized groups. When political activists and observers size up the value and impact of different forms of political participation, deliberation often lands toward the bottom, having been ranked below voting, protesting, volunteering, and other forms of political and civic behavior. For instance, one of the most comprehensive and valuable studies of political participation makes no mention of public talk (Verba, Schlozman, and Brady 1995).

Action-oriented political participation monopolizes much discussion of what citizens do for a simple reason—its consequences for citizens and the community are readily observable. For instance, voting and contributing leads to institutionally guaranteed outcomes—namely, the election of one candidate instead of another.

By contrast, public deliberation, it is charged, is literally "just talk" because it is cut off from government decision making. As one review of deliberative theory and practice asked, "What real purpose does deliberation serve?" (Button and Mattson 1999, 629). Its impact on political participation and political knowledge has been reported as slight, if evident at all (Denver, Hands, and Jones 1995). Diana Mutz goes a step further to argue that deliberation may actually *decrease* participation (especially voter turnout and engagement) in contexts where differences and oppositional viewpoints are aired. In contexts of conflict, she argues that "the prospects for truly deliberative encounters may be improving while the prospects for participation and political activism are declining" (2006, 3).

Although proponents of deliberation emphasize its potential importance within civil society for setting the terms of discourse, some democratic theorists insist that the dominant discourse is deeply entrenched in the existing economic and political system and generally resistant to challenge. "Dominant discourses and ideologies, [which are] often intertwined with structural economic forces," are "agents of distortion that cannot easily be counteracted" (Dryzek 2000, 21). Indeed, some suggest

Table 1.1   Theoretical dimensions of public deliberation

DEMOCRATIC TENDENCIES	DIMENSIONS	UNDEMOCRATIC TENDENCIES
Universal: All individuals affected by the issue participate in deliberation.	Access	**Elitest:** Public deliberation is infrequent and participation in it is selective.
Inclusive: All relevant viewpoints and arguments are equitably expressed.	Voice	**Exclusive:** Expressed viewpoints and arguments are skewed in favor of entrenched social and economic hierarchies.
Reason-Based: Relies on logic and facts.	Type of discourse	**Emotion and coercion-based:** Unreasoned appeals that are easily manipulated and that disadvantage marginalized groups.
Agreement-Oriented: Leads to consensus based on common understandings of the public good and/or acceptance of the legitimacy of whatever disagreements linger.	Effect on cohesion	**Disagreement-oriented:** Intensifies divisions and disagreements or stifles genuine differences.
Strengthens democracy: Increases citizens' efficacy, political knowledge, and future participation, and can lead to better, more legitimate policy outcomes.	Effect on politics	**No or negative effect on democracy:** Exerts little impact on citizen knowledge and participation and can reinforce cynicism and disengagement while leading to harmful or short-term policy outcomes.

that the political ineffectiveness of public deliberation may actually reinforce a sense of disconnection from government decision making among citizens who already feel marginalized (Button and Mattson 1999; Sanders 1997).

In short, the five conditions upon which theories of deliberative democracy rest have been challenged as unattainable, undesirable, or both. This fundamental disagreement and the underlying dimensions upon which it is based are summarized in table 1.1. As the table shows, each dimension is anchored on one end by the views of advocates of deliberation and on the other by its critics. The advocates envision a democracy in which all relevant views on important public issues are present, expressed, and argued from evidence and logic. They also envision a democracy in which this process creates greater consensus, acceptance of difference when consensus is not possible, and, as a result, better, more legitimate policy. Critics of deliberation see this notion as naive at best and dangerous at worst, leading to greater elitism, the reification of existing hierarchies, false consensus or heightened disagreement, increased disillusionment and disengagement, and poor policy decisions.

THE ANALYTIC KNOT CONCERNING DELIBERATION

The debate among political theorists regarding the possibilities, promises, and pitfalls of deliberative democracy has reached something of an impasse. Proponents of public deliberation set out to provide a vision of democracy in which citizens' participation is universal, inclusive, rational, agreement-oriented, and politically significant. In turn, critics of this vision have questioned both the criteria of democratic deliberation that citizens are expected to meet and whether the results would be as positive as imagined. The irony is that in responding to their critics, many deliberationists have unwittingly "adopt[ed] these objections as the standards for how democratic political discussions should range or be restricted" (Sanders 1997, 356), adding to the sense that deliberative democracy is unattainable.

The critics of deliberation suffer from a similar tendency toward absolutist approaches to democratic citizenship. Where deliberationists herald the classical ideal of the Athenian citizen or the New England town hall meeting, their critics reject *any* notion of deliberative democracy, absent assurances that *all* impediments to meeting the standards set by proponents are met (see, e.g., Dryzek 2000; Fraser 1992; Sanders 1997). For example, Sanders states that she is "against [deliberation] for now [because] . . . it is premature as a standard [given the inequalities in American society]" (1997, 369). And Dryzek dismisses prevailing approaches to public deliberation as "not well equipped to respond to the challenges presented by deep plurality and difference in the political composition of society; by ecological crisis; by economic transnationalization and globalization" (2000, 30). Instead, he offers "insurgent democracy" that transforms civil society and is "suspicious . . . [of] inclusion of as many interests as possible in the state" (30, 93).

Largely absent from both sides of this debate is a systematic understanding of the actual behavior of citizens. Whether and how real citizens engage in discursive participation; the nature, settings, and impact of this public talk; and when and if "talk" rises to the level of "democratic deliberation"—each of these is ignored or, at best, occasionally introduced by way of illustration or anecdote. In short, *the idea of deliberation draws far more attention than its actual practice*.[1] This shortcoming hinders efforts to develop robust but implementable theories of discursive politics, democratic deliberation, and, ultimately, deliberative democracy.

From Theory to Practice: Researching Deliberation

Understanding deliberation requires two innovations: we need to know much more about whether and how citizens participate in public talking; and we need a framework for mapping citizen deliberation. Our analyses of the public deliberation of Americans reveal two consistent findings. First, deliberation is varied and heterogeneous. Americans' public talk defies uniform characterization as either democratic or undemocratic. We need to develop more complex conceptualizations of deliberation than this either/or dichotomy and welcome nuanced research findings.

Second, the practice of deliberation by citizens exhibits democratic tendencies but is marked by areas of ambiguity that defy sweeping conclusions. We find evidence that the central tendency of Americans' deliberative experience leans toward being accessible and open to a range of diverse voices, relying on reason and evidence and the pursuit of agreement, and augmenting political influence. Nonetheless, the public talking of citizens falls notably short of the ideals of deliberation. There is consistent evidence of forms of participation, though not dominant ones, that are undemocratic—deliberation is not fully universal and inclusive, and there are some signs that those in the minority feel intimidated and perceive their views as being given short shrift. The political effects of public talk are evident but not as all-encompassing as some suggest.

Learning about Citizen Deliberation

Few areas of American public life have received as much attention with as little actual on-the-ground study as citizen deliberation. As one set of case studies of citizen deliberation observes, "A great deal of work has tried to define what scholars mean by deliberation. Not enough has been said about how deliberation actually works among citizens" (Button and Mattson 1999, 612). Political theorists who have been active in debates about public deliberation concede that research on its actual practice is skimpy. One summary of recent political theory on deliberation concedes that "theories of deliberative democracy contain many empirical claims and assumptions" that lack supporting evidence, and that "empirical research can be invaluable in keeping normative theorists on their toes" (Chambers 2003, 219, 222).

Research on citizen deliberation has been largely limited to a series isolated studies. These islands of analysis include studies of decision making in town hall meetings (Mansbridge 1983); group meetings (Gamson 1992; Gastil 2000); informal neighborhood and city conversations (Walsh 2004 and 2007; Leighninger 2006; Sirianni and Friedland 2001); political talk that includes oppositional perspectives (Mutz 2006); public hearings in towns that are racially integrated and racially segregated (Mendelberg and Oleske 2000); "deliberative polls" and the National Issues Forums (Luskin and Fishkin 1998 and 1999; Fishkin 1995; Gastil and Dillard 1999a and 1999b); on-line communication (Price and Cappella 2001); and experiments on individuals in laboratory settings (Sulkin and Simon 2001; see reviews in Gastil and Levine 2005; Button and Ryfe 2005).

One of the few areas of sustained research involves the mass media and its impact on the process of citizen opinion formation (e.g., Graber 2001; Comstock and Scharrer 2005). Taking a different approach, Page analyzes the role of the media in facilitating "mediated deliberation": the "reasoning and discussion about the merits of public policy [in the press]," he suggests, "trickle out through opinion leaders and cue givers to ordinary citizens, who can deliberate about [them] in their own small, face-to-face groups of family, friends, and co-workers" (Page, 2, 7, 123). The implicit conclusion of this work is that deliberation continues but in a form mediated through the mass media rather than through serious face-to-face deliberation. The notion of individuals meeting to talk in public about issues of concern to their community may be merely a relic of European salons in the eighteenth century or ancient Greece and Athens (e.g., Habermas 1989).

Finally, some groups of policymakers and policy analysts have examined public deliberation. For instance, planners who manage and administer programs and projects have sponsored and studied citizen deliberation (Forester 1999). Fung (2004) documents the redesign of Chicago's policing and public education bureaucracies to foster structured and deliberative community dialogue and shared decision making.

There has been no systematic and comprehensive effort, however, to gauge the overall extent to which Americans engage in discursive participation generally and public deliberation more specifically, the specific forms this participation takes, the traits of those who do and do not participate, or its relationship to other forms of political engagement. This is a sobering conclusion, given the extensive debates among political theorists about deliberation and the enormous amount of survey research on Americans that is conducted every year by scholars, the media, and other organizations. Bryan laments that "we know much more about the Greek democracy of twenty-five hundred years ago than we do about real democracy in America today" (2004, 13).

This book addresses this substantial deficit by conducting a comprehensive study of the extent and nature of discursive participation and public deliberation in the United States. Taking the contending analyses discussed earlier and summarized in table 1.1 as our starting point, we begin to provide empirical answers to key questions. How many Americans are engaging in various forms of public talking, and who are they? Is participation equitable, or is it skewed in favor of those who already disproportionately vote, volunteer, and engage in other political activities? What form does their public talking take? Is this largely limited to informal settings as opposed to the more time-consuming and cognitively taxing, organized, face-to-face meetings? Do all those who show up in these various settings get included in the discussion, or are some discouraged or excluded from meaningful participation? Does reason and the search for agreement predominate or not? Finally, does public deliberation matter in politically significant ways? Answering these questions is a crucial first step in resolving the theoretical debate over the possibilities and pitfalls of deliberative democracy.

MAPPING CITIZEN DELIBERATION

Before turning to a description of our data and an overview of subsequent chapters, we need to clarify the scope of our study. We take a broader perspective than do many scholars, placing the specific concept of "deliberation" in the more general context of "discursive participation." Our definition of the latter is characterized by five traits. First, the primary form of activity we are concerned about is *discourse with other citizens*—the collective process of citizens talking, discussing, and debating with each other. We study deliberation that is public and done with others; the form of deliberation we examine consists of public exchanges of ideas and arguments rather than the private internal thoughts of an individual (Lindeman 2002, 199; Gunderson 1995, 199) or conversations about strictly personal issues or concerns (such as group therapy).

Second, we study citizen deliberation in a *variety of settings*, including but not limited to the formal institutions and processes of civic and political life. It can involve private individuals in informal, unplanned exchanges; those who convene for public purposes but do so outside the normal processes of government operations (for example, in such places as libraries, schools, homes, churches, and community centers); and those who are brought together in settings such as town hall meetings of political representatives and their constituents.

Third, we examine discursive participation in a *variety of formats*, including face-to-face exchanges, phone conversations, e-mail exchanges, and Internet forums. Fourth, we study discursive participation that focuses on local, national, or international issues of public concern; it does not include meetings or conversations about personal lives that are *unrelated* to issues of broader public concern.

Fifth, we define public talking as a *form of participation* that reflects and contributes to American politics. As the analysis of civic and political participation (from voting to participating in voluntary associations) has become more sensitive to the variety of ways in which citizens can act, there has not been the same level of attention to talk as a measure of engagement (Brady 1999; Ladd 2000; Putnam 2000; Skocpol and Fiorina 1999). This book, however, takes a different approach; we treat public talk as a form of political participation, one that provides the opportunity for individuals to develop and express their views, learn the positions of others, identify shared concerns and preferences, and come to understand and reach judgments about matters of public concern. Such exchanges can clarify deep divisions over material interests and moral values; they are also critical for publicly airing disagreements that have not been articulated or have been incompletely stated because so many citizens have withdrawn from electoral and legislative politics (Benhabib 1992a, 1992b; and 1996a, 1996b; Dryzek 1990; Elster 1998; Etzioni 1997; Gutmann and Thompson 1996; Habermas 1989; Michelman 1988). The nature and extent to which public talking affects political processes remains a critical question that we analyze.

The five components that define the parameters of our research include a broad range of public talking but they also *exclude* a number of legitimate "talk-centric" activities. Elite-to-elite discussions, such as campaign debates, congressional hearings and debates, and television talk shows (e.g., *Meet the Press*) fall outside our definition of active citizen participation. We also exclude both citizen-to-elite communications that were one-shot exchanges (such as call-in radio or television shows, letters to the editor, and op-eds) and elite-to-citizen communications (such as press conferences or speeches) because they exclude sustained and active participation by citizens.

SURVEYING DISCURSIVE POLITICS

The bulk of our analysis is based on a national telephone survey of American adults age eighteen and over that explores the prevalence, types, distribution, sources, and impact of public deliberation in the United States. Conducted by the Center for Research and Analysis at the Roper Center of the University of Connecticut, the survey consisted of a random sample of 1,001 respondents and an over sample ($N = 500$) of what we call "face-to-face deliberators"—those who had attended a formal or informal meeting to discuss a local, national, or international issue of public importance.

The few systematic studies of deliberation have tended to focus narrowly on certain aspects of deliberation. For instance, Mutz adopts what she defines as a "minimalist conception of what it means to deliberate" and limits her study to informal talk (often in workplaces). Her focus is on tracking the impact of "cross cutting exposure or diverse political networks" (2006, 6) on electoral behavior; she does not aim to map the extent and form of discursive politics as a potentially general phenomenon. Although Mutz's study offers valuable insights into possible impacts of a certain type of public talk, it reveals little about the content, nature, and conditions of discursive participation and public deliberation in American society more generally.

Our national survey offers a comprehensive analysis of the extent to which individuals engage in distinct types of discursive participation: face-to-face deliberation, traditional talk, two forms of Internet deliberation, and Internet talk. We devote particular attention to studying face-to-face deliberation, which many observers consider the epitome of citizen participation and which comes closest to most formal definitions of public deliberation or street-level deliberation. As Page notes, the "exemplars of deliberation, and many of the ideals and normative standards that we associate with it, are based on situations involving face-to-face talk among small numbers of people" (1996, 2–3). Participation in face-to-face group discussions may be the quintessential form of public deliberation, but it also imposes high costs on individuals in terms of their time (i.e., travel, preparation, and participation) and psychological commitment, which might include public speaking and the tension associated with disagreeing with another person in public.

We also investigated five additional (albeit, less demanding) forms of public talking. The first—what we call "traditional talkers"—involves participation in informal conversations about public issues. The next two involve efforts to persuade someone to adopt one's own view regarding a public issue or candidate for office. The Internet has been heralded as a promising means for reengaging a disconnected and atomized citizenry in political life. For this reason, the fourth type of discursive participation we investigated is "Internet deliberation"—chat rooms, message boards, or other on-line discussion groups organized specifically to discuss a public issue. Finally, we also examined whether Americans are "Internet talkers"—namely, those who report using e-mail or instant messaging to talk informally about issues of public concern at least several times a month.

As we will see in chapter 2, public talk is far more extensive than many political theorists and researchers presumed. Although it does not always conform to the idealized standards posed by the advocates (or critics) of democratic deliberation, public talking is a vibrant and surprisingly widespread process by which citizens form opinions about civic life.

ORGANIZING A COMMUNITY OF DELIBERATORS

Deliberation is a public activity that requires a community of participants. This kind of collective activity rarely, if ever, results from the spontaneous and uncoordinated decision of individuals; it usually springs from widespread or systemic conditions that motivate, recruit, and enable disparate individuals to come together. Chapter 7 examines one factor that might facilitate deliberation—an infrastructure of organizations and associations that conduct civic dialogues. In the first large-scale effort to examine the organizational infrastructure of public deliberation, we conducted a mail survey of 396 associations that hold civic forums. We used this survey to investigate who organizes public deliberation and how it is done.

Our survey of civic conveners suggests that the firms and groups who organize citizen deliberation have created an infrastructure for civic forums that casts deliberation as normatively positive and subsidizes the significant costs of deliberative activity that would otherwise fall on individuals. Although this organizational infrastructure may not necessarily "cause" deliberation, it may create favorable conditions for individuals, groups, and government units to foster it.

We use the term *discursive capital* to refer to the collective resources of a talking citizenry—the summary measure of the collective social process of communication between citizens. In addition to encompassing the deliberative nature of social relations among individuals, the notion of discursive capital also recognizes the importance of normatively reinforcing the values and organizational infrastructure that facilitate public talking.

Looking Ahead

The following four chapters (2 through 5) are organized around the questions posed by table 1.1. How many Americans participate in public deliberation? Who deliberates? How do Americans deliberate? And what are the civic and political effects of deliberation? Chapter 2 considers the extent of discursive participation in the United States. We present evidence from our survey of Americans that public talk is more extensive than previously assumed. Although participation is not universal, eight out of ten Americans engage in some form of public talking, and one-fourth participate in face-to-face forums. This is a much more robust level of engagement than that suggested by warnings that deliberation is elitist. The participation of Americans extends from informal conversations to the most taxing and structured form of deliberation—face-to-face interactions.

Chapter 3 investigates who deliberates, especially in face-to-face forums. Our findings indicate notable differences regarding which Americans engage in public deliberation. What is striking is that these differences do not support the dire conclusion that citizen deliberation replicates entrenched social and economic status. Indeed, our analysis suggests that the discursive participation of Americans is less directly tied to the traditional social and economic correlates of political behavior than are other forms of political participation.

Chapter 4 examines how Americans deliberate, with a particular focus on face-to-face forums and street-level deliberators. Our survey provides strong evidence of a decisive tendency toward inclusive, reason-based, and agreement-oriented discourse. There are, however, some notable contradictions of the democratic expectations of deliberationists. For example, participants in civic forums tend to be drawn from somewhat higher levels of income and education and to perceive other participants as more active than themselves.

Chapter 5 examines the political effects of participation in face-to-face forums. Analysis of our national survey indicates that face-to-face deliberation increases subsequent participation in civic activities, except for participation in electoral activities such as voting or working for a party or a candidate. These findings appear to support the expectation of deliberationists that public talking would invigorate civic life, though its apparent irrelevance to electoral politics may suggest an important limitation.

Chapter 6 reports an in-depth case study of a national effort to foster public deliberation about Social Security. Our purpose here is to make concrete the general analyses in previous chapters and to examine in detail who deliberates, how, and to what effect. The results reveal the complexities of public deliberation in ways that both confirm and challenge our more general findings and raise important questions for further analysis.

Chapter 7 draws on our survey of civic conveners—in conjunction with other research—to reveal the organizational infrastructure that facilitates public deliberation. Identifying and analyzing this organizational infrastructure helps to explain the surprisingly wide scope and public nature of civic deliberation. The concluding chapter connects our findings about deliberation to broader debates about democracy.

Part 1

DISCURSIVE PARTICIPATION
AND PUBLIC DELIBERATION
BY AMERICANS

TWO

How Much Deliberation?

How extensive are discursive politics in general and public deliberation more specifically? How many Americans voice their preferences on public issues by talking in public about issues that affect localities, states, and the nation? In what ways do Americans publicly communicate? How often do they talk about public issues in informal, one-on-one conversations, e-mail exchanges, and meetings that have been formally organized to facilitate face-to-face discussions? How do these diverse forms of discursive participation compare with better-known types of political participation such as voting, signing a petition, or writing a government official?

Although political theorists have long debated the nature of public deliberation, there is little actual research about the extent and form of public talking about policy issues. The research that has been conducted generally reports that public deliberation is not extensive, especially the more elaborate forms that involve citizens meeting face-to-face to discuss issues of concern to the community. Past research has accepted these results as a natural outcome of a process that is laborious, taxing the time and cognitive capacities of busy citizens.

This chapter presents evidence from our survey of American adults, which reports a level of discursive participation that is more extensive than previously assumed. The participation of Americans extends from informal one-on-one discussions of public issues to the most taxing and structured form of deliberation—face-to-face interactions in public forums. Eighty percent of Americans engage in some form of public talking and a quarter participates in face-to-face forums. Although there is not universal participation, this is a much more robust level of engagement than suggested by common warnings that deliberation is elitist and exclusive.

What We Do Not Know

The limited research conducted on public talk and deliberation concludes that it is uncommon. Nina Eliasoph (1998) offers a sober assessment in her book *Avoiding Politics*. She reports that members of volunteer groups (such as high school parent associations) and recreational groups (e.g., fraternal associations) assiduously avoid "public-spirited political conversation." According to Eliasoph's participant observation and in-depth interviews, even members of activist groups were initially skeptical regarding the payoff and value of political deliberation (e.g., preventing the construction of a toxic incinerator in the neighborhood). If they perceived a payoff, they were still more likely to deliberate in the safety of their own company than in more public settings (see also Conover et al. 2004 on the dominance of "private" over "public" discussion). Eliasoph attributes Americans' limited engagement in deliberation to the country's poorly developed public sphere rather than an inherent or natural aversion to politics. Hibbing and Theiss-Morse reach a starker conclusion: Americans' limited engagement in the political process reflects a genuine disinterest and deference to "largely invisible and unaccountable elites" (2002, 239).

A smattering of survey data portrays a similarly withdrawn citizenry (Brady 1999). According to Barnes et al. (1979), 16% of U.S. adults said they discussed politics with friends "often," and another 37% reported doing so "sometimes." National Election Studies (NES) and General Social Survey (GSS) data collected in the late 1980s show that 28%–32% of Americans say they have tried to persuade someone how to vote "often" or "sometimes" (Brady 1999, 750–51). NES data from 1984 to 1992 indicate that between one-third and one-half of the American public had had *no* discussions about politics in the past week; the average number of weekly discussions ranged between about 1.5 and 2.5 (Bennett, Fisher, and Resnick 1995).

Some survey research does point to a somewhat more discursively active public. According to Verba, Schlozman, and Brady, 51% of American adults attended meetings of voluntary associations from time to time during the course of a year (1995, 62–63), and 48% attended a meeting where decisions were made (Brady, Verba, and Schlozman 1995, 274). Moreover, Wuthnow (1994) found that 40% of adults reported belonging to "a small group that meets regularly and provides caring and support for its members." Sixty percent of these participants (or 24% of the adult population) described their group's primary purpose as including "discussion." A more recent survey by Zukin et al. (2006) found that 60% of Americans age fifteen or older reported talking "very often" about "current events or things you have heard on the news with your family or friends" and that another 32% did so "sometimes." In a separate survey item, 12% reported that "politics" was discussed "very often" in their homes, and another 35% reported it was discussed "sometimes." In addition, 33% of those interviewed said that during elections they "generally" tried to persuade people whom to vote for, and that 11% have done door-to-door canvassing for a political or social group or a candidate at some point in their lives (3% reported having done so in the past year).

Overall, research on public deliberation is limited, and the available evidence on discursive participation has not received serious attention. Indeed, the leading books on political behavior rarely, if ever, even mention public deliberation or political talk. It is easy to get the general impression that talk about public issues is not common in the United States and certainly lags far behind common forms of political participation like voting and joining organizations in frequency and importance.

A Survey of Discursive Participation in America

In order to understand the extent and nature of discursive participation in the United States, we developed a national telephone survey of American adults age eighteen and over. Conducted by the Center for Research and Analysis at the Roper Center of the University of Connecticut, the survey consisted of a random sample of 1,001 respondents and an over sample ($N =$ 500) of what we call "face-to-face deliberators"—those who had attended a formal or informal meeting to discuss a local, national or international issue of public importance within the last year.[1]

Our survey was explicitly geared to study the extent and types of conversations (whether informal or formal, and whether online or in person) that individuals engaged in when discussing local, national, or international issues. We specifically focused on discussions about issues related to public life, rather than more general discussions of, for instance, personal matters. (The questionnaire appears online at http://www.press.uchicago .edu/books/jacobs.)

The survey was in the field from February 10 to March 24, 2003. We asked respondents about their discursive participation during the time since January of the preceding year (January 2002). This period included not only the 2002 election cycle and debates about state and national budgets, but also a number of post–September 11 issues such as the ongoing war against terrorism, follow-up from the invasion of Afghanistan, and the build-up and beginning of the war against Iraq. The possible effects of September 11 on interpreting our survey results are complicated and interactive. On the one hand, September 11 and the subsequent U.S. government responses stimulated unusually spirited debates about local, national, and international issues, which may have produced levels of discursive participation that created what evaluators call a "best case study." On the other hand, where our data overlap with previous research (such as the incidence of face-to-face meetings), they are comparable to previous findings (Verba, Schlozman, and Brady 1995; Wuthnow 1994). If our study was affected by a lingering "September 11 effect," the greatest impact was most likely on the topics that received attention.

Our survey allowed us to study patterns in the general public as well as to investigate in detail the nature and impact of face-to-face deliberation—a particular focus of theoretical and case study analyses. For the analyses in this chapter, chapter 3 and most of chapter 5, we create a combined sample of 1,501 cases and weighted it to be representative of the general population of adults residing in the United States. We use this weighted sample to report on distributions relating to the general population. For regression analyses using tests of statistical significance, we did not weight the sample. In chapter 4 and part of chapter 5, we primarily study face-to-face deliberation by analyzing the 756 cases of respondents who had attended a face-to-face forum during the past year. For both the general population sample of 1,501 cases and the face-to-face deliberation sample of 756 cases, the effective number of cases often varies due to missing cases in the independent variables that are included in the regression analyses.

Much of our analysis focuses on the organization and content of Americans' discursive and deliberative experiences. For instance, we explored the structure of deliberative forums (e.g., what issues were discussed, where the forum was held, how many people attended) as well as respondents' reactions to them (e.g., their perception of whether or not the discussions were balanced and their motivation to take any action as a result of the meeting). Our study's use of the respondents' self-reported recall of political behavior is a standard technique in survey research on a range of analyses from voter turnout to petition signing. For our purposes, we focused respondents on discursive experiences that were more recent and therefore more likely to be recalled (e.g., Cobb and Kuklinski 1997). In particular, we asked respondents to describe "the last meeting" they had attended during the past year. There are possible drawbacks to this approach: the last meeting attended may have been atypical, and respondents' recall may be incomplete or inaccurate. With regard to possibly highlighting uncommon deliberative experiences, this may occur for an individual respondent but there are no grounds for expecting this to hold for the full range of experiences across respondents: the "last meeting" attended by all respondents should be a random sample of such meetings. With regard to relying on the self-reported recall of respondents, we asked respondents about their most recent meeting, which they should most easily recall, and we extensively use open-ended questions to discourage arbitrary or forced responses that might be inflated by faulty memory or an interest in impressing the interviewer. (If there were significant recall problems, we would expect spikes in "Don't know" responses to more taxing questions and a drop-off in responses to detailed questions on the meeting—patterns that did not emerge.)[2]

As a general rule, we excluded missing data—questions on which respondents did not provide an answer. This allows us to focus on analyzing the attitudes that respondents did possess.

Six Types of Discursive Participation

Our survey asked Americans about six different types of public deliberation that they might engage in—one-to-one talking about public issues; one-to-one discussions on the Internet via e-mail; Internet communications that involved chat rooms, message boards, or other on-line discussion groups; participation in more collective conversations (i.e., participation in a "formal or informal meeting organized by the individual, by someone else who is a personal acquaintance, or by a religious, social, civic, governmental, or political group); attempts to persuade another person about a particular stance on a public issue; and attempts to persuade another person about whom to vote for.

Opening our analysis to a range of discursive activities has several advantages. First, it allows us to inventory the multiplicity of discursive activities. Second, studying a wide range of discursive forms makes it possible to assess a broader extent of public talking than is possible by simply examining one type.

For many observers, face-to-face deliberation is the gold standard of discursive participation (e.g., Page 1996, 2–3). Respondents in our survey fell into this group of "face-to-face deliberators" or "street-level deliberators" if they indicated that they had "attended a formal or informal [organized] meeting" in the past year to discuss a local, national, or international issue.[3]

Participation in face-to-face group discussions may be the epitome of public deliberation, but it also imposes particularly high costs in terms of time (i.e., travel, preparation, and participation) and psychological commitment, which might include public speaking and the tension associated with disagreeing with another person in public (Mutz 2006). Past research has found that political participation relies on the skills, experience, and comfort with public activity and speaking that arise from occupation and organizational memberships (Verba, Schlozman, and Brady 1995).

To capture a more extensive range of discursive activities and put face-to-face deliberation in context, we asked respondents about five less demanding forms of discursive participation. The Internet has been heralded as a promising means for reengaging a disconnected and atomized citizenry with political life (Iyengar, Luskin, and Fishkin 2003; Cappella, Price, and Nir. 2002; Price and Cappella 2002; Price et al. 2003). We measured this form of discursive participation—what we call "Internet deliberators"—by asking respondents to indicate if they participated since January 2002 in "Internet chat rooms, message boards, or other on-line discussion groups organized specifically to discuss a local, national, or international issue." We designate as "Internet talkers" those who report having used e-mail or instant messaging to talk informally about issues of public concern at least a few times a month.[4]

"Traditional talkers" participate in informal conversations about public issues either in person or on the phone. Respondents in our survey fell into this category if they indicated that they had "informal face-to-face or phone conversations or exchanges with people you know about public issues that are local, national, or international concerns" at least "a few times a month."[5]

Finally, people engage in political discussion when they try to persuade someone to see an issue their way or when they try to persuade someone to vote for their candidate. "Issue persuaders" are those who have tried to persuade someone to adopt their views on a public issue,[6] and "vote persuaders" are those who have tried to persuade someone to vote for a candidate in a local, state, or national race.[7] Our Discursive Participation Survey allows us, then, to map the extent of citizen participation in six quite different forms of discursive participation.

The Frequency of Discursive Participation

In the remainder of this chapter we examine the extensiveness and nature of citizen participation in the six types of discursive politics identified above. Public talk is often considered relatively limited and infrequent. Even advocates of civic dialogue acknowledge that "deliberation is difficult to achieve and sustain over time" (Ryfe 2005, 49) and that it is rare to "involve a critical mass of citizens" (Leighninger 2006, 7). Despite these low expectations, our national survey suggests that a sizable portion of Americans are engaging in various forms of discursive participation.

EXTENSIVENESS OF PUBLIC DELIBERATION

As a first look at the extent of discursive participation in the United States, we present the frequencies of reported engagement in our six measures (table 2.1). Informal conversation about public issues (what we refer to as traditional talking) is the most common form of discursive participation.

Table 2.1   Reported levels of discursive participation in the United States

TYPE OF DISCURSIVE PARTICIPATION	PERCENTAGE (%)	N
Public deliberation		
"Face-to-face deliberation" about a public issue	25	379
"Internet deliberation" (communication via Internet chat rooms, message boards, or other online discussion groups about a public issue)	4	61
Informal public talk		
"Traditional talking" (phone or in-person conversation about a public issue)	68	1018
"Internet talking" (e-mail or instant messaging about issues of public concern)	24	360
Political persuasion		
Persuade someone about your view on a public issue	47	698
Persuade someone about whom to vote for	31	458

Source: Discursive Participation Survey. Total sample: N = 1,501 (weighted general population sample).

Two-thirds of our respondents reported that they had informal conversations about public issues at least several times a month. Of these, the vast majority said they frequently had discussions of five minutes or longer.

One-quarter of Americans reported engaging in the most difficult and time-consuming type of discursive participation—attending a formal or informal meeting in the past year to discuss a local, national, or international issue. Given the effort required to participate in formal, face-to-face deliberation, this is an impressive proportion that substantially exceeds earlier expectations. It also appears that if more Americans were given an opportunity to attend such meetings, the proportion might be even higher. Eighty-four percent of those who said they had not attended such a meeting reported they had never been *invited* to meetings like this.

Despite the widespread attention given to Internet forms of communication, this medium was not a central vehicle for public deliberation. Only 4% of our respondents reported engaging in what we call "Internet deliberation"—chat rooms, message boards, or other online discussion groups organized to discuss a local, national, or international issue. However, a much larger proportion (24%) reported e-mailing with others about policy issues several times a month or more ("Internet talking").

Finally, we found that two other forms of political talking—namely, efforts to persuade another individual about whom to vote for or about where to stand on a public issue—were quite common. Nearly half (47%) reported having tried to convince someone to adopt a particular stance on a public issue, and nearly a third (31%) reported having tried to convince someone how to vote.

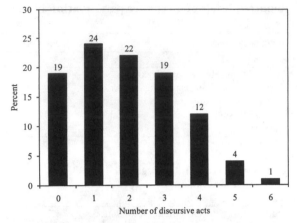

FIGURE 2.1 AGGREGATE LEVELS OF DISCURSIVE PARTICIPATION

Source: Discursive Participation Survey. Total sample: N = 1,501 (weighted general population sample).
Note: Additive index of the six forms of discursive participation (see text for more details).

FREQUENCY OF DISCURSIVE PARTICIPATION

Recurrent public talking is a second way of gauging the extent of discursive participation. We constructed a simple additive index of the six forms of discursive participation described above. Figure 2.1 shows the frequency distribution of our respondents on this index. Fully eight in ten (81%) reported having engaged in at least one form of discursive participation in the last year, and more than one in three (36%) reported engaging in three or more such activities.

It is sobering and worth further analysis that 19% of Americans reported *never* discussing a public issue. Nonetheless, we find it impressive that a relatively large proportion of Americans engage in some form of public talk. Public deliberation and discursive participation are robust and certainly more widespread than many have assumed.

COMPARING DISCURSIVE PARTICIPATION AND POLITICAL AND CIVIC PARTICIPATION

A third way to assess the extent of discursive participation is to compare it to other, more intensively studied forms of citizen engagement. Our survey asked respondents about their engagement in nine forms of political and civil participation that fall into three broad categories: "elite contacting" (boycotting a product or company, signing a petition, contacting a public official, contacting the media); "civic participation" (volunteering for community service, working informally with others to solve a com-

Table 2.2 Types and measures of discursive, political, and civic participation

CATEGORY	MEASURES	
Discursive participation	Face-to-face deliberation	Yes = 1
	Internet deliberation	Yes = 1
	Traditional talker	Every day to few times a month = 1
	Internet talker	Every day to few times a month = 1
	Persuade issue	Yes = 1
	Persuade vote	Yes = 1
Electoral participation	Voting 2002	Yes = 1
	Volunteer for campaign	Yes = 1
Elite contacting	Boycott	Yes = 1
	Petition	Yes = 1
	Contact official	Yes = 1
	Contact media	Yes = 1
Civic participation	Community service	Yes = 1
	Work informally to solve community problem	Yes = 1

Note: All measures are coded 0 or 1. Question wording is contained in the appendix.

munity problem); and "electoral participation" (voting in 2000, voting in 2002, working for a party or candidate).[8]

Our Discursive Participation Survey contains a number of measures for various forms of public talking as well as related political and civic attitudes and behaviors. Table 2.2 summarizes four forms of traditional political and civic participation and discursive participation: (1) measures of six types of discursive participation and public deliberation; (2) two measures of electoral participation; (3) four measures of elite contacting; and (4) two measures of civic participation. (Complete questions and coding for each measure appear in the appendix.)

Table 2.3 reports the percentages of citizens engaging in discursive participation compared to the levels of engagement in more commonly studied forms of political and civic participation. As this comparison shows, discursive participation is quite extensive and a more common feature of democratic life than is often assumed: political talk forms a kind of discursive equivalent to the more traditional indicators of political engagement. Table 2.3 shows that the frequency of informal conversations about public issues parallels the level of reported voting and is more extensive than a number of activities related to contacting elites such as joining a boycott, signing a petition, or contacting an officeholder or the media.

Table 2.3 Comparison of frequency of discursive participation with that of other forms of civic and political engagement

PERCENTAGE (%)	DISCURSIVE PARTICIPATION	ELITE CONTACTING	CIVIC PARTICIPATION	ELECTORAL PARTICIPATION
70				Voting in 2000
68	Traditional talker			
61				Voting in 2002
55			Community service	
47	Persuade someone on an issue			
46			Work informally with others	
44		Boycotting		
32		Sign a Petition		
31	Persuade someone whom to vote for			
28		Contact an official		
25	Face-to-face deliberation			
24	Internet talker			
21		Contact the media		
10				Volunteer for campaign
4	Internet deliberation			

Source: Discursive Participation Survey. Total sample: $N = 1{,}501$ (weighted general population sample).

The most taxing and illustrious type of deliberation (formal face-to-face deliberation) is comparable to well-known types of political participation such as contacting an officeholder and is only a bit less common than signing a petition.

In short, the overall amount and range of citizen engagement in various forms of discursive participation compare well to those of other kinds of self-reported civic and political activities. The classic form of deliberation—organized person-to-person forums—is certainly not common, but it is as extensive as other well-known and well-studied forms of political participation. This is an impressive finding, given its demands on people's time and effort.

Reconsidering the Frequency of Discursive Participation

Public talking takes time, effort, skill, and nerve. These demands and risks make discursive talking more of a personal challenge than many other political actions such as pulling a lever in the privacy of a voting booth. The high costs of public deliberation pose a barrier to participation. Given these daunting costs, why are large numbers of Americans gathering together to talk about public issues?

The explanation for discursive participation does not rest on one factor; it emerges from a number of processes and developments. Four factors, which we examine in subsequent chapters, contribute to the surprisingly extensive amount of discursive participation in America.

The first of these is the emergence of professional networks and community organizations committed to convening public forums—a development that we consider in chapter 7. The effect has been to lower the costs to individuals of discursive participation. In addition to this organizational infrastructure for public forums, technological change has widened access to the Internet and instilled the requisite skills in using the Web among a growing number of Americans, especially the young (Iyengar, Luskin, and Fishkin 2003; Cappella, Price, and Nir 2002; Price and Cappella 2002; Price et al. 2003).

The second factor is that Americans see discursive participation as a meaningful form of political expression and a pathway to other forms of political participation. One possibility is that people may view public talk as a way to influence policy by reaching government officials or by other means. In addition, Americans may be discursively active for reasons not directly connected to influencing government policy; instrumental calculations about immediate means-ends payoffs may not be the only or even principal source of perceived reward. Instead, Americans may be engaging in public talk because they value discursive participation as educative (i.e., it delivers information and improved understanding), morally rewarding (it fulfills a sense of responsibility to the community), and socially gratifying (it offers a format for political expression and interaction with individuals) (Button and Mattson 1999, 631–37). We explore some of these possibilities in chapter 5.

Third, Americans may be drawn to public talk because they enjoy it. As Walsh (2004) found in her qualitative study of groups who met regularly and discussed politics from time to time, they *enjoyed* their interchanges about politics. Similarly, when Fishkin examined the reactions of a national sample of Americans who participated in his deliberative polling discussions, he found that 73% gave the deliberative experience a perfect score of nine ("an extremely valuable experience") instead of one ("generally a waste of time") (1995, 187).

Finally (and more like other forms of civic and political engagement), discursive participation may be affected by the differences in the resources available to individuals that arise from different levels of education, income, social networks, and political interests. The variation in these resources may lead to differentiation in the political participation and discursive participation of individuals. Public talking may, however, open up opportunities to reduce some of these barriers to fuller participation. We explore this possibility in the next chapter.

Discursive Participation in Theory and in Context

Public talking about issues of concern to the broad community falls short of the optimistic expectations of democratic theory. Participation in the different forms of discursive engagement—from informal talking and Internet communications to formal, face-to-face deliberation—is far from universal. The most common form of discursive participation (informal talking) was engaged in by two-thirds of Americans, and one-fourth took part in the most taxing form of public deliberation (face-to-face deliberation).

Nonetheless, public talk of various kinds is more extensive than imagined by many critics, who dismiss it as infrequent and selective. Discursive participation rivals other forms of civic and political engagement in frequency. In an era in which Americans have been called loners with low social capital (Putnam 2000), it is significant that millions of Americans are discursively engaged. Sixty-eight percent informally discussed issues of concern to their community or to the nation. Eighty-one percent had engaged in at least one form of discursive participation in the last year, and 36% reported taking part in three or more such activities. That one in four individuals engaged in face-to-face deliberation is impressive, given what it requires, and exceeds the impression that it was restricted to a small enclave of elites.

At a minimum, the findings presented in this chapter suggest that discursive participation deserves more scholarly attention and empirical study than it has received to date. While this chapter has investigated and challenged the sweeping conclusion of skeptics that few citizens engage in public talking and deliberation, this is only one of several criticisms requiring investigation. Of equal or greater concern is the charge that public deliberation and discursive participation are "exclusive" forms of participation that are reserved for the segments of citizens who have the requisite time, resources, and skills.

THREE

Who Deliberates?

Evidence that two-thirds of Americans are engaging in traditional talking and one-fourth are engaging in more time-intensive, formal, face-to-face deliberation is impressive. Yet, the sheer scope of deliberation does not reveal *who* is deliberating. What matters is not only the amount of discursive participation but also its distribution. Who is talking in public about issues of concern to the community? Are talkers representative of the general population? Or is public talk—like political activity more generally—disproportionately engaged in by advantaged social and economic status groups that enjoy higher levels of education and income?

Consistent and strong evidence that public talk was systematically unrepresentative would confirm the strong criticisms of deliberation for reproducing and even exacerbating economic and social inequalities in American society. It would also deepen the sobering reality of American democracy. Research already shows that electoral and legislative politics are dominated by the advantaged who convey consistent and effective messages to government officials (Verba, Schlozman, and Brady 1995). Evidence of social and economic disparities in public talk would suggest that the bias in American democracy extends beyond formal politics to the interactions and relations within communities themselves, how neighbors talk and treat each other. This would introduce still another layer of unequal voice in American society.

The relative representativeness of discursive participation is embedded in broader patterns in American society and politics that appear to reinforce the criticisms of deliberation. One of the enduring features of American political life is that political participation is highly uneven across the population. People with higher levels of education and income and who are white and male tend to participate more often in a full range of political activities than those with lower levels of income and education who are African American, Latino, and female (Verba, Schlozman, and Brady 1995; Schlozman et al. 2005). Generations of research have demonstrated that participation in most forms of civic and political activity by individuals from socially and economically advantaged groups is systematically greater than their proportion of the population. This "bias" toward individuals with higher social and economic status (SES) is most striking with regard to "more difficult" political acts—for example, contacting a public official, working on a political candidate's campaign, or making campaign contributions (Verba and Nie 1972; Verba, Nie, and Kim 1978; Schlozman et al. 2005).

The SES bias in American politics prompted E. E. Schattschneider to conclude in 1960 that "the flaw in the pluralist heaven is that the heavenly chorus sings with a strong upper class accent" (1960, 35). A recent task force of the American Political Science Association (2004), entitled "Inequality and American Democracy," not only confirmed Schattschneider's observation but also concluded that inequalities in political life have been reinforced or widened in the wake of growing economic inequities since the 1970s.

The general pattern of stratification in American civic and political participation may be evident in discursive activities as well. Some past studies on public deliberation have indicated that people with the most time, resources, expertise, and information appear to participate most extensively in public forums (Susskind and Ozawa 1984, 257; Forester 1999 and 1989). Research on juries reports that income, education, gender, race, and ethnicity affect the level of participation and influence. Jury members with higher-status jobs, greater education, and higher income talk more and are more likely to be (often incorrectly) perceived as more accurate (Hastie, Penrod, and Pennington 1983; Strodtbeck, James, and Hawkins 1957). Women and African American jurors have also been found to be less likely to talk and participate (James 1959; Nemeth, Endicott, and Wachtler 1976; Strodtbeck and Mann 1956; Strodtbeck, James, and Hawkins 1957) and more generally to be less influential in group decisions (Ridgeway 1981; Mendelberg 2002, 165; Bowers, Steiner, and Sandys 2001). These studies, however, have relied on uncommon forums (such as juries), individual case studies, or anecdotal evidence. Whether discursive participation is systematically unrepresentative and reproduces systematic inequalities in SES remains a critical unanswered question.

Despite the patterns of SES bias, four dynamics challenge and modify a simple deterministic model in which inequalities in social and economic conditions directly cause political disparities. First, strongly held ideological and partisan identities may motivate political participation (Delli Carpini and Keeter 1996; Patterson 2002). For instance, Thomas Frank's book, *What's the Matter with Kansas?* (2004), argues that socially conservative attitudes have prompted lower-income groups to support candidates who favor economic policies that advantage the affluent (see also Brooks and Manza 1997; but cf. Bartels 2008). The implication is that ideology and partisanship may prompt individuals to participate politically in ways that contradict or, less directly, condition simple predictions based on their economic and social interests.

Second, political attitudes about politics and the political process—especially expressions of psychological engagement with politics such as interest, efficacy, knowledge, and attention—may contribute directly to greater participation than expected among well-resourced groups (Verba and Nie 1972; Verba, Nie, and Kim 1978). Third, economic and social conditions are not the only factors that affect the resources and motivations of individuals to participate in civic and political activities. Recent research suggests that government policies also help to construct the "environment" in which individuals reach decisions about whether and how to participate. Inclusive public policies (such as Social Security and the GI bill) have been found to encourage participation among beneficiaries, offsetting the influence of SES (Campbell 2003; Mettler 2002; cf. Soss 1999 on the differential effects of AFDC and Social Security Disability).

The fourth dynamic that may modify or offset the direct impact of SES on civic and political participation is affiliation with organizations that mobilize their communities (Verba and Nie 1972). Membership and participation in civic organizations like churches, volunteer associations, and unions are not closely related to SES. Belonging to these organizations and attending their meetings may equip, motivate, and facilitate the civic and political participation of individuals from lower and middle SES.

Civic organizations may contribute to participation in two ways. First, they serve as a training ground and setting for life-long learning and confidence-building that is valuable for civic and political participation—whether it relates to the planning of meetings or to public speaking (Verba, Schlozman, and Brady 1995). Second, civic organizations also create a context of activity and a web of relations that can set expectations, facilitate interactions among individuals, and subsidize the activities of middle and lower SES groups that may lack the skills or inclination to participate in political and nonpolitical activities. Churches and other community organizations contribute to learning but also establish opportunities and platforms for their members and even for nonmembers to meet, talk, and act together.

Community networks and organizations may be especially important for facilitating discursive participation across SES groups. Public talking is inextricably grounded in social relations and the interchanges among individuals; bringing people together is a primary mission of most organizations. In addition, public talking has directly benefited from targeted investments in new organizational capacity. The development of deliberative organizations and a professional deliberative association—as discussed in chapter 7—are aimed at subsidizing the cost of public talking to expand its incidence and to improve its quality. Communities with significant civic organizations can facilitate public deliberation not only by teaching skills and building confidence in public talking but also by broadly distributing the opportunities and resources for people to come together to exchange ideas and viewpoints. Membership in organizations and attendance at their meetings potentially generates dynamics for public talking that offset the stratifying effects of SES.

This chapter offers the first survey-based analysis of the social, economic, and political characteristics of the individuals who deliberate and engage in other forms of discursive participation. Investigating the distribution and determinants of discursive participation allows us to address a central dispute related to deliberation: Is it sharply stratified?

Studying Who Deliberates

Our National Survey of Discursive Participation in America was designed to gather data on a variety of characteristics that might stratify discursive participation or offset it. We collected data on four sets of independent variables that directly measure the competing explanations for political and civic participation. First, our survey gathered standard demographic traits of individuals that measure SES (income, education, gender, age, and race). Second, it assembled data on political characteristics related to ideological and political party identification. Third, it collected measures of the attitudinal model of participation—what we call "political capital"—through a series of questions related to such things as political interest, efficacy, knowledge, and attention. Fourth, we measured "social capital" through questions related to organizational membership, length of residence in the respondent's current community, and religious attendance. (The appendix describes the variables and their construction.)

We constructed eight dependent variables to study the differential influences on discursive participation. These include the six types of discursive participation presented in the previous chapter—face-to-face deliberation, Internet deliberation, traditional talk, Internet talk, issue persuasion, and vote persuasion. The seventh dependent variable, *nondiscursive participation*, measures non-engagement in any form of the six types

Table 3.1   Measures of political and social capital and demographic indicators

CATEGORY	MEASURES	
Political capital	Political efficacy	10-point scale
	Political trust	5-point scale
	Social trust	4-point scale
	Political knowledge	6-point scale
	Political interest	11-point scale
	Political attention	4-point scale
	Ideological strength	3-point scale
	Partisan strength	2-point scale
	Political tolerance	3-point scale
Social capital	Belong to organization	Belong = 1
	Religious attendance	7-point scale
	Length of residence	No. of years
Demographics / background	African American	African American = 1
	Latino	Latino = 1
	Other ethnicity	Other ethnicity = 1
	Education	5 categories
	Gender	Female = 1
	Age	5 categories
	Income	5 categories

Note: Question wording is contained in Appendix 1.

of discursive participation. These seven variables are measured as 0 or 1. Finally, we used an additive index of what we call *discursive intensity*. This summary variable measures the extent to which respondents engaged in multiple forms of discursive participation. It is measured on a scale from 0 to 6, with 0 indicating that the respondent did not engage in any of the six types of discursive participation, and 6 indicating that the respondent participated in all six types. Table 3.1 presents the measures of our political and social capital variables as well as demographic indicators that have often been found to influence political and civic participation; the remaining variables used in this and later chapters are summarized in table 2.2. (Full question wording and coding for each measure appear in the appendix.)

Who Deliberates?

Our investigation is divided into three sets of analyses. The first offers the "big picture" of who engages in various forms of discursive participation. It examines the demographic and political characteristics of those who engage in the six types of discursive participation and allows us to assess the proportion of subgroup discursive participation relative to their share in the general population. The second element of our research uses regression analyses to examine the relative impact of the four competing potential influences—demographic characteristics of SES, political characteristics, political attitudes, and organizational capacity—on the different forms of discursive participation and on the intensity of discursive participation. Finally, our third set of analyses examines the perceptions and reactions of face-to-face deliberators with regard to the diversity of the meetings they attended.

THE BIG PICTURE

Previous research on civic participation would lead us to expect disproportionately lower discursive engagement among socially and economically disadvantaged citizens—for example, African Americans, women, and young adults. To what extent do the results of our survey support or refute this expectation?

Table 3.2 shows the level of discursive participation across racial, educational, gender, age, income, and political groups. The first column presents the proportion of each demographic and political category in the general population (as measured by our weighted sample). The other seven columns present the characteristics of those who participate in various forms of discursive participation as well as those who never talk about public policy issues (i.e., nondiscursive participants). The closer the percentages for discursive and nondiscursive participation are to those of the sample as a whole, the more representative discursive participants are of the general population.

There are two consistent types of variations in discursive participation that mirror the most pervasive differences in other forms of political participation—education and income. First, the better-educated are overrepresented among those who engage in each type of discursive participation. Whereas 25% of our sample had a college or postgraduate degree, 39% of face-to-face deliberators and 42% of Internet deliberators were college educated. In addition, those with a college or postcollege education are more likely to be found in the ranks of those who try to persuade others on issues (33%) and on voting (34%). This is consistent with previous research on other forms of civic and political engagement; education equips individuals with the skills and confidence to participate in a number of different activities (Nie, Junn, and Stehlik-Barry 1996; Verba, Schlozman, and Brady 1995).

Second, there are also differences by income subgroups, but they are less striking in certain respects; those in the lowest income group (those earning below $30,000) tend to be less discursively active. Compared to the 33% of the general population in the lowest income group, only 21%

Table 3.2   Differences across individuals in discursive and nondiscursive participation

DEMOGRAPHIC CHARACTERISTICS	WHOLE SAMPLE	FACE-TO-FACE DELIBERATORS	INTERNET DELIBERATORS	INTERNET TALKERS	TRADITIONAL TALKERS	PERSUADE ON ISSUE	PERSUADE ON VOTE	NONDISCURSIVE PARTICIPANTS
	PERCENTAGES (%)							
Race								
African American	8	9	5	7	6	7	9	9
Latino	7	4	5	2	4	4	3	14
White	78	78	84	81	82	82	84	69
Other	7	10	6	9	8	7	4	8
	(N = 1,454)	(N = 362)	(N = 60)	(N = 348)	(N = 984)	(N = 681)	(N = 449)	(N = 269)
Education								
< HS degree	10	5	15	5	5	7	6	24
HS degree only	37	26	5	23	32	27	28	49
Some college	28	30	38	35	32	33	32	15
College degree	16	22	19	22	19	20	21	9
Postgrad degree	9	17	23	16	12	13	13	3
	(N = 1,466)	(N = 368)	(N = 61)	(N = 355)	(N = 996)	(N = 690)	(N = 452)	(N = 268)
Gender								
Male	48	46	58	49	48	54	55	48
Female	52	54	42	51	52	46	46	52
	(N = 1,501)	(N = 379)	(N = 61)	(N = 360)	(N = 1,018)	(N = 698)	(N = 458)	(N = 279)
Age								
18–29	23	24	31	32	24	26	24	21
30–39	17	18	12	16	17	16	13	15
40–49	22	24	33	19	23	24	22	20
50–64	21	22	20	21	22	22	25	19
65+	16	12	4	11	14	12	17	24
	(N = 1,460)	(N = 365)	(N = 61)	(N = 350)	(N = 994)	(N = 684)	(N = 449)	(N = 266)

Table 3.2 (*Continued*)

DEMOGRAPHIC CHARACTERISTICS	WHOLE SAMPLE	FACE-TO-FACE DELIBERATORS	INTERNET DELIBERATORS	INTERNET TALKERS	TRADITIONAL TALKERS	PERSUADE ON ISSUE	PERSUADE ON VOTE	NONDISCURSIVE PARTICIPANTS
	PERCENTAGES (%)							
Family income								
< $30k	33	21	21	23	27	26	27	52
$30k–$50k	21	23	20	21	21	18	16	22
$50k–$75k	23	24	29	27	25	26	25	12
$75k–$100k	12	17	16	16	13	14	15	9
> $100k	12	14	13	13	14	16	17	5
	(N = 1,128)	(N = 307)	(N = 53)	(N = 299)	(N = 791)	(N = 547)	(N = 371)	(N = 179)
POLITICAL CHARACTERISTICS								
Ideology								
Strong liberal	8	14	15	16	9	8	12	1
Liberal	13	11	12	11	14	13	11	7
Moderate	42	42	49	43	42	38	36	50
Conservative	20	16	8	16	19	18	17	31
Strong conservative	17	17	16	15	16	23	24	11
	(N = 1,302)	(N = 350)	(N = 60)	(N = 341)	(N = 919)	(N = 646)	(N = 433)	(N = 201)
Party ID								
Democrat	35	33	43	41	34	35	38	40
Independent	39	39	32	31	37	34	28	42
Republican	26	28	25	28	29	31	34	18
	(N = 1,481)	(N = 375)	(N = 61)	(N = 359)	(N = 1,007)	(N = 693)	(N = 453)	(N = 270)
Belong to organization (%)	37	62	60	48	44	48	50	18
	(N = 1,495)	(N = 378)	(N = 61)	(N = 360)	(N = 1,015)	(N = 697)	(N = 457)	(N = 277)

Variable								
Religious attendance (mean: 0–6)	3	3	3	3	3	3	3	2
	(N = 1,455)	(N = 367)	(N = 61)	(N = 351)	(N = 995)	(N = 687)	(N = 452)	(N = 258)
Length of residence (mean; years)	21	19	14	16	20	20	22	27
	(N = 1,454)	(N = 367)	(N = 61)	(N = 350)	(N = 990)	(N = 679)	(N = 446)	(N = 263)
Political efficacy (mean: 0–9)	4	5	5	5	5	5	5	3
	(N = 1,409)	(N = 362)	(N = 61)	(N = 351)	(N = 975)	(N = 675)	(N = 442)	(N = 236)
Political trust (mean: 0–3)	2	2	2	2	2	2	2	2
	(N = 1,290)	(N = 336)	(N = 58)	(N = 321)	(N = 903)	(N = 612)	(N = 402)	(N = 214)
Social trust (mean: 0–3)	2	2	2	2	2	2	2	1
	(N = 1,336)	(N = 346)	(N = 56)	(N = 329)	(N = 918)	(N = 613)	(N = 403)	(N = 243)
Political knowledge (mean: 0–5)	3	4	4	4	3	4	4	2
	(N = 1,501)	(N = 379)	(N = 61)	(N = 360)	(N = 1,018)	(N = 698)	(N = 458)	(N = 279)
Political interest (mean: 0–10)	6	7	7	7	6	7	7	4
	(N = 1,492)	(N = 379)	(N = 61)	(N = 360)	(N = 1,018)	(N = 698)	(N = 458)	(N = 270)
Political attention (mean: 0–3)	2	2	2	2	2	2	2	1
	(N = 1,492)	(N = 379)	(N = 61)	(N = 360)	(N = 1,015)	(N = 695)	(N = 456)	(N = 273)
Political tolerance (mean: 0–2)	2	2	2	2	2	2	2	1
	(N = 1,312)	(N = 340)	(N = 57)	(N = 324)	(N = 906)	(N = 625)	(N = 419)	(N = 229)

Source: Discursive Participation Survey. Total sample: N = 1,501 (weighted general population sample).

of those engaged in face-to-face deliberation were in the lowest income group; higher proportions of those engaging in traditional talking (27%) and issue- and vote-focused persuasion (26% and 27% respectively) came from this group. Not surprisingly, Americans who did not engage in any of the six forms of deliberation (i.e., nondiscursive participants) were disproportionately from the lowest income (and education) subgroups.

In addition to education and income, other differences related to social and economic status emerged (though less consistently). Compared to their presence in the general population, women were less engaged in Internet deliberation and efforts at persuasion on issues and voting. The participation of Latinos also fell somewhat short of their population share in terms of Internet talking, traditional talking, and persuasion on issues and voting. African Americans were a bit less engaged in Internet deliberation.

Table 3.2, however, presents two patterns that explain but also complicate the simple bivariate relationship with social and economic status. First, the disparities that do exist in discursive participation appear to be most related to participatory *formats*. For example, the two deliberative formats connected to the Internet—Internet deliberation and Internet talking—showed a consistent pattern of subgroup variation. Internet-based discourse varies by education and age: the better-educated (some college or more) and younger (ages 18–29) are more likely to engage in Internet discourse than their proportion in the general population would suggest. These are precisely the subgroups that are best-trained and most exposed to and comfortable with computers and the Internet. By contrast, those least familiar with the Internet—the older (65 and older) and less well educated (high school degree or less)—are the least predisposed to engage in Internet discourse. Age may also help to explain the disproportionate tendency of Democrats and strong liberals to participate in Internet talking and Internet deliberation; young adults are somewhat more likely to be Democrats and liberals. In general, the most costly forms of discursive participation—Internet deliberation and face-to-face deliberation—are characterized by the largest differences based on SES.

The second and most impressive pattern is related to organizational membership—a measure of social networks and community involvement—and its impact in countering the effects of SES. While 37% of the whole sample belonged to an organization, far higher proportions of those engaging in face-to-face deliberation (62%), Internet deliberation (60%), and other forms of public talking belonged to organizations; only 18% of those who did not engage in any form of deliberation were members of organizations.

In summary, our first, broad-gauged analysis suggests that the advantages of SES do affect discursive participation to some degree but that social and political capital may mitigate or condition their impact.

A Closer Look at Who Engages in Discursive Participation

Initial evidence suggests that education and income, among other variables, appear to be related to levels of discursive politics. If this pattern held, it would confirm the penetrating criticisms of public deliberation for reproducing social and economic inequalities (Fraser 1997; Sanders 1997). There are, however, potentially counteracting influences due to generational acclimation to new technology as well as social and political capital. Does SES sort discursive participation to generate further inequalities in voice, or are there processes that enable discursive participation to escape the tongs of SES to engage social and economic subgroups in ways that represent their presence in the community?

The SES Model

To investigate the relative effects of competing influences on discursive participation, we regressed our six measures of discursive participation (plus our measure of nondiscursive participation) on a traditional set of demographic variables and measures of political orientation (ideology and party identification). We use logit regression because the dependent variables are dichotomous. Table 3.3 provides the unstandardized coefficients from these analyses.

Not surprisingly, the familiar impact of SES evident in table 3.2 remains in these regressions. Education has a consistent, positive impact on all forms of discursive participation. In addition, income has an effect, though it is less consistent and limited to issue and vote persuasion: lower-income groups are less likely than the more affluent to attempt to change other people's minds on issues and candidates. African Americans and, more consistently, Latinos and females, also tend to be less likely to engage in discursive participation.

Table 3.3 also suggests that the relationship between certain demographic characteristics and discursive participation varies somewhat by the format of public talking. Unsurprisingly, younger people continue to appear more likely than older ones to participate in Internet deliberation and Internet talking. This seems to indicate that discursive participation by youth may be tied to the Internet and new technology—a finding that revises previous research on the disproportionate political participation of

Table 3.3 Influences on discursive and nondiscursive participation (Model 1, demographic and political characteristics)

	FACE-TO-FACE DELIBERATORS	INTERNET DELIBERATORS	INTERNET TALKERS	TRADITIONAL TALKERS	PERSUADE ON ISSUE	PERSUADE ON VOTE	NONDISCURSIVE PARTICIPANTS
Demographic characteristics							
African American	.19 (.25)	−.41 (.50)	−.44 (.27)	−.61 (.29)*	−.49 (.25)*	−.29 (.26)	.27 (.43)
Latino	−.52 (.36)	−.15 (.64)	−.86 (.42)*	−1.14 (.36)**	−.60 (.35)+	−.91 (.42)*	1.46 (.44)***
Other ethnicity	.12 (.25)	−.45 (.49)	−.18 (.26)	−.52 (.29)+	−.37 (.25)	−.16 (.25)	1.03 (.38)**
Education (5 cat.)	.38 (.06)***	.29 (.12)*	.34 (.07)***	.38 (.08)***	.33 (.07)***	.24 (.06)***	−.36 (.12)**
Gender (F = 1)	.01 (.13)	−.52 (.24)*	−.23 (.14)+	.11 (.17)	−.51 (.13)***	−.48 (.13)***	.11 (.25)
Age (in years)	−.03 (.05)	−.32 (.10)***	−.26 (.05)***	−.10 (.06)	−.05 (.05)	.09 (.05)+	.11 (.10)
Income (5 cat.)	.06 (.05)	.10 (.09)	.08 (.05)	.10 (.07)	.14 (.05)**	.12 (.05)*	−.28 (.11)**
Political characteristics							
Ideology	−.07 (.06)	−.29 (.11)**	−.24 (.07)***	−.24 (.08)**	.00 (.06)	−.02 (.06)	.27 (.12)*
Party ID	−.03 (.09)	−.04 (.17)	−.00 (.10)	.16 (.12)	−.03 (.09)	−.11 (.09)	−.20 (.18)
Constant	−.54 (.32)+	−1.26 (.57)*	.12 (.34)	1.27 (.41)**	−.04 (.33)	−.81 (.33)**	−2.46 (.62)***
N	1,080	1,080	1,080	1,080	1,080	1,080	1,080
Pseudo R^2	0.056	0.032	0.082	0.067	0.074	0.054	0.052

Source: Discursive Participation Survey. Total sample: N = 1,501 (unweighted sample).

Notes: The first numbers are logit coefficients. The numbers in parentheses are robust standard errors. Ideology is coded such that 1 = strong liberal and 5 = strong conservative.

+ $p < .10$; * $p < .05$; ** $p < .01$; *** $p < .001$.

seniors (Verba, Schlozman, and Brady 1995; Campbell 2003). In addition, liberals continue to appear somewhat more likely than conservatives to engage in traditional talking and both Internet deliberation and Internet talking despite controls for age and other demographic and political characteristics. This may also be related to the familiarity of youth with the Web.

Table 3.3 offers, however, an incomplete analysis because it omits important potential influences—notably social and political capital. The omission of potentially significant influences may be reflected in the relatively weak pseudo R-squared, which indicates that relatively little of the variance in our dependent variables is explained by our independent variables.

The Social and Political Capital Model of Discursive Participation

Having explored the collective effects of SES and political orientations on discursive participation, we turn to a more fully specified model that includes our various measures of social capital (organizational membership, religious attendance, and length of residence in the community) and political capital (political efficacy, political trust, social trust, political knowledge, political interest, political attention, and political tolerance). Our analyses in this chapter of the "social and political capital model" use individual-level measures on the assumption that organizational and political resources may be refracted through individuals; chapter 7 uses community-level variables to augment the analyses and more directly examine contextual variables that may influence individual behavior and attitudes (see Schlozman et al. 2005 for a previous examination of individual- and community-level analyses).

The unstandardized coefficients from our logit models appear in table 3.4. Confirming the empirical value of including critical additional variables, the expanded model explains a notably larger percentage of the overall variance (as indicated by the higher pseudo R-squared).

Social capital and, especially, organizational membership are powerful forces propelling discursive participation and notably diminish the impact of SES. Organizational membership has the most consistent and strongest effects, exerting a significant effect on five of the six forms of discursive participation. The networks and resources of organizations facilitate public talking.

Political attitudes—what we call "political capital"—also have some effects on discursive participation. Controlling for other factors, political interest is especially effective in boosting discursive participation. In addition, having high levels of political efficacy—that is, thinking that public

Table 3.4 Influences on discursive and nondiscursive participation (Model 2, demographics, political characteristics, social capital, and political capital)

	FACE-TO-FACE DELIBERATORS	INTERNET DELIBERATORS	INTERNET TALKERS	TRADITIONAL TALKERS	PERSUADE ON ISSUE	PERSUADE ON VOTE	NONDISCURSIVE PARTICIPANTS
Demographic characteristics							
African American	−.05 (.32)	−.28 (.55)	−.06 (.33)	−.94 (.36)**	−.76 (.32)*	−.13 (.32)	.74 (.56)
Latino	−.03 (.43)	.13 (.71)	−.39 (.47)	−.53 (.45)	−.18 (.44)	−.25 (.47)	.72 (.62)
Other ethnicity	.20 (.34)	−.72 (.59)	−.12 (.33)	−.56 (.39)	−.19 (.34)	.02 (.33)	.86 (.58)
Education (5 cat.)	.05 (.09)	−.09 (.15)	.11 (.09)	.28 (.11)**	.12 (.09)	−.03 (.09)	−.01 (.18)
Gender (F = 1)	−.01 (.17)	−.69 (.29)*	−.17 (.17)	.19 (.21)	−.23 (.17)	−.30 (.17)+	−.05 (.33)
Age (in years)	−.09 (.07)	−.42 (.13)**	−.18 (.07)**	−.07 (.09)	−.17 (.08)*	−.07 (.07)	.14 (.15)
Income (5 cat.)	−.01 (.07)	.13 (.11)	.00 (.07)	−.16 (.09)+	.07 (.07)	.05 (.06)	.02 (.14)
Political characteristics							
Ideology	−.14 (.08)+	−.37 (.14)**	−.21 (.08)**	−.35 (.11)***	−.02 (.09)	.04 (.08)	.42 (.17)*
Party ID	−.16 (.12)	.10 (.21)	−.05 (.12)	.21 (.15)	−.05 (.12)	.01 (.12)	−.16 (.23)
Social capital							
Belong to organization	1.11 (.17)***	1.46 (.36)***	.35 (.18)*	.69 (.22)***	.42 (.18)*	.24 (.17)	−.63 (.36)+
Religious attendance	.12 (.04)**	.03 (.07)	−.01 (.04)	−.04 (.05)	−.01 (.04)	−.03 (.04)	−.05 (.08)
Length of residence	.00 (.01)	−.01 (.01)	−.02 (.01)**	.00 (.01)	.01 (.01)+	.00 (.01)	.01 (.01)
Political capital							
Political efficacy	.15 (.04)***	.20 (.08)**	.16 (.04)***	.06 (.05)	.06 (.04)	−.02 (.04)	−.04 (.08)
Political trust	.09 (.09)	−.49 (.17)**	−.02 (.09)	−.11 (.11)	−.01 (.09)	−.22 (.09)*	−.12 (.18)
Social trust	−.05 (.08)	−.16 (.14)	−.01 (.08)	.06 (.10)	−.11 (.09)	.02 (.08)	.09 (.17)
Political knowledge	.02 (.07)	.08 (.13)	.15 (.07)*	.10 (.08)	.18 (.07)**	.22 (.07)**	−.21 (.12)+
Political interest	.08 (.04)*	.15 (.08)+	.09 (.05)*	.10 (.05)*	.19 (.04)***	.21 (.04)***	−.17 (.07)**
Political attention	.29 (.15)+	.19 (.29)	.20 (.16)	.25 (.17)	.38 (.15)**	.36 (.15)*	−.49 (.25)*
Political tolerance	.20 (.12)	−.44 (.22)*	−.09 (.13)	.05 (.15)	−.01 (.13)	.07 (.13)	−.05 (.23)
Constant	−2.33 (.53)***	−2.04 (.95)*	−1.57 (.54)**	.22 (.60)	−2.21 (.54)***	−2.97 (.56)***	−1.15 (.93)
N	795	795	795	795	795	795	795
Pseudo R²	0.175	0.103	0.144	0.118	0.188	0.160	0.085

Source: Discursive Participation Survey. Total sample: N = 1,501 (unweighted sample).

Notes: Logit models were used to generate unstandardized beta coefficients. Robust standard errors are in parentheses.

Ideology is coded such that 1 = strong liberal, and 5 = strong conservative.

Party is coded so that 1 = Democrat, 2 = Nonidentifier (includes Independent; Other; Don't Know), and 3 = Republican.

+ p < .10; * p < .05; ** p < .01; *** p < .001.

officials care what people like you think, that people like you understand what is going on in government, and that you can have a say in what government does—increases the likelihood of public talking. The likelihood of Internet deliberation increases among individuals with low levels of political interest, political trust, and political tolerance (i.e., they believe that some groups such as members of the Ku Klux Klan and radical Islamic fundamentalists should not be guaranteed rights of speech and organization). While this finding may seem surprising, it is consistent with the argument that the Internet may be a refuge for people who are intolerant and distrustful of others and disconnected from their communities. Surprisingly, low social trust (i.e., those who think most people cannot be trusted, would take advantage of others, and are just looking out for themselves) has no effect, challenging the assumption that communication with others relies on confidence in others.

The addition of political capital and, especially, organizational membership notably diminishes the direct effects of SES influences. All but one of the effects of education in the initial model in table 3.3 disappeared; where education initially affected six of the six forms of participation, it only affects traditional talking in table 3.4 after variables for political capital and, especially, organizational membership are introduced. Income no longer has statistically significant effects apart from its marginal impact on traditional talking.

In addition, political capacity and, particularly, organizational membership also weaken the direct effects of other SES factors. The direct effects of race, ethnicity, and gender are weak or reduced: these variables registered only five statistically significant effects in table 3.4 as compared to seventeen in table 3.3. Gender's impact all but disappears; all of the effects associated with being a Latino fade. Finally, in the more fully specified model, the effects of ideological predisposition increase; being liberal (rather than conservative) increases the likelihood of talking about public issues.

In short, discursive participation is shaped by the social and political repertoire that individuals bring to public dialogues. Although conversations are bilateral, the broader social and political context is quite influential.

Intensity of Discursive Participation

Our analysis to this point has focused on explaining the influences on participation in different types of discursive activity. As a final cut at our data, we replicate the analyses presented in table 3.4 but use our sum-

Table 3.5   Determinants of deliberative intensity

	DELIBERATIVE INTENSITY			
	MODEL 1		MODEL 2	
	UNSTANDARDIZED	STANDARDIZED	UNSTANDARDIZED	STANDARDIZED
Demographic characteristics				
African American	-.36 (.17) *	-.06 *	-.39 (.18) *	-.07 *
Latino	-.84 (.24) ***	-.10 ***	-.23 (.24)	-.03
Other ethnicity	-.24 (.17)	-.04	-.13 (.18)	-.02
Education (5 cat.)	.37 (.04) ***	.26 ***	.08 (.05)	.06
Gender (F = 1)	-.29 (.09) ***	-.09 ***	-.16 (.09) +	-.05 +
Age (in years)	-.09 (.04) **	-.07 **	-.14 (.04) ***	-.12 ***
Income (5 cat.)	.11 (.03) ***	.10 ***	.01 (.04)	.01
Political characteristics				
Ideology	-.13 (.04)**	-.09**	-.14 (.05) **	-.10 **
Party ID	-.02 (.06)	-.01	-.02 (.07)	-.01
Social capital				
Belong to organization			.63 (.10) ***	.20 ***
Religious attendance			.01 (.02)	.02
Length of residence			.00 (.00)	.01
Political capital				
Political efficacy			.09 (.02) ***	.14 ***
Political trust			-.08 (.05)	-.06
Social trust			-.04 (.05)	-.03
Political knowledge			.12 (.04) ***	.11 ***
Political interest			.13 (.02) ***	.23 ***
Political attention			.31 (.08) ***	.15 ***
Political tolerance			.01 (.07)	.00
Constant	2.64 (.23) ***		.98 (.29) ***	
N	1,079		794	
R^2	0.142		0.350	

Source: Discursive Participation Survey. Total sample: N = 1,501 (unweighted sample).
Notes: OLS regression was used to generate standardized and unstandardized beta coefficients. Standard errors are given in parentheses. Ideology is coded such that 1 = strong liberal, and 5 = strong conservative. Party is coded so that 1 = Democrat, 2 = Nonidentifier (includes Independent, Other, Don't Know), and 3 = Republican.
$^+ p < .10$; $^* p < .05$; $^{**} p < .01$; $^{***} p < .001$.

mary measure of "discursive intensity" as our dependent variable. Table 3.5 gives the results of two OLS regression analyses—the first using only demographic and political characteristics, and the second adding the social and political capital variables.

Our analysis of discursive intensity replicates the pattern of earlier findings. Absent other controls, individuals with higher levels of income and, especially, education are more discursively active. Ethnicity and gender continue to depress discursive participation: being African American and, especially, female or Latino decreases the number of discursive activities in which individuals engage.

Age continues to be negatively related to discursive participation. The young tend to be engaged in more discursive activities. This may be related to the greater familiarity of younger people with the Internet. In addition, liberals continue to participate in more discursive activities.

Confirming earlier results, Model 2 in table 3.5 demonstrates the impact of social and political capacity in mitigating the direct effects of SES. Organizational membership is the strongest influence on the degree of public talking. Political interest and, to a lesser extent, political attentiveness, political efficacy, and political knowledge similarly drive engagement with multiple forms of talking. Finally, where six of the seven demographic traits associated with SES had significant effects on discursive intensity in Model 1, only three of these variables remain significant in Model 2, with one only marginally significant. The twin engines of SES sorting—education and income—have no direct effects once the social and political capital variables are added.

Indirect Effects of Social and Economic Status

Although SES has little direct impact on deliberation, it has an indirect effect on public talking through organizational membership and other influences. In other words, higher levels of education and income may not directly lead individuals to be more deliberatively active, but they may guide them to join organizations that foster political and civic participation.

We find evidence of the indirect effects of SES on deliberation in the experiences and perceptions reported by Americans who attended face-to-face forums. We also find, however, that Americans perceive some degree of diversity (especially in larger meetings) and see greater diversity among individuals who tend to speak out in the forums. These reactions suggest that some face-to-face deliberators do not view public talking as an enclave of the elite

Diversity and Representativeness

Although SES fails to exert a consistent effect on deliberation after controlling for a number of factors, public talking does not appear to be fully representative of the country according to deliberators. As we report below, Americans who deliberated reported that civic forums were not especially diverse or representative of their communities. The perceptions of public talking as not particularly diverse may appear to echo criticisms of deliberation as skewed. There are, however, a number of indications that deliberative forums are not simply the gated salons imagined by critics.

Table 3.6 shows ratings of diversity on five distinct dimensions—income, race and ethnicity, gender, age, and points of view. Respondents generally rated the diversity of their forums around the midpoint—a score of 5 or 6 on an 11-point scale, with 0 designating "not at all diverse," and 10 indicating "very diverse." The forums were generally perceived as a bit less diverse in terms of race and ethnicity (mean of 4.6) and a bit more diverse on gender and age (mean of about 6), with quite a bit of variation.[1] (Although assessing ascriptive diversity for Internet chat rooms is more difficult than for face-to-face meetings, Americans generally perceived similar levels of gender, income, and age diversity.)[2]

In what may reflect a commitment to representativeness, larger meetings were generally perceived as being more diverse in terms of race, ethnicity, income, age, gender, and, to a lesser extent, point of view (table 3.7). (Deliberators reported that meetings were attended on average by 83 individuals, with a median of 40.) Attending larger meetings was correlated with reports of greater diversity with regard to race and ethnicity ($r = .10$ at .01 level of significance), income ($r = .13$ at .001 level of significance), and a bit more strongly with gender and age ($r = .16$ and .17, respectively, at .001 level of significance).[3] Larger meetings were not significantly associated with perceptions of a wider range of viewpoints; people who attend larger civic forums do not seem particularly more likely to report divergent perspectives. When all five measures of perceived diversity were combined into an additive index, the correlation with meeting size was .21 (.001 level of significance).

Table 3.6 Face-to-face deliberators rate diversity

TYPE OF DIVERSITY	MEAN RESPONSES	N	DON'T KNOW (%)
Race or ethnicity[1]	4.6 (3.3)	745	1.3
Income[2]	5.6 (2.6)	689	8.9
Age[3]	6.0 (2.6)	748	1.1
Gender[4]	5.7 (3.0)	748	0.8
Points of view[5]	5.1 (2.9)	746	1.3

Source: Discursive Participation Survey. Face-to-face deliberation sample: $N = 756$ (unweighted).
Notes: Entries are based on diversity ratings, an 11-point scale ranging from 0 ("not diverse at all") to 10 ("very diverse"). The second column contains mean scores with standard deviations in parentheses. Respondents who refused to answer or responded "Don't know" were excluded when calculating the means, and the effective N for each type of diversity rating is listed in the third column. The fourth column shows the percentage (based on all 756 face-to-face deliberators) of "Don't know" responses for each type of diversity.
1 "How racially or ethnically diverse would you say the people at the last meeting you attended were?"
2 "How diverse were the people attending this meeting by income?"
3 "How diverse were the people attending this meeting by age?"
4 "How diverse were the people attending the meeting by gender?"
5 "How diverse were the points of view expressed during the meeting?"

Table 3.7   Ratings of diversity by face-to-face deliberators across meeting size

	NUMBER OF PARTICIPANTS				
TYPE OF DIVERSITY	0–19	20–39	40–99	100+	DON'T KNOW (%)
Race or ethnicity[1]	4.3	4.3	4.4	5.2	1.3
Income[2]	5.2	5.5	5.9	6.0	8.9
Age[3]	5.2	5.9	6.0	6.9	1.1
Gender[4]	4.6	5.7	6.1	6.5	0.8
Points of view[5]	4.9	4.8	5.5	5.2	1.3

Source: Discursive Participation Survey. Face-to-face deliberation sample: $N = 756$ (unweighted).
Notes: Entries are based on diversity ratings, an 11-point scale ranging from 0 ("not diverse at all") to 10 ("very diverse"). Respondents who refused to answer or responded "Don't know" were excluded when calculating the means. The last column shows the percentage of "Don't know" responses for each type of diversity. This percentage is based on all 756 face-to-face deliberators.
1 "How racially or ethnically diverse would you say the people at the last meeting you attended were?"
2 "How diverse were the people attending this meeting by income?"
3 "How diverse were the people attending this meeting by age?"
4 "How diverse were the people attending the meeting by gender?"
5 "How diverse were the points of view expressed during the meeting?"

Participation by Others

Americans perceive the participation of other citizens in face-to-face forums as more active than their own (a potentially worrisome sign that the more advantaged dominate public conversations). But they also report that participation by others widens diversity. The perceived diversity of deliberative forums was positively correlated with participant perceptions of how often other attendees engaged in the discussion. The average rating of personal participation was 4.8; the rating of participation by others was a full point higher, at 5.8.[4] (Contrary to the impression that the Internet invites greater participation, personal participation in chat rooms was rated only slightly higher—mean of 5.03.)

Higher participation by others could indicate an indirect effect of SES. Higher levels of education and income as well as occupational success are believed to contribute to stronger confidence and skill in public talking (Brady, Verba, and Schlozman 1995). Americans' reactions to their deliberative experience suggest, however, that their perception of elevated participation by others may actually contribute to greater representativeness. Specifically, our findings indicate that the more respondents perceived others as active in discussion, the more likely they were to perceive the meeting as diverse in terms of age ($r = .14$), points of view ($r = .17$), race and ethnicity ($r = .11$), and income ($r = .16$) (at or above .01 levels of statistical significance). In contrast, reports by respondents regarding their own participation were generally not related to perceived diversity (with the exception of viewpoints).

In short, the absence of consistent direct effects of SES on deliberation does not mean that public talking is representative of the general population. The perceptions of Americans who deliberate suggest that public talking is not especially diverse. Nonetheless, there are consistent signs that deliberation is not "owned" or dominated by the better off, as the critics of deliberation have warned. Participation extends beyond personal networks, with larger face-to-face forums reaching out to a wider array of Americans. Relatively less diverse forums do not appear to inhibit less well represented groups from participating.

Conclusion

The practice and promise of public deliberation have been sharply challenged on the grounds that such deliberation merely reproduces and reinforces economic and social inequalities. According to critics, public talk parades as a friend of open and inclusive democracy, but it is little more than the latest Trojan Horse that further locks in or perhaps expands the advantage of those who enjoy higher levels of education and income and hail from the dominant racial, ethnic, and gender groups.

To the extent that such arguments assume a direct and deterministic effect of SES, the analyses presented in this chapter suggest that they are wrong. While SES-based and other group biases exist, discursive participation by more marginalized groups is significant, as indicated by both the characteristics of the discursive participants in our survey and respondents' self-reports regarding their last deliberative experience. And the finding that those forums where participants were regarded as most active were perceived as more diverse than the group as a whole is an encouraging indication.

Further, the effects of SES appear to flow largely through the benefits of social and political capital that accrue to the better off, rather than resulting from more direct and insidious forms of exclusion. Our multivariate analyses demonstrate that income is, at best, only weakly related to discursive participation and that after the introduction of measures of social and political capital, the effects of education, income, ethnicity, and gender moderated or disappeared. New media for talking about politics such as the Internet can help counter some of the biases in other forms of political participation associated with age (Wattenberg 2002; Campbell 2003; Zukin et al. 2006).

The most optimistic finding in this chapter is the positive influence of organizational membership on discursive participation. This finding is consistent with the work of scholars such as Putnam (2000), Skocpol and Fiorina (1999), Skocpol, Ganz, and Munson (2000), and Verba, Schlozman, and Brady (1995), all of whom note that organizational membership brings with it social networks and other resources that can enhance the resources, motivations, and opportunities that fuel political and civic participation.

Nonetheless, social and economic status bias discursive participation. The regression analyses demonstrate that while the effects of SES are largely not direct, they are real. In addition, the self-reports of face-to-face deliberators indicate that they perceived modest diversity in the forums they attended.

As with efforts to understand those other forms of engagement, we must move beyond deterministic theories and models in favor of explanations that appreciate the conditionality of discursive participation. Verba, Schlozman, and Brady's (1995) resource model suggests that the three resources that define individual capacities for civic and political participation (time, money, and civic skills) are differentially related to SES stratification. Contributing money and certain civic skills are closely connected to SES, while committing time and other civic skills are less dependent on SES and so less stratified. Discursive politics appears to be one form of engagement that relies on the opportunities created by community organizations and other factors that are less directly shaped by sharp SES stratification.

The significance of organizational capacity and the muted direct impact of SES appear to open the door to expanding the equitable involvement of citizens in public life. Our finding that 85% of those who had not attended a deliberative meeting *had never been asked to do so* seems to suggest that discursive participation may be increased still further with appropriate community intervention. Although discursive participation is certainly not free of the distorting effects of SES, the dire warnings about the unrepresentativeness of deliberation do not appear to be justified.

Discursive participation does appear to be more extensive and inclusive than commonly assumed, but we know little about the process and quality of these exchanges. Knowing more about the content of discursive participation is critical to evaluating the nature of communications in civic forums and discovering whether their outcomes generate agreement or disagreement.

FOUR

How Do Americans Deliberate?

Understanding how much deliberation is occurring in the United States and who is discursively engaged is critical. Equally important is the quality of the deliberative experience itself. What do the millions of Americans who report attending civic forums actually do, think, and feel during these meetings? Do the internal dynamics of deliberative forums facilitate a democratic openness to different perspectives or merely create another arena in which society's social and economic stratifications are reproduced in ways that benefit already powerful individuals and groups? Is the method of communication and interchange based on reason, collective considerations, and the search for agreement or on manipulation, coercion, self-interest, and disagreement? Do deliberators perceive their fellow interlocutors as tolerant or as trampling on the viewpoints, interests, and values of individuals who are in the minority? Evaluating these fundamental questions about public talk requires an in-depth understanding of the actual experience of deliberators—the Americans we refer to as "street-level deliberators."

We need to investigate the detailed contours of deliberation that inform and shape how individuals experience public talking—the size of the forums, whether and how they are mediated or facilitated, the familiarity of participants with each other, whether and how participants are recruited, and the degree to which conflict is aired or discouraged.

Research on the structure and experience of deliberative forums is limited and largely dominated by case studies (e.g., Gastil 1993; Karpowitz and Mansbridge 2005; Rosenberg 2007; Sokoloff, Steinberg, and Pyser 2005; Walsh 2007). Such case studies are quite valuable, allow for nuanced, qualitative analyses, and can collectively produce the beginnings of broader generalizations about the nature of deliberation in contemporary America. Similarly, less common experimental (e.g., Price, Nir, and Capella 2002) and quasi experimental (e.g., Fishkin and Luskin 1999a, 1999b, 1999c) research can provide carefully controlled analyses of the effects of specific characteristics of the deliberative experience such as the number or diversity of participants, or the style of facilitation. For all their strengths, however, these approaches also have drawbacks; the most significant limitation is the inability to make valid and reliable generalizations to a larger population that are based upon actual (rather than artificially constructed) deliberative experiences (but cf. Fishkin and Luskin 1999a, 1999b, and 1999c).

This chapter takes a different approach than most previous research. Our "observations" regarding the deliberative experience are based on a large survey of respondents who told us they had participated in at least one face-to-face meeting organized to discuss a public issue of local, national, or international import. In particular, we evaluate two critical dimensions of the deliberative experience—the method of communication (reason-based or manipulative) and the discursive outcome (agreement or disagreement). Given research on "recency effects" (e.g., Cobb and Kuklinski 1997), we asked respondents—as noted in chapter 2—about their most recent deliberative experience. Although there is potential for selective recollection, respondents provided detailed information to open-ended questions and generally answered the questions, despite the investment of time and energy required to fashion responses. Even with potential limitations, the survey provides valuable, detailed information about how deliberators were recruited, who facilitated their sessions, the nature of their interactions with forum participants, and other detailed features of Americans' deliberative experience. (Complete question wording appears online at http://www.press.uchicago.edu/books/jacobs.)

Our survey results provide strong evidence of a decisive tilt toward reason-based and agreement-oriented deliberation. Face-to-face deliberation tends to be geared toward discussions based on expert information, logic, and toleration, and is oriented toward reaching agreement and addressing concerns about the larger community. There are, though, some notable warning signs. Although large majorities report that deliberative forums were structured to be tolerant and welcoming, there are indications that a (small) segment of participants experience intolerance and undemocratic dynamics. This is a worrisome subtheme that we explore. The next section discusses previous theorizing and research about the actual experience of deliberation. We then report the experiences of Americans who participated in civic forums.

What Is the "Deliberative Experience"?

Advocates of public deliberation tend to laud it as an engine of democracy that deepens citizen knowledge, participation, and moral self-development.

Critics charge that deliberation may actually undermine democracy by producing a false consensus that submerges the interests and the voices of the less well established, becoming yet another vehicle for exercising power and domination (Barber 1984; Benhabib 1996; Bickford 1996; Bohman 1996; Chambers 1996; Cohen 1989; Fishkin 1995; Gutmann and Thompson 1996; Mansbridge 1983 and 1996; Sunstein 1993; Warren 1992 and 1996.). Addressing these debates requires a detailed cataloguing of how the deliberative interactions of citizens are organized and how they are perceived and experienced by their participants. Four components of deliberation are especially important in understanding the nature and quality of public talking.

ORGANIZING DELIBERATION

First, the quality of deliberation depends on its basic organization—its publicness, recruitment strategy, and orientation to collective as opposed to individualistic perspectives. Deliberation can be a private affair limited to a preselected set of stakeholders or a public event that is open to any who wish to attend. Recruitment of participants accordingly varies: private forums rely on invitations, and public events are open to the broader community.

The public or private nature of forums and their corresponding recruitment strategies reflect two contrasting perspectives. One perspective views private interest as insuperable: even well-intentioned efforts to search for the community's common good invariably submerge real differences in interest and values (Sanders 1997). Instead of obscuring or wishing away unavoidable and conflicting interests, this perspective suggests that deliberation should foster negotiation and bargaining over individual interests, often in private settings among identifiable stakeholders (Fisher and Ury 1981).

The second perspective suggests that a broader community of individuals can be gathered in public forums and transcend their differences to focus on their shared, collective considerations. This perspective rests on the assumption that collective decisions are better than individual ones, that groups tend to use information that is commonly shared and accepted rather than the self-interested claims of individuals, and that individuals can set aside a fixation with winning or losing to focus on how their fate is linked to others and search for outcomes that will benefit the larger collectivity (for a review of related research see Delli Carpini, Cook, and Jacobs 2004).

A critical question, then, in studying actual deliberation is whether street-level deliberators experience and perceive public talking as a private affair to achieve personal gain or a public affair intended to benefit the broad community. Are the deliberative forums that Americans attend eliciting a focus on private interests or on collective considerations?

REASON-ORIENTED DELIBERATION

The second component of the deliberative experience relates to the type of discursive activity by citizens. Advocates of deliberation insist that public talking should rely on reason—offering evidence, advancing claims grounded in logic and facts, and listening and responding to counterarguments (Benhabib 1996, 69; Gutmann and Thompson 2004, 12–21; Cohen 1998, 186; Warren 1992, 8). For many deliberationists, the giving of reasons is the principal distinguishing feature and strength of deliberation because it diminishes the impact of naked uses of power, false empirical claims, morally offensive views, and narrow self-interest.

The critics of deliberation warn that the cognitive capacity to engage effectively in reasoned debate is substantially lower for some individuals than for others, that it is unrealistic to expect rational deliberation from ordinary citizens untrained in policy issues and too busy or distracted to equip themselves, and that it invites passive dependence on experts and on the discursively skilled rather than active engagement by other participants (Honig 1996, 258, 272–73; Mouffe 1996, 254). It also discredits other legitimate forms of communication, including passionate appeals and boisterous expressions through rallies and other forms of public gatherings. The critics warn that deliberative forums are liable to become vehicles for promoting one narrow perspective, enabling motivated and well-versed advocates to manipulate and indoctrinate participants (Sanders 1997, 370; Dryzek 2000, vi, 4–6).

The moderator is a critical organizational figure in deliberation. The moderator's most direct responsibility is to create a "space" for talking and listening and to establish a process that is fair and is perceived as fair. John Forester (1999) argues that moderators are the "creators of public space . . . in which disputants as citizens meet and seek to refashion their lived worlds" (192). Leighninger (2006) reports that organizers of civic forums were "successful if [the facilitator] remained impartial: giving everyone a chance to speak, helping the group manage the allotted time, helping the group use discussion materials, and trying to manage conflicts within the group." By contrast, the efforts of facilitators who attempted to "direct the group toward a particular conclusion . . . would backfire" (6).

For many deliberationists, the effectiveness of moderators depends on their ability to remain independent and impartial and to enjoy the respect of deliberators for their detachment. An effective moderator facilitates the public expression of divergent perspectives and fosters respect for differences. Moderators may need to serve a more protective function—namely, to block the imposition of inappropriate arguments or attempts to wield power that intrudes on the ability or willingness of others to participate.

Research suggests that deliberative settings that give individuals the opportunity to express their views—a critical responsibility of the moderator—have positive effects. Such settings have been found to increase consideration for arguments made by others as well as perceptions by participants that the process is fair and the outcome legitimate, regardless of whether they agree substantively with the outcome (Thibaut and Walker 1975; Lind and Tyler 1988; Tyler 1994 and 2001; Tyler and Blader 2000).

Reaching Agreement through Deliberation

The third component of the deliberative experience concerns the effect of public dialogue on the opinions of participants—the generation of agreement and narrowing of differences or the airing of disagreement and conflict. The proponents of deliberation emphasize that vigorous citizen deliberation leads to reflection and learning, awareness of similarities and appreciation of differing perspectives, and convergence toward a "common shared perspective" and support for joint gains (Benhabib 1985, 348–49, and 1992; Chambers 1996; Smith and Wales 2000; Gutmann and Thompson 1996). One study of fiscal policy discussions found, for instance, that increased deliberation among rival groups of partisans increased consensual decision making that identified which taxes to raise and which government programs to cut to reduce the federal budget deficit (Gaertner et al. 1999). Research on small groups indicates that discussion moves collective opinion in the direction of the preexisting views of the majority (Moscovici and Zavalloni 1969; Myers and Lamm 1976; Schkade, Sunstein, and Kahneman 2000). The conversion to the majority perspective has been attributed to the greater capacity of the majority—owing to its larger size—to formulate more novel, valid, and convincing arguments that genuinely change the opinions of those in the minority (Burnstein, Vinokur, and Trope 1973; Burnstein and Vinokur 1977; Vinokur and Burnstein 1978). Where disagreements remain, deliberationists expect that the process of "reason-giving" and public "justifications" will help citizens to narrow their differences with opponents and will foster continuing efforts to find common ground (Gutmann and Thompson 2004, 7, 20, 36, 93–94).

Deliberationists suggest that the organization, mission, and use of moderators trained in building consensus and resolving disputes contribute to the "joint search . . . for newly fashioned agreements" (Forester 1999, 196; Susskind and Ozawa 1984). Rules or expectations that deliberation should reach agreement have been found to increase the amount of deliberation, the search for agreement, and satisfaction with the process as fair (Kameda 1991; Kaplan and Miller 1987; Nemeth 1977; Davis, Bray, and Holt 1977; Davis et al. 1989).

Critics of deliberation have posed several negative (though distinct) effects on public opinion from public talking. Some warn that airing different perspectives in public forums can intensify disagreements and further polarize citizens by exacerbating and reinforcing existing social divisions (Mansbridge 1996; Sunstein 2002). One experiment that varied the level of participation in political decision making concluded that deliberation creates "dislike" and can "exacerbate already present divisions," and that the pursuit of agreement can increase polarization, especially in the face of genuinely conflicting interests and values (Morrell 1999, 318; Mendelberg and Karpowitz 2000; Mansbridge 1983). Other critics offer an alternative interpretation: deliberation may produce "false" agreement that sublimates genuine disagreements and differences (Young 1996, 126, 133; Sanders 1997). Some research has shown that individuals in the minority continue privately to harbor dissenting views but publicly acquiesce in the face of majorities (Davis, Bray, and Holt 1977; Davis et al. 1988; Davis et al. 1989; Penrod and Hastie 1980).

Tolerating Difference

The fourth component of the deliberative experience is toleration of difference. Research shows that the majorities in deliberative settings respect and even seek out new perspectives and new information presented by individuals in the minority and become more open and empathetic with their views (Walsh 2007; Nemeth 1986; Nemeth and Kwan 1985; Nemeth and Wachtler 1983; Turner 1991; Nemeth and Mayseless 1987; Nemeth and Rogers 1996; and Moscovici 1980). Open-mindedness and tolerance of minority views appear to be tied to the presence of objective information and credible alternative arguments from those perceived as experts. Tolerance has also been attributed to rules and expectations (such as a requirement to seek agreement) that encourage respect for difference (Bottger 1984; Kirchler and Davis 1986; Ridgeway 1981 and 1987; Maass and Clark 1984; Moscovici 1980; Wood et al. 1994; Kameda 1991).

Although deliberation appears to elicit tolerance, there are grounds for caution regarding rejection and hostility toward those in the "out group." Some research suggests that individuals who expect to be in the majority ignore opposing views, though, in fairness, members of the minority also consciously ignore information that contradicts their perspective (Levine and Russo 1995; Zdaniuk and Levine 1996).

THE CONDITIONALITY OF DELIBERATION

The deliberative experience is conditioned by several factors that our survey allows us to examine. First, the size of forums (i.e., how many people attended) may interact with several deliberative elements. For instance, face-to-face deliberation in small groups may foster participation, toleration, and positive emotional reactions that are absent in larger forums. Respondents to our survey indicated, however, that face-to-face deliberation occurred in relatively large meetings in which participants were not particularly well acquainted. Deliberators reported that, on average, 83 people attended meetings, with a median of 40 participants. Only half of face-to-face deliberators indicated that they were acquainted with all or most of the other people attending—a surprising figure, given the expectation that face-to-face meetings typically involve family, friends, and neighbors. One-quarter reported knowing only a few or none of the other participants; the other quarter indicated that they were familiar with "some" of the other attendees. (Not surprisingly, chat rooms are more anonymous than in-person meetings; almost one-half of respondents knew no one in the chat room, and about 90% believed that participants were from outside their local community.) Second, the selection of topics for public discussion and their differential salience may interact with perceptions of diversity and emotional reactions. For example, "racialized" domestic issues may give rise to perception of more ethnically and racially diverse forums.

Given the complexity of deliberation and diversity of contexts, many might expect *discursive heterogeneity*—namely, that Americans might report a wide array of deliberative experiences and perceptions rather than coalescing around strong central tendencies. This would mean that the actual deliberation of Americans may well be characterized by a mixture of both public meetings that recruit widely, search for agreement grounded in reason, and foster toleration and more private meetings that draw more narrowly, accept disagreement, and are marked by close-mindedness.

Studying Street-Level Deliberation

This chapter examines in detail the actual experiences and perceptions of Americans in what is often touted as the quintessential deliberative forum—the face-to-face meeting. In particular, we concentrate on an unweighted sample of 756 respondents who indicated that they participated in face-to-face deliberation—a sample large enough for quantitative analysis. We did not weight this sample because our principal concern is to describe what face-to-face deliberators encounter rather than to generalize about the U.S. population as a whole. We also believe that it is plausible to consider this sample of 756 respondents as a random draw of forum participants in the population. This sample includes respondents in our full sample who were forum participants as well as an oversample, which was drawn by contacting a random sample of the adult population and then using a screen question to select forum participants for additional questions.

We also occasionally examine a smaller, unweighted sample of 105 respondents who reported using the Internet to discuss local, national, and world issues in chat rooms. Although we find the Internet exchanges in chat rooms to be intriguing, we focus our analysis on the larger sample of face-to-face deliberators. We refer to both groups as "street-level deliberators."

Our analysis of deliberative experiences relied in particular on the reactions of respondents to two series of questions. The first asked about the purpose of the deliberative forum that they attended.[1] The second focused on the respondent's own experiences and perceptions of the forum.[2]

Although we expected the actual experiences and perceptions of deliberators to be quite diverse, their reports on face-to-face deliberation were remarkably similar. There is a central tendency toward the democratic outcomes that deliberationists herald.

ORGANIZING THE COMMUNITY

Americans reported that they attended deliberative forums geared toward community—that is, the forums recruited widely and focused on shared, collective considerations.

Convening a Public Sphere

Civic forums are generally public rather than private or exclusive events. Deliberators reported that they pitched in to help organize forums and that community organizations sponsored them. Forty-six percent reported that they or someone they knew personally helped to organize face-to-face forums, and three-quarters indicated that an organized group like a religious or civic body sponsored or organized the event. The most frequently mentioned organizations were civic or community organizations (26%), government bodies (23%), church or religious groups (22%), and schools (13%). It is telling that a business or business organization was rarely mentioned (3%).

The public nature of face-to-face forums is also evident in their placement in familiar and accessible community locations. Deliberators reported that only 11% of meetings were in a personal home. By contrast, 87% of deliberators reported that the meetings were held in public spaces. Of these forums in public spaces, 29% were in schools and colleges, 18% were in churches, synagogues, or other religious facilities, 16% were in a government building, and another 15% assembled in other public buildings.

Recruiting the Wider Community

Fitting with the public character of deliberation, deliberators report that the forums they attended recruited widely rather than simply drawing on tightly knit circles of friends. Sixty-five percent pointed to organizations, the media, or some other form of communication and recruitment. Only 22% said they found out about the meeting they attended from a friend, neighbor, or family member. Deliberators did not put a particularly strong premium on the importance of being personally asked to participate: when asked to rate the importance of a variety of potential factors to their decision to attend a deliberative forum, 36% scored having been personally contacted between 8 and 10 in importance, with only 24% giving this reason the highest score (i.e., a 10 on a scale from 0 to 10). Clearly, recruitment is important, even though the invitation does not have to be personally delivered by a friend. Recruitment to Internet chat rooms follows a similar pattern. Only one-fifth of respondents learned of the chat room from a familiar person.

Deliberators tend to be drawn into civic forums, then, through public rather than private means. This pattern in face-to-face meetings and Internet-based chat rooms suggests that public deliberation may deserve more attention as a means for "socializing" debate on matters of concern to the broader community (Schattschneider 1960).

Community Concerns Motivate Participation

Whether deliberators are motivated by self-interest or by more genuinely collective considerations is a critical and hotly debated question. According to our survey, public deliberation in America consistently tilts toward collective as opposed to personal considerations. This is evident in the convening of meetings, recruitment of participants, and motivation for attending.

Deliberators mostly attend public meetings because of concerns about others as well as their own situation. Table 4.1 shows the mean scores for six reasons that might motivate Americans to participate in face-to-face forums. The most highly rated motivation is that the topic under discussion at the meetings "affected other people who live in my community": the

Table 4.1   Reasons for participating in civic forums

REASONS FOR PARTICIPATING IN LAST MEETING	MEANS
Affect others in community[1]	8.2 (2.7)
Duty[2]	7.7 (2.9)
Affect me and my family[3]	7.5 (3.2)
Sounded interesting[4]	6.5 (3.5)
Chance to meet other people[5]	6.0 (3.5)
Personally asked[6]	4.8 (4.0)

Source: Discursive Participation Survey. Face-to-face deliberation sample: N = 756 (unweighted).
Notes: Entries are based on reason-for-participation scores: 11-point scales ranging from 0 ("not important at all") to 10 ("very important.") The second column contains mean scores, with standard deviations in parentheses. Respondents who refused to answer or responded "Don't know" were excluded when calculating the means.
1 "The issue under discussion directly affected other people who live in my community."
2 "I felt it was my duty as a citizen or member of the community."
3 "The issue under discussion directly affected me and my family."
4 "The issue under discussion just sounded interesting to me."
5 "It was a chance to meet or talk to other people who share my interests."
6 "Because I was personally asked by someone to participate."

mean was 8.2, with 77% scoring this between 8 and 10 in importance, and more than half (53%) giving it the highest score (10). The second strongest motivation for attending a deliberative forum was the sense of "duty as a citizen or member of the community": the mean was 7.7, with 66% scoring this between 8 and 10, and 45% giving it the highest score.

Research on sociotropism and self-interest has found, though, that collective and personal considerations often coexist. Indeed, concern that the meeting "directly affected me and my family" was also a major reason for participation: the mean was 7.5, with 66% scoring this between 8 and 10, and 46% giving it the highest score. This suggests that personal circumstances also motivated participation.

Personal gratification and recruitment were notably less important reasons for respondents to participate in face-to-face meetings. In the context of other considerations, deliberators were not especially drawn by genuine intellectual curiosity—namely, for the reason that the meeting "sounded interesting to me." The mean score for this question was 6.5, with 52% scoring this between 8 and 10. Nor were they drawn centrally by a "chance to meet or talk with other people who share my interests" (mean 6.0; only 44% scored this between 8 and 10). Deliberators reported that attending because of being "personally asked" exerted even less pull (mean of 4.8).

In sum, concerns about how issues in communities affected individuals, their families, and others were reported as the strongest motivations for participating in civic forums. Personal edification was a weaker draw. Deliberation by Americans appears to be a public activity motivated by collective considerations (along with attention to one's personal circumstances) rather than by a single-minded focus on advancing personal interests.

DELIBERATING WITH REASON

The results of our survey suggest that public deliberation tends to be cognitive, relying on reading, evidence, and reasoned argument.

Preparing for Deliberation

Equipping deliberators with unbiased information was a common practice. Face-to-face deliberators assigned a mean rating of 7.5 to the importance that their forum placed on the goal of "teach[ing] people about the issue in a neutral, factual way" (s.d. 2.8). The distribution of responses was clustered toward agreeing that this goal was "very important": 60% scored this between 8 and 10, with 37% indicating the latter). Visitors to chat rooms gave lower ratings for the importance of neutral education (mean 5.4, s.d. 3.5).

In addition, 41% of face-to-face deliberators reported that their meeting had a guest whose role was to "serve as a neutral expert . . . and to help educate participants." The tendency to equip deliberators with the empirical tools to engage in reasoned debate and to use experts reflects a commitment to pursuing a cognitive approach to deliberation.

Reading to Deliberate

Two-thirds of face-to-face deliberators reported receiving reading materials to help them "better understand or think about the issue" under discussion, with most receiving it before (60%) or during the meeting (28%). Written material was less common for the Internet forums; 24% of Internet deliberators received reading material, most before (57%) or during (17%) their session.

The reading materials were a tool for explaining different perspectives or neutrally describing the facts rather than pushing a slanted outlook. A third of face-to-face deliberators who received reading materials said they offered a balanced account of different perspectives, and 30% more responded that the materials were "neutral and objective." By comparison, a smaller proportion (37%) indicated that the reading materials were "biased in favor of a particular point of view," and 44% of Internet deliberators who received written materials said they were biased.

Moderating for Reason

Moderators are a common feature of public deliberation in America. Eighty-three percent of face-to-face deliberators indicated that someone was responsible for leading or facilitating the meeting (only 36% of Internet deliberators reported a moderator).

Facilitators tended to be neutral agents. Deliberators rated their discussion leaders well on an 11-point scale for "trying to educate the meeting's participants about the issue being discussed in a neutral, balanced way" (mean 6.9, s.d. 2.9). The distribution of responses was clustered toward agreeing that their facilitators were balanced "very often" (the ratings of 50% fell between 8 and 10, with 27% indicating the latter).

Deliberation in America appears to be consistently grounded in the use of balanced information and fairly moderated reason-giving. Indeed, the pillars of this cognitive approach—fair moderation and balanced information—are strongly associated: neutral, balanced facilitation is highly correlated ($r = .52$) with neutral and factual teaching as a meeting goal (sig. at .001).

In short, fears that deliberation is a vehicle for promoting one narrow perspective—allowing advocates to indoctrinate participants and advance self-serving claims—do not appear to be supported by the experiences reported. Instead, public talking appears to be anchored in a process that provides fair opportunities for assembling information and for offering reasoned argument from multiple and competing perspectives. Although this does not prohibit attempts at manipulation and coercion or the internalization of ideological positions, there is a surprising convergence toward norms, expectations, and organizational features that diminish the naked uses of power, false empirical claims, morally offensive views, and narrow self-interest.

TALKING TOWARD AGREEMENT

Respondents reported that the face-to-face forums they attended were largely focused on reaching agreement. The reactions of deliberators suggest that these forums tend to be organized to balance the aim of generating agreement with respect for individual perspectives and an apparent hesitance to use facilitators to impose a false consensus, as critics of deliberation have worried.

Seeking Agreement and Moderating Difference

Deliberators indicated that the purpose of the last forum they attended was to allow people to reach agreement. The mean rating of whether the goal of civic forums and its facilitators was to reach agreement was 7.3 (on a scale from 0 to 10). Thirty-two percent ranked this at 10—that is, the highest possible score. Facilitators were not necessarily an engine for forcing consensus: deliberators gave weaker ratings for facilitators helping the group reach agreement on an issue (mean 5.8). Ratings of facilitators in forging agreement were widely dispersed (s.d. 3.4), and the ratings of agreement as the purpose of meetings were less so (s.d. 2.8).

Reaching agreement is a central organizing principle of face-to-face deliberation. The orientations of the meeting and the facilitator toward agreement were highly correlated (r = .48 at .001 level). Deliberation in America appears geared, then, toward generating agreement, but it does not seem to rely on facilitators trying to force consensus where it does not exist.

Americans' experience with Internet chat rooms helps to underscore the distinctive commitment of face-to-face forums to reaching agreement. Coming to agreement was far less important in chat rooms (mean 5.4, s.d. 3.5). This is consistent with conventional assumptions about Internet talk.

Publicly Airing Differences

While reaching agreement is a central organizing principle of the forums attended by our respondents, these meetings also appear to have avoided the risk of suppressing disagreement out of a dogged pursuit of agreement. Large majorities of face-to-face deliberators agreed that their meetings were organized to "air differences of opinion and discuss different points of view." The mean rating was 7.7 (s.d. 2.8). The ratings of 66% of deliberators fell between 8 and 10, with 42% indicating the latter.

The airing of differences is encouraged by the organization of forums and the roles assigned to discussion leaders. There is a strong correlation of .49 between a forum's airing of differences and facilitators hearing all opinions (sig. at .001).

Publicly discussing differences apparently connects to the broader search for commonalities. We found that the tendency of facilitators to "help the group come to agreement" is correlated (sig. at .001 level) with the commitment of the forum to "air[ing] differences" (r = .16).

The public discussion of differences in deliberative forums does not appear to involve a concerted effort to strong-arm or channel the views of participants—a pattern that could discourage or silence dissent and conflict. Face-to-face deliberators did not commonly report efforts by facilitators to "convince people of a particular point of view." The mean rating was 5.0 (s.d. 3.5), with responses distributed in nearly equal thirds. Attempts at persuasion by forum leaders were a bit more likely in larger meetings: the efforts of facilitators to convince people were correlated (albeit weakly, r = .16, sig. at .001 level) with large meetings (i.e., meetings with more than 30 attendees).

In another sign that advocacy was not prevalent, participants in civic forums infrequently encountered "people whose roles were to formally advocate for or debate different points of view." Only 35% reported the presence of an advocate in their last meeting. Where advocates or different points of view were present, they were weakly associated with the airing of differences (r = .16 at .001 sig. level).

Overall, then, face-to-face deliberation does not appear to rely persistently on stereotyped arm twisting by a dogged advocate. Instead, public talk in face-to-face meetings tends to rely on raising differences and allowing the discussion of these differences to convince people, with some encouragement by facilitators. These findings are consistent with the optimistic appraisals of deliberation and its democratic potential.

In summary, we found no consistent and strong evidence that deliberation intensifies disagreement, as deliberation critics fear. In addition, the fear that deliberation suppresses disagreement is also not directly evident. The critics of deliberation may pose a false dichotomy between agreement and disagreement on the assumption that the two are inversely related—that is, that an orientation toward seeking agreement would invariably suppress disagreement. Our findings suggest that disagreements have been aired even as face-to-face forums move toward finding areas of shared interests and concerns.

The Norm of Toleration and the Unease of the Minority

One of the most persistent questions about public deliberation is whether it breeds toleration by broadening understanding of different perspectives or generates disrespect or neglect of the perspectives of minorities. The lived experiences of Americans in face-to-face forums offer two bodies of evidence that seem to support the more optimistic scenario, though the reactions of a small minority hint at sobering possibilities.

A Central Tendency toward Toleration

Toleration is evident in two main themes. First, most deliberators report that the forums create a kind of marketplace of ideas. Most face-to-face deliberators report that facilitators were committed to "making sure that everyone's opinions were heard." The mean score was 8.1 (s.d. 2.4), with 42% scoring this role of discussion leaders at the highest possible level (10), while 2% scored it as 0, or "not often at all." Similarly, deliberators recorded that "allow[ing] people to air differences of opinion and discuss different points of view" was also quite important; the mean score was 7.7 (s.d. 2.8), with 42% scoring it 10, and 4% scoring it 0. Internet deliberators reported a similar respect for allowing people to discuss different perspectives (mean 8.1, s.d. 2.8).

Agreement flows from awareness and respect. The organization of face-to-face forums to give participants the opportunity to reach agreement and decide on concrete actions is robustly correlated in the .28–.36 range, with facilitators working to ensure that everyone's opinion is heard and to make the airing of differences a goal of public meetings.

Second, most face-to-face deliberators did not express emotional reactions and feelings that suggested a significant sense of anxiety or anger that might be associated with intimidation and intolerance. They indicated feeling little anger during the last meeting attended; the mean score was among the lowest recorded (2.9; s.d. 3.1): 36% indicated "not often at all" (0), with a much smaller proportion (5%) describing it as "very often" (10). Deliberators also expressed little anxiety. The mean score for anxiety was 3.7 (s.d. 3.3); 28% said they felt this "not often at all," and 7% registered a 10, which may reflect discomfort with talking in public.

The articulation of different perspectives in an environment that was not threatening to most participants contributed to somewhat broader understanding and agreement as well as a general sense of improved well-being during the forums. The public forums did not appear to force decisions on participants. More than 90% of deliberators reported that they agreed with the decision of the forum (94%) and that other participants agreed as well (95%); about 6% disagreed with the decision of their group. Most deliberators expressed a sense of "more understanding of different points of view" during the meeting; the mean was 6.2 (s.d. 2.7), and 37% of the ratings were between 8 and 10. Moreover, deliberators emerged from civic forums with a sense of well-being and satisfaction; the mean score for feeling "enthusiastic" during the meeting was 6.6 (s.d. 2.6).

Warnings from the Minority

Although most deliberators found civic forums to be tolerant, a critical indicator of how opposing ideas are received lies in the reactions of the minority. Although they were few, those who expressed concerns deserve attention in evaluating toleration within face-to-face forums. Six percent of face-to-face deliberators reported disagreeing with the forum's decisions. This may not warrant alarm in itself, but similar proportions noted that making sure everyone's opinions were heard was not often a priority for facilitators, that the forum did not make airing differences an important goal, and that they felt anger during the last meeting. (It may also be of concern that the standard deviations for these ratings tended to be greater than the mean or fairly close to them.)

Although the views of a minority may point to intolerance, there may be less ominous explanations. The small numbers may reflect statistical "noise" in the survey. They may also be the natural result of vibrant discussions. In addition, individual ease with public talking varies; some of the discomfort with the deliberative experience may reflect unease among some respondents about engaging in discursive activities, especially face-to-face forums, rather than coercive or intolerant civic forums.

CONTINGENCY AND CONDITIONALITY

The context of public deliberation matters. Organizational decisions and the real-world contexts of public talking may significantly affect deliberation. In particular, we explore two conditions that may influence deliberation—the size of forums and the selection of specific topics for public talking.

Deliberation Comes in All Sizes

Size has long been considered a potential influence on deliberation. The ideal deliberative forum is often described as a small gathering where participation, reason, and tolerance are expected to be most likely (Bryan 2004).

Our analysis of face-to-face deliberation finds, however, that size does not have a consistent influence on deliberative interactions. Smaller size is associated with more participation, and facilitators are a bit more prone to attempt to convince deliberators of a particular point of view in meetings of more than thirty participants.

The impact of meeting size is not pervasive, however, which contradicts the claims of some previous research (e.g., Bryan 2004). Meeting size did not influence a set of crucial organizational characteristics, from the tendency to listen to all opinions to various characteristics of the forums. Meeting size was also not associated with a range of emotional reactions by deliberators; reports of enthusiasm, anger, and anxiety were not affected by whether the groups were large or small. These nonfindings appear to contradict the expectation that the ideal small meeting will systematically produce qualitatively different dynamics.

The Topic Matters

The selection of the topic for deliberation may be a particularly important contextual factor. The subject matter—its salience, and connection to the values and interests of deliberators and Americans more generally—may affect perceptions regarding the distribution or concentration of costs and benefits and the identity and motivation of deliberators.

In our study of face-to-face deliberators, 69% reported attending forums that discussed principally one topic. (We gave respondents an opportunity to identify multiple topics.) The forums tended to focus on a group of six topics. Table 4.2 shows that local issues and international issues related to terrorism and the war in Iraq were the most common topics, accounting for 24% and 23%, respectively, of the topics identified by deliberators. Children's issues were the third most commonly cited topics (18%), followed by social policy (14%), social welfare and economic policy issues (6%), economic development policy (5%), and a cluster of miscellaneous topics (10%). Local issues accounted for 24% of the topics mentioned by deliberators. The findings in Table 4.2 contradict a suspicion that public deliberation tends to be myopic and excessively oriented toward disconnected neighborhood issues. Three-quarters of the topics addressed in civic forums concerned broad, interrelated policies.

Our study indicates that the topic matters. The selection of social welfare and economic policy as the subject of deliberation tended to increase perceptions of racial and ethnic diversity. For all other issues, perceptions of racial and ethnic diversity were relatively low. The elevated perceptions of ascriptive diversity may reflect a genuine change in turnout—discussion of social welfare and economic policy may generate a higher turnout of racial and ethnic minorities—or it may heighten sensitivity among deliberators to racial and ethnic differences. Although we lack evidence to sort out the likely explanation, there are hints that topic selection may prime elevated perceptions of diversity. We did not find evidence that racial and ethnic group turnout was heightened during discussions of social welfare and economic policy. In addition, deliberators attributed their attendance at meetings concerning these issues to a sense of "duty as a citizen or member of the community." Moreover, social welfare and economic policy were also associated with reports of enthusiasm and elevated anxiety, hinting at the role of acute perceptions.

Deliberation over the set of issues related to terrorism and the Iraq war generated higher than average levels of anger, anxiety, and participation by respondents. These discussions were also marked by proportionately fewer meetings that included an advocate; Americans were apparently sufficiently informed and did not want (or need) an advocate to help them articulate their views. Moreover, deliberators addressing these topics were more motivated by their "interest" in the topic than their commitment to issues that "directly affect other people who live in my community."

In contrast to social welfare and national security policies, the sometimes technical nature of economic development policies appeared to depress engagement. Discussion of these issues stands out a bit for lower

Table 4.2   Number and percentage of topics by policy category

TOPIC	FREQUENCY	PERCENTAGE (%)
Local issues	177	24
War/Terrorism/Iraq/Middle East	175	23
Children's issues	133	18
Social policy	107	14
Other issues	73	10
Social welfare and economic policy	46	6
Economic development	37	5

Source: Discursive Participation Survey. Face-to-face deliberation sample: N = 756 (unweighted).
Notes: Entries are frequencies and percentages of responses to the question, "What public issue did you discuss [in the most recent meeting you attended]?" Up to four responses were allowed. Respondents were asked subsequent probes for additional topics (see questions 6b, c, and d in the questionnaire available online at http://www.press.uchicago.edu/books/jacobs).

than average enthusiasm and participation by respondents; there were also higher reports that advocates were present, which organizers may consider necessary to generate full discussion. Not surprisingly, personal motivation was also higher than for other issues: the significance of economic development for living standards tended to motivate Americans to attend because the topic "directly affected me and my family"; it also provoked higher anxiety and a greater diversity of points of view. Perhaps because of the focus on class rather than identity, perceptions of racial and ethnic diversity tended to be lower for economic development policy than for other policy issues.

Social issues (namely, crime, safety, and religion) were also associated with unique deliberative features. Discussion of these issues tended to draw people who were personally recruited to attend. The connection of crime, safety, and religion to discrete neighborhoods and distinct communities may have provided concrete motivations to bring people out to meetings that discussed them.

Conclusion

The argument over deliberation among scholars and practitioners often boils down to what actually happens inside civic forums. The experiences and perceptions of the actual deliberators are critical to assessing the importance of deliberation for democracy. The general thrust of our findings indicates that deliberation is generally supportive of two democratic dynamics. The first concerns the quality of interactions. Face-to-face deliberators consistently report that the forums they attended relied on expert information, reason-giving, and toleration. This argues against the fear that deliberation would breed substantial coercion and intolerance.

The second theme to emerge from street-level deliberators is their regular focus on collective considerations—talking with members of their community about how their fate is linked to others and searching for outcomes that will benefit the larger collectivity. Deliberators consistently reported that face-to-face forums were genuinely public spaces where a wide spectrum of the community could gather to talk about their shared interests and pursue broad areas of agreement. Deliberators did not report the kind of fixation with winning or losing an advantage that is sometimes attributed to American public life.

Even with these broad themes, though, the deliberative experience was contingent on size and, especially, the topic chosen for discussion. We also found that small numbers of deliberators did report dissatisfaction that pointed to the potential of intolerance. Although this potential deserves careful scrutiny, there are several explanations for the critical responses that may not be related to systematic intolerance—such as personal discomfort with public speaking and the nature of survey research.

Knowing more about the lived experiences of Americans in public deliberations expands our understanding of a critical component of civic life in the United States. We now turn to an important question that remains: What difference does deliberation make in the civic and political life of Americans?

FIVE

The Civic and Political Impacts of Discursive Participation

What impact, if any, do public talk and deliberation have on subsequent civic and political behavior? Deliberation and other forms of public talking have been persistently downgraded as "just talk," ineffective and perhaps a cause of citizen disengagement. A variety of research studies report that deliberation's impact is slight or nonexistent and may actually prompt a decline in civic and political participation (Mutz 2006; Ryfe 2005; Button and Ryfe 2005). One review of deliberative theory and practice was moved to ask, "What real purpose does deliberation serve?" (Button and Mattson 1999, 629).

Doubts about the value and impact of deliberation stem in part from unfavorable comparisons with other forms of citizen participation that involve citizens taking concrete and observable action. Voting, protesting, volunteering, and other forms of political and civic behavior produce observable consequences for the individual and the community—from changes in local government policy to new state and federal government laws. Such actions reward citizens who participate and thus encourage their continued engagement. Typical of the unfavorable comparison of discursive participation with action-oriented participation, one of the most comprehensive studies of political participation completely leaves out public talk in its catalogue of citizen engagement (Verba, Schlozman, and Brady 1995).[1]

Researchers, political theorists, and community organizers continue to insist, however that deliberation does have a positive impact on civil and political engagement. In particular, public talk may directly influence the deliberation of government through appointed bodies or the transmission of citizen views in ways that may "blu[r] the line between governors and the governed" (Leighninger 2006, 15–18). For instance, deliberative efforts have been a part of such diverse policy areas as forest management, urban planning in Philadelphia, and Social Security reform (Gastil and Keith 2005). In addition, some insist that "deliberation shapes participants' opinions." This impact of deliberation can have indirect effects on government by influencing citizen resources and motivations. They may also exert broader affects on society's civic culture and discourse—the assumptions, language, and shared meanings that set the boundaries for civil and political action (Gastil 2008, xii, chaps. 2 and 8). Katherine Cramer Walsh (2007) reports that civic dialogues can contribute to improved race relations among citizens, and other analysts point to Philadelphia's project, Citizen Voices; the National Issue Forums; and Citizen Juries as improving the public's judgment (Gastil and Keith 2005).

One of the most important and telling questions, therefore, remains unanswered: Does deliberation increase other forms of political and civic participation? This chapter offers the first systematic analyses of the effects of deliberation on political attitudes and on civic and political participation. It begins by specifying the direct and indirect paths by which deliberation might (or might not) exert an impact and then draws on a variety of data and quantitative methods to disentangle the relationships between deliberation and citizen engagement.

Understanding the Effects of Discursive Participation

There are at least four challenges to understanding the political impact of discursive participation. First, we need a conceptual framework that allows us to parse the direct and indirect ways in which discursive participation may affect public life. If we do not specify the paths by which deliberation can affect politics, we cannot investigate them. Researchers may thus fail to examine critical connections and falsely conclude that discursive participation has no tangible effect.

Second, if public talk and deliberation do exert direct or indirect influences on civic and political life, we need to explain the mechanisms by which this occurs. As part of this, we must explain why such effects might vary for different types of civic and political engagement. Third, we need valid and reliable data that allow us to investigate systematically the potential effects of public talk. Past research has largely relied either on in-depth case studies or on experimental or quasi-experimental designs. Examples of such studies include analyses of courtroom juries, of the Kettering Foundation's National Issues Forums, and of the Deliberative Polls designed by James Fishkin (1995; cf. Cook, Barabas, and Jacobs 2003). Although instructive, these case-specific studies examine discrete and often self-selected sets of participants or (in the case of Deliberative Polls or laboratory experiments) are better at demonstrating potential more than actual effects. As a result, they are less able to provide a basis for drawing

Policy	Issue-specific engagement	General engagement	Political capital	Shared meanings
(1)	(2)	(3)	(4)	(5)
Impact on policy agenda and outcomes	Increased political (e.g., voting, contacting) and civic (e.g., volunteering) participation around specific issue (e.g.,crime)	Increased political (e.g., voting contacting) and civic (e.g., volunteering) participation in general	Increased motivation (e.g., political interest) and ability (e.g., political knowledge) to participate	Greater agreement on foundational issues (e.g., what constitutes the public interest, community, citizenship)

Direct effects	← ——————————————————————— →	Indirect effects

FIGURE 5.1   HYPOTHESIZED EFFECTS OF DISCURSIVE PARTICIPATION

conclusions about the real-world effects of public talk and deliberation on the general public.

The fourth challenge is to address the complicated issue of causality. Public talk and public action may be correlated, but does engaging in the former *lead to* more of the latter? This is a particularly daunting challenge, but meeting it is essential for isolating the effects of deliberation. Accordingly, this chapter devotes special attention to this challenge, beginning with a mapping of direct and indirect effects of deliberation on civic and political behavior.

POTENTIAL EFFECTS OF DISCURSIVE PARTICIPATION

Political theorists and researchers have identified a wide range of potential impacts of discursive participation in general and of public deliberation more specifically. These hypothesized effects vary in their degree of explicit and direct connection to the public policy process.

Figure 5.1 outlines some of these connections. At one extreme, deliberation can be a means for directly influencing legislative and executive processes and outcomes. At the other extreme, it can exert a more indirect civic and political influence through the formation of new socially constructed and shared meanings, understandings, and discourses. While our data only allow us to examine part of this larger array of hypothesized effects, it is important to situate our work in this larger context.

Direct Effects of Discursive Participation on the Public Policy Process

Discursive participation may directly affect the policy process (see fig. 5.1, column 1). There are two potential direct paths. The first and most concrete direct impact occurs when political talk—most commonly in the form of formal deliberation—is explicitly tied to the policy process itself. The most obvious examples are local, state and national regulations requiring "public input" in the creation, implementation, or assessment of policies regarding issues such as economic development, urban planning, land and energy use, the location of hazardous waste sites, health insurance, and the like. But less formal connections to the policy process, as when public officials attend or support public forums focusing on particular issues, can also exert a direct impact on policy agendas and outcomes.

A second potential direct (albeit, lesser) impact involves formally organized deliberative processes by, for example, a nonprofit, advocacy group, newspaper, or television station that is independent of explicit government involvement or support. Even less formal or organized public talk, when its volume reaches a threshold point, can in theory directly influence local, state, and even national policy agendas, forcing public officials to address previously neglected issues. Based on his organization of Deliberative Polls, Fishkin (1991) argues that the citizen preferences resulting from deliberation have a "recommending effect" on lawmakers, who feel pressure to respond to this educated opinion. In all these cases, the impact of discursive participation is ultimately manifested within the formal institutions of representative government and involves the direct, observable influence of citizen deliberators over official government policy (Dahl 1956).

There is at least some evidence that deliberative forums can have a direct effect on policy. For example, Gastil (2000) found that a 1984 "community visioning process" in Chattanooga, Tennessee, which involved fifty community activists and volunteers meeting over a twenty-week period, produced a list of priorities and solutions that included a shelter for abused women and a riverfront park. Spurred by these deliberative forums, the organizers developed a series of neighborhood associations and new nonprofit organizations, and by 1992 most of the solutions proposed in the forums had been implemented. Gastil also found that from 1980 to 1990 a nonprofit organization in Oregon organized hundreds of neighborhood forums across the state in which citizens discussed the state's health care problems. As a result, in 1990 the state legislature created the Health Services Commission, which adopted the same citizen forum model to provide more official guidance and input. Within a year these forums contributed to a list of statewide health care priorities that were used to guide government action in this area.

Sirianni and Friedland (2001) point to similar cases in which organized, community-based deliberation led to policy change. Moreover, in the aftermath of Hurricane Katrina, several affected communities instituted formal and informal neighborhood forums that played a direct role in developing and implementing recovery plans (Tierney 2006).

Not all the evidence is positive, however. For example, Lindeman (2002) found that citizen deliberation contributed to building support for health care reform and environmental regulation during the 1990s, but that the federal government failed to act on these issues in ways consonant with public opinion (cf. Jacobs and Shapiro 2000).

The Indirect Effects of Discursive Participation on the Public Policy Process

Deliberation may have a number of indirect effects on political and civic participation.

Increasing Issue-Specific and General Political and Civic Participation

An indirect but still powerful potential impact of discursive participation may be to increase the likelihood that participants will follow up their talk with action *on the specific issue under discussion* (fig. 5.1, column 2). Deliberation may motivate and equip individuals to act on behalf of specific policy issues through political avenues such as financially supporting, campaigning for, or voting for candidates who share their views; contacting or lobbying public officials; signing petitions; and participating in rallies and protests.

Some research indicates that public deliberation can have such mobilizing effects. In the next chapter we discuss a concerted national effort to engage participants in discussions about reform options proposed for Social Security and then to encourage them to influence elected officials and become involved in the political process. Similarly, though in a way that is less connected to the formal mechanisms of government, discursive participation can provide citizens with the motivations and resources to take action on particular issues in the civic rather than the explicitly political sphere (fig. 5.1, column 2). Examples of such civic participation might include following up an informal discussion or deliberation on the issue of homelessness by volunteering time at a soup kitchen, or contributing to or joining an organization devoted to this issue. Wuthnow (1994) provides evidence of such effects; he found that participants in small group discussions about social justice and peace issues reported increasing the amount of time and money they subsequently devoted to organizations committed to these issues.

An even more indirect but possibly more important outcome of discursive participation is that it may increase citizens' general (rather than issue-specific) political or civic participation (fig. 5.1, column 3). For example, Gastil, Dees, and Weiser (2002) found that participants in jury deliberations were subsequently more likely to vote in elections. Delli Carpini (1997) found that citizens who participated in a series of deliberative discussions about the role of money in politics reported being more likely to participate in a variety of other forms of political and civic participation. Gastil (2000, 118–19) found that participants in the Kettering Foundation's National Issues Forums increased their general level of political activity. Moreover, Wuthnow (1994) found that participants in "the small group movement" who deliberated were subsequently moved to pursue a range of activities, including the following: help others in the group (74%); help others outside of the group (62%); donate money to a charitable organization (57%); volunteer in their community (43%); participate in a political rally; or work for a political campaign (12%).

Increasing Political Capital

Another step removed from a direct effect on policy outcomes is the possibility that deliberation equips individuals with the motivations, skills, and attitudes—the political capital—that are known precursors to participation in the political and civic spheres (Verba, Schlozman, and Brady 1995; see fig. 5.1, column 4). In particular, discursive participation may increase political and civic attributes such as knowledge, interest, attention, efficacy, and trust, which can generate greater engagement. Prior research provides some (though not uniform) evidence for such indirect effects. For example, research suggests that participation in the Kettering Foundation's National Issues Forums increased interest in politics and knowledge of the issues directly under discussion (and a greater flexibility and sophistication about these issues), as well as a higher frequency of political information-seeking and a stronger sense of political efficacy (Gastil 2000, 118–19; Doble and Richardson 1991; Gastil and Dillard 1999a and 1999b; Loyacano 1992; Delli Carpini, Cook, and Jacobs 2004). Moreover, 56% of respondents in a survey of individuals who engaged in small-group discussions reported that they subsequently became more interested in social justice or peace issues, and 45% reported taking greater interest in general political and social issues (Wuthnow 1994). The next chapter reports that deliberative forums on Social Security increased interest in and knowledge about the program. Furthermore, some research on Deliberative Polls found that participation in the forums increased political learning, led to some changes in opinion that appeared to show the influence of greater knowledge (as compared to the "spur-of-the-moment" responses tapped by opinion surveys), and increased political efficacy (Fishkin 1999; Fishkin and Luskin 1999a, 1999b, and 1999c; Luskin and Fishkin 1998; Luskin et al. 1999; Luskin, Fishkin, and Plane 1999; Luskin et al. 2000, and Luskin, Fishkin, and Jowell 2002).

Despite these studies, doubts and questions remain about the nature and scope of the impact of public deliberation on the development of political capital. Some research reports that the influence of deliberation on increasing political participation and political knowledge has been slight, if not nonexistent (Denver, Hands, and Jones 1995). One study highlighted the ineffectiveness of efforts to increase citizen involvement in policy decisions (Berry, Portney, and Thomson 1993). The generalizability and durability of the effects of Deliberative Polls have also been challenged (e.g., Traugott 1992).

In addition to questions about the magnitude and staying power of the effects of public deliberation, several studies warn that public talking may heighten (rather than reverse) political disengagement and civic withdrawal. Public deliberations on race heightened the perception of the issue's complexity and its intractability while reinforcing divisions and suspicions (Walsh 2003; Mendelberg and Oleske 2000). Mutz (2006) reports that political conversations (a form of public talking short of deliberation as commonly defined) are not only ineffective but may actually *decrease* participation (especially voter turnout and engagement). In contexts where differences and oppositional viewpoints are aired, she reports that "the prospects for truly deliberative encounters may be improving while the prospects for participation and political activism are declining" (Mutz 2006, 3).

Research using controlled experiments offers similarly mixed findings. On the one hand, laboratory experiments have discovered that face-to-face communication can increase the likelihood of cooperation—the mortar of political and civic life (Bornstein 1992; Dawes, van de Kragt, and Orbell 1990; Ostrom 1998; Sally 1995). Talking allows group members to demonstrate their genuine willingness to cooperate and to determine others' willingness to do so (Bornstein and Rapoport 1988; Kerr and Kaufman-Gilland 1994; Orbell, van de Kragt, and Dawes 1988). Public deliberation helps participants see the connection between their individual interests and those of the group (Dawes, van de Kragt, and Orbell 1990; Orbell, van de Kragt, and Dawes 1988). The agreement that emerges from public talking appears to lead to actual cooperative behavior, with more talk leading to more cooperation (Bouas and Komorita 1996). On the other hand, however, some studies have found that in certain settings, deliberation and other forms of public talk can exacerbate group differences in opinion (Insko et al. 1993; Bornstein 1992; Bettencourt and Dorr 1998; Miller and Davidson-Podgorny 1987).

Creating Shared Meaning and Understanding

The most indirect effect of public deliberation is on socially shared meanings and understandings (fig. 5.1, column 5). Democratic theorists suggest that deliberation invigorates citizens, educates them about their interests, and focuses their expectations of government. "Talk-centric democratic theory," Simone Chambers explains, "focuses on the communicative processes of opinion and will-formation that precede voting" (2003, 310).

Deliberation may improve the confidence of citizens in their own efficacy by helping them see the relevance of government and politics to their private lives and by increasing their political knowledge, participation in voting, volunteer work for elections, attendance at rallies, letters to officials, and other forms of political participation (Gastil and Dillard 1999a; Kim, Wyatt, and Katz 1999; Knoke 1990; McLeod, Scheufele, and Moy 1999; Walsh 2004). By heightening citizen participation, deliberation may improve the quality and responsiveness of government (Gutmann and Thompson 1996; Chambers 1996). In this way, public talk may have a feedback effect by increasing deliberators' perception of their relevance and influence, which in turn boosts their motivation for political and civic participation (Mettler and Soss 2004; Pierson 1993; Campbell 2003).

Although deliberation may motivate citizens and help form the discourse that structures debates during elections and policy discussions, some political theorists argue that the impact of deliberation on discourse is more fundamental and thorough-going in shaping the "contestation of discourses in civil society" (Dryzek 2000, 5). They place more faith in fostering discourse in civil society than in influencing the electoral process, which they criticize as myopic in its preoccupation with direct political or legislative results and as narrowly instrumental in treating the preferences of voters as fixed.

The "shared terms of reference" are the building blocks for forming coherent narratives or accounts that set the expectations to which political representatives must respond. Martin Luther King's protests and speeches in the 1950s and 1960s contributed, for instance, to the formation of a discourse about race relations that prefigured a shift in civil society and policy. This emphasis on discourse and civil society redefines politics from an instrumental means for achieving the fixed goals of isolated and anonymous individuals to a process of collective and public communication for expressing and reconciling deep moral differences and reconnecting individuals to what they share (Habermas 1989; Gutmann and Thompson 1996).

Deliberation, for these theorists, takes on particular importance by setting the boundaries of government policy decisions and, more fundamentally, by shaping the "shared means of making sense of the world embedded in language . . . [and its] assumptions, judgments, contentions, dispositions, and capabilities" (Dryzek 2000, 18). Benhabib insists that "we cease thinking of the public realm solely in terms of . . . legislative or state activity. . . . Power is not only a social resource to be distributed say like bread or automobiles. It is also a sociocultural grid of interpretation and communication. Public dialogue is not external to but constitutive of power relations" (1989, 155). Michelman adds that "much of the country's normatively consequential dialogue occurs outside the major, formal channels of electoral and legislative politics . . . [in] what we know as public life, . . . in the encounters and conflicts, interactions and debates that are in and around town meetings, local government agencies, civic and voluntary associations, social and recreational clubs, [and] schools" (1988, 1531). Dryzek suggests that "the communicative power that the public sphere can exert over the state is diffuse and pervasive, felt in the way terms are defined and issues framed, not in the direct leverage of one actor over another" (2000, 87, 101).

Despite the thoughtful and energetic exchanges among political theorists, there is limited research on whether participation in public deliberation influences the discourse of participants or wider communities, either as an end in itself or in a way that ultimately affects more formal government decision making. An analysis of the Kettering Foundation's National Issues Forums suggests that participation in deliberative forums can make participants more "deliberative" in their political conversations (Gastil 2000, 118–19). A report on several different efforts at public deliberation found that some participants in civic forums did not treat them in instrumental terms but as opportunities for engaging in "intelligent discussion about weighty matters, sensing that the mass media and political pundits [were] not doing a good enough job at directing public discourse." The experiences of these individuals, one review surmised, point to the "public formulation of values through civic discourse and the formation of articulate citizens" (Button and Mattson 1999, 636–37).

But some democratic theorists question whether deliberation can exert much influence on the dominant discourse owing to its grounding in the economic and political systems. "Dominant discourses and ideologies, [which are] often intertwined with structural economic forces," are "agents of distortion that cannot easily be counteracted" (Dryzek 2000, 21). Indeed, some suggest that the political ineffectiveness of public deliberation may actually reinforce a sense of disconnection from government decision making among citizens who already feel marginalized (Button and Mattson 1999; Sanders 1997).

The general evaluation of deliberation's effect on the discourse of civil society is hindered by the lack of research: there are only a few sustained empirical and theoretical analyses. The scarcity of analysis stems in part from the difficulty of measuring the discrete effects of one or more civic forums on something as diffuse as socially shared meanings and understandings. At best, political theorists have pointed to the long-term impact of major social movements (e.g., civil rights) on civic discourse (Michelman 1988, 1531; Dryzek 2000). Indeed, some participants in civic forums have complained about the diffuse effects of deliberation, insisting that "political talk must be followed by some kind of practical activity or representation in actual decision making" (Button and Mattson 1999, 630–34; see also Chambers 2003).

MODELING THE IMPACT OF DISCURSIVE PARTICIPATION

In the past, deliberative theorists and researchers tended to focus exclusively on one or more of these direct or indirect effects. For instance, some theorists singled out the effect of deliberation on the creation of shared meanings while minimizing or altogether ignoring other direct or indirect pathways. In our view, however, discursive participation is plausibly entangled in a host of relationships.

Figure 5.2 provides a heuristic model for conceptualizing the various hypothesized effects of discursive participation and their interrelationships. Discursive participation has direct and positive effects on the creation of shared meaning, the development of political capital, levels of civic and political engagement, and policy outcomes.[2] Public talking also has indirect effects, including, for example, the path running from discursive participation through political capital to political engagement.

In principle, understanding the full impact of discursive participation would require examining *all* the direct and indirect pathways illustrated in figure 5.2. In practice, however, our data limit our analysis to the direct and indirect impacts of discursive participation on political capital and on civic and political engagement. Figure 5.3 provides a reduced version of the model presented in figure 5.2; it includes only those paths that we focus on in our analyses. Although our analysis falls short of investigating

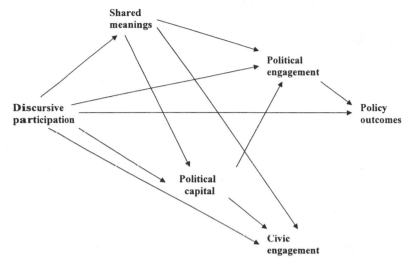

FIGURE 5.2   A HEURISTIC MODEL OF THE EFFECTS OF DISCURSIVE PARTICIPATION

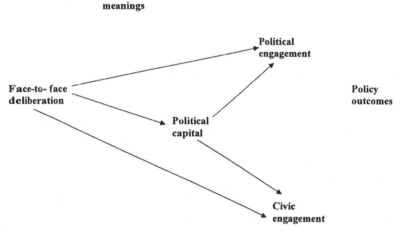

FIGURE 5.3   A REDUCED MODEL OF THE EFFECTS OF DISCURSIVE PARTICIPATION

deliberation's full set of impacts, it is the most comprehensive examination of deliberation's political and civic effects to date and opens the door to future research.

Our investigation of deliberation's political and civic effects examines several ways in which people talk about politics. Our primary analysis of the causal impact of public talking focuses, though, on the effects of face-to-face deliberation on political capital and civic and political engagement.

The Political and Civic Impacts of Discursive Participation

Our analyses of the political effects of deliberation are sequenced. We begin with a descriptive examination of the purpose of deliberative forums and the simple relationships between discursive participation and civic and political behavior and attitudes before moving on to use regression analyses to explore the potential effects of public talking. (The appendix describes the variables examined in these analyses and how they were constructed.)

DESCRIPTIVE ANALYSES OF DELIBERATIVE EFFECTS

Talking with a Purpose

Deliberation in America is often purposive, aimed at promoting changes in attitudes and behaviors. Participants in face-to-face forums reported to us that "giv[ing] people an opportunity to decide on concrete actions" was an important goal of the forum they attended. The mean rating was 7.1 (s.d. of 2.8), with 30% scoring it a 10 as "very important." In-person deliberation appears more intended to connect talk to action than deliberation on the Internet, where the mean score for providing remedial concrete actions was 5.4 (s.d. 3.7).

The orientation of meeting organizers toward translating talk into action is also reflected in the efforts of the facilitators. Face-to-face deliberators reported that the work of discussion leaders to "convince people to do something about the issue [under discussion]" was an important part of their role (mean 6.8, s.d. 3.2), with 30% scoring this purpose as "very important." Indeed, facilitators were identified as catalysts for moving civic forums from talk to action: the role of discussion leaders in convincing people to act is strongly correlated with the importance that forums place on taking concrete action ($r = .45$ at .001 sig. level), allowing people to come to agreement ($r = .43$ at .001 level), and the leader's role in encouraging agreement ($r = .50$ at .001 level).

Deliberators indicated that the commitment of forums to take concrete action was connected to their reliance on encouraging participants to reach agreement through talking. The organization of forums to allow people to agree is very highly correlated ($r = .64$ at .001 level) with giving people the opportunity to decide on concrete action. In addition, the role of facilitators in encouraging agreement is associated with the organization of forums to decide on concrete action ($r = .42$ at .001 level).

The Association of Deliberation with Political and Civic Attitudes and Behaviors

A range of different forms of deliberation are related to civic and political motivations, skills, attitudes and behaviors. Table 5.1 shows that individuals who engage in any of the six types of discursive participation that we measure are consistently more likely than are those who do not to have political capital such as political knowledge, interest, efficacy, attention, and tolerance; to participate in the electoral process; to contact elites about their public concerns; and to engage in civic behavior such as community service. Indeed, these differences are often quite sizeable. The few exceptions to this pattern are political trust generally (which shows no consistent relationship to our measures of discursive participation, though face-to-face deliberators appear more trusting, and Internet deliberators appear less so); the relationship between Internet deliberation and social trust, with online deliberators expressing less trust; and the relationship between face-to-face deliberation and partisan strength (i.e., identification with either major political party), in which deliberators are no more likely to be partisan than non-deliberators.

The specific patterns captured in Table 5.1 are presented in more summary fashion in Figure 5.4, which uses an additive index of discursive participation and an additive index of our four categories of civic and political engagement. The results are clear and consistent: as the number of types of discursive participation in which citizens engage increases, their levels of political capital and their propensity to vote, to contact the media or public officials, and to participate in civic activities also rises.

STUDYING THE CAUSAL CONNECTION OF DELIBERATION AND POLITICAL AND CIVIC LIFE

Thus far our data suggest—perhaps unsurprisingly—that citizens who participate in public talk are also likely to have key civic and political skills, motivations, and attitudes (political capital), and to engage in a variety of political and civic behaviors. There is, however, a critical question regarding causality: Do these positive associations simply show that citizens who are more engaged *also* tend to be more likely to participate in public talk, or does discursive experience actually *lead to* changes in civic and political attitudes and behaviors? A definitive answer to this important question is difficult to confirm under ideal research conditions, and the limits of our date make such an answer even more elusive.

Table 5.1 Relationship between discursive participation and political capital and participation

	FACE-TO-FACE DELIBERATION		INTERNET DELIBERATION		TRADITIONAL TALKER		INTERNET TALKER		PERSUADE ISSUE		PERSUADE VOTE		SUMMARY MEASURE	
	YES	NO	YES	NO	YES	NO	YES	NO	YES	NO	YES	NO	HIGH	LOW
Political capital	PERCENTAGE (%)													
Political efficacy	68	42	61	48	55	35	65	43	58	41	58	44	63	41
Political trust	62	55	41	57	57	56	61	55	57	56	54	58	56	57
Social trust	69	55	50	59	66	43	69	56	62	56	65	56	67	55
Political knowledge	62	39	59	44	54	27	59	40	61	31	64	37	64	35
Political interest	74	46	74	52	62	33	67	49	70	38	75	44	75	41
Political attention	88	68	84	73	82	56	85	70	85	64	89	67	90	64
Ideological strength	31	22	32	24	25	24	31	23	32	18	36	19	32	20
Political tolerance	71	60	63	63	67	53	71	60	68	58	68	60	71	58
Partisan strength	61	62	67	61	63	58	69	59	66	57	72	57	69	57
Electoral participation														
Voting 2002	76	56	72	60	65	52	67	59	69	54	77	54	73	54
Volunteer for campaign	22	6	21	10	13	5	17	8	15	6	22	5	20	5
Elite contacting														
Boycott	58	40	66	44	50	33	52	42	59	31	58	38	61	35
Petition	52	26	56	31	41	14	55	25	47	20	49	25	55	20
Contact official	53	20	57	27	35	14	40	24	41	17	45	21	49	16
Contact media	39	14	51	19	27	8	36	16	29	13	35	15	36	12
Civic participation														
Community service	80	46	74	54	62	40	69	50	66	45	65	50	72	46
Work informally	73	37	64	45	51	34	60	42	57	36	58	41	62	37

Source: Discursive Participation Survey. National adult sample: N = 1,501 (weighted sample).
Note: For information on the dichotomized coding of the variables in this table please see table 2.2 and appendix (page 176).

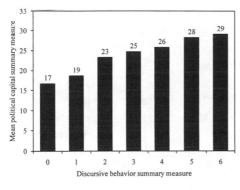

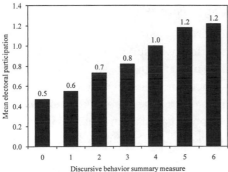

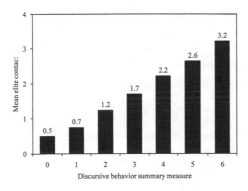

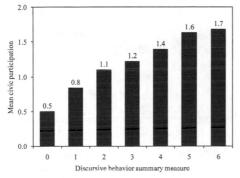

FIGURE 5.4   A SUMMARY OF THE RELATIONSHIP BETWEEN DISCURSIVE PARTICIPATION AND POLITICAL CAPITAL, POLITICAL BEHAVIOR, ELITE CONTACTING, AND CIVIC BEHAVIOR

Source: Discursive Participation Survey. National adult sample: N = 1,501 (weighted sample).

Notes: Discursive Behavior Summary Measure ranges from 0 to 6 and is an additive index of the following variables: face-to-face deliberation, traditional talker, Internet talker, Internet deliberation, persuade issue, and persuade vote.

Our best analytic line of attack to specify the causal connection between deliberation and civic and political activities is to concentrate on face-to-face deliberation. We use three approaches to analyze the political and civic effects of participating in face-to-face forums: (1) self-reports on the civic and political effects of participating in forums; (2) multivariate ordinary least squares regression analyses; and (3) two-stage least squares regression analyses. The first approach offers the perspective of the participants themselves, while the last two approaches allow us to control for potential confounding influences and bidirectional effects.

Self-Reported Effects of Participating in Face-to-Face Deliberative Forums

A substantial proportion of deliberators report that they were moved by their face-to-face forums to take action. Our survey asked the following question of respondents who had participated in a face-to-face deliberative forum in the last year: "People sometimes follow up their participation in public meetings with other kinds of activities intended to address the problem that was discussed. Have you engaged in any charitable, civic or political activities AS A DIRECT RESULT of the last meeting you attended about a public issue?"

Respondents who answered yes were then asked, "What activity or activities did you do?" These answers (allowing for up to four open-ended responses) were then recoded into separate categories. One-third (33%) of face-to-face deliberators reported having engaged in some form of charitable, civic, or political activity as a direct result of the last meeting they attended. This is a fairly straightforward indicator that discursive participation does indeed lead to other forms of public involvement.

Table 5.2 provides a breakdown of the kinds of follow-up activities in which face-to-face deliberators engaged. Among these deliberators who did follow-up activities, they report that their experience prompted them to engage in a range of "traditional" civic and political activities, including discussing public issues with others (18%) or trying to persuade someone to agree with their policy views (7%), contacting a public official or candidate (16%), volunteering or participating in other community activities (15%), signing a petition (8%), and helping to raise funds (7%) or making charitable and political contributions (7%).

Ordinary Least Squares Regression Analysis of the Effects of Deliberation

It is impressive that one-third of citizens report that they followed-up their deliberative experience by engaging in other activities. This suggests that public deliberation can indeed be a pathway to more traditional forms of civic and political engagement. These findings, however, remain ambigu-

Table 5.2   Self-reported activities as direct result of the last deliberative forum attended

ACTIVITY	PERCENTAGE (%)
Discussed public issues with others	18
Contacted or visited a candidate for office or public official	16
Volunteered or participated in own community	15
Signed an e-mail or written petition	8
Tried to persuade someone about your views	7
Fund-raising	7
Gave money to a charitable or political cause	7
Wrote, called, or e-mailed a newspaper, magazine, or television show	7
Protest/rally	7
Joined a political or civic organization	4
Distributed information	3
Followed public affairs more closely in the media	3
Volunteered to work for a political candidate or party	3
Voted in an election for local, state, or national office	2
Walked, ran, or bicycled for a charitable cause	2
Refused to buy something because you disliked the conduct of manufacturer	2
Tried to persuade someone else about whom to vote for	1
Refused to buy something because of conditions	1
Called in to a radio or television talk show	1
Purchased a certain product or service	1
Other (PLEASE SPECIFY)	21
Refused (volunteered)	1
Don't know (volunteered)	4

Source: Discursive Participation Survey. Face-to-face deliberators sample: $N = 756$ (unweighted sample).
Notes: Percentages add up to more than 100% due to multiple (up to four) responses. Proportions listed in table are based on the 33% of the 756 face-to-face deliberators who indicated that they subsequently took an action.

ous. Self-reported activities, while often valuable, run the risk of being inaccurate. They may also be inflated owing to potential social desirability effects—respondents may have sensed an expectation of continued engagement. While these limitations may be shortcomings of any survey design that relies exclusively on "self reports," our analysis is additionally hampered by our tendency to ask about both behavior and motive in the same set of questions.

We work to avoid the potential pitfalls associated with self-reported motivation by pursuing a second approach, which uses ordinary least squares regression (OLS) to examine the relationship between participation in face-to-face deliberative forums and in other forms of civic and political engagement. In particular, OLS regression allows us to treat political capital as both a dependent variable and a control or intervening variable.

We investigate three empirical models. We begin by investigating a standard model (Model 1), which uses social and economic status to explain political participation (SES Model). We use a summary measure of political capital as the dependent variable, with several demographic variables normally associated with civic and political engagement as the independent variables. Second, Model 2 expands the SES Model by adding three "social capital" variables that are also hypothesized to increase civic and political engagement (SES plus Social Capital Model). Finally, and most centrally to our purpose, Model 3 adds participation in a face-to-face deliberative forum as an additional independent variable (SES, Social Capital, and Deliberation Model). This third model allows us to gauge the "value added" of this form of deliberation to increasing civic and political motivation, skills, and attitudes. We then rerun these three models using summary measures of electoral participation, elite contacting, and civic participation as dependent variables, and shifting political capital from a dependent to a set of independent variables. We do this because such prior motivations, skills, and attitudes might confound any apparent impact of deliberation on our measures of civic and political engagement.

Table 5.3 presents three models to explain political capital—the model of socioeconomic status (Model 1) as well as the models adding social capital (Model 2) and face-to-face deliberation (Model 3). Among our variables, education and income have the strongest positive effects on political capital, while being female and being Latino are less strong and have significant negative effects (being African American also has a negative effect but is of only marginal statistical significance). Model 1 has modest explanatory power, accounting for 20% of the variance in political capital.

Adding the three social capital measures slightly increases the variance explained (from 20% to 22%) (Model 2). The SES variables continue to exert similar effects. The major changes are the emergence of religious attendance and belonging to an organization as positive and significant influences on the level of political capital reported by deliberators. Nonetheless, the powerhouse SES tag team of income and, especially, education continue to exert the strongest impact, notably larger than that of the social capital variables. Somewhat surprisingly, length of residence (a presumed measure of social capital) has a statistically insignificant relationship with political capital. Overall, though, Model 1 and Model 2 tell a familiar story. Social capital and, especially, SES are dominant influences on political capital.

Of greater interest to us is the effect of adding participation in face-to-face deliberation into the mix (Model 3 in table 5.3). The most notable result is that deliberation emerges as significant and among the strongest influences on political capital (standardized beta = .21), stronger than that

Table 5.3   Effects of public deliberation on political capital

	MODEL 1		MODEL 2		MODEL 3	
	UNSTANDARDIZED	STANDARDIZED	UNSTANDARDIZED	STANDARDIZED	UNSTANDARDIZED	STANDARDIZED
Demographic characteristics						
African American	-1.30 (.75) +	-.06 +	-1.5 (.75) *	-.07 *	-1.58 (.73) *	-.07 *
Latino	-3.41 (1.03) ***	-.11 ***	-3.42 (1.0) ***	-.11 ***	-3.34 (1.0) ***	-.11 ***
Other ethnicity	-.56 (.80)	-.02	-.66 (.80)	-.03	-.77 (.78)	-.03
Education (5 cat.)	1.64 (.20) ***	.29 ***	1.46 (.20) ***	.26 ***	1.35 (.20) ***	.24 ***
Gender (F = 1)	-1.12 (.39) **	-.09 **	-1.16 (.39) **	-.09 **	-1.13 (.38) **	-.09 **
Age (5 cat.)	.12 (.15)	.02	.07 (.17)	.02	.12 (.17)	.03
Income (5 cat.)	.78 (.15) ***	.18 ***	.74 (.15) ***	.17 ***	.72 (.15) ***	.17 ***
Social capital						
Belong to organization			1.12 (.42) **	.09 **	.45 (.43)	.04
Religious attendance			.26 (.09) **	.09 **	.21 (.09) *	.07 *
Length of residence			-.00 (.01)	-.00	-.00 (.01)	-.01
Deliberation					2.62 (.40) ***	.21 ***
Constant	19.54 (.73) ***		18.76 (.76) ***		18.07 (.74) ***	
N	800	800	794	794	794	794
R^2	.20	.20	.22	.22	.26	.26

Source: Discursive Participation Survey. National adult sample: $N = 1,501$ (unweighted sample).
Notes: OLS regression method. Standard errors in parentheses. Dependent variable: Political capital summary measure ranges from 0 to 39. It is an additive index of the following variables: political efficiency, political trust, political knowledge, political attention, ideological strength, party identification strength, and political tolerance.
+ $p < .10$; * $p < .05$; ** $p < .01$; *** $p < .001$.

of income (beta = .17) and comparable to the effect of education (beta = .24). Moreover, the addition of deliberation increases the explained variance to 26%, a boost of nearly one-quarter over the fit of Model 1.[3] Participating in even a single deliberative forum is positively related to political capital, even when controlling for demographic characteristics. In other words, discursive participation seems to provide civic and political fitness training, bolstering the knowledge, interest, attention, efficacy, and trust that are known precursors to participation (Verba, Schlozman, and Brady 1995).

Can we say the same for the relationship of face-to-face deliberation to civic and political behavior? We replicated the analyses presented in table 5.3, with two differences. First, we use as dependent variables our measures of electoral participation (table 5.4), elite contacting (table 5.5), and civic participation (table 5.6). Second, we expand the roster of independent variables by including in Model 3 and Model 4 our nine measures of motivations, skills, and attitudes upon which our summary index of political capital is based.

The results in tables 5.4 through 5.6 reveal some interesting patterns and differences regarding the civic and political effects of SES, social capital, and political capital, but the important and consistent finding is the strong and significant influence of deliberation across the different models. Looking across tables 5.4 to 5.6, the SES variables (especially education) largely generated the predicted (positive) effects on electoral participation, elite contacting, and civic participation (Model 1). Higher levels of education and, less consistently, income and age led to greater participation, while Latino status depressed engagement. Model 1 reveals that SES has only modest explanatory power (as measured by the R^2), accounting for 17%, 11%, and 6% of the variance.

Model 2, which adds social capital variables, similarly produces the expected results. Tables 5.4 to 5.6 show that belonging to an organization and, a bit less consistently, attending religious services increase political and civic participation. The results also confirm that social capital (especially organizational membership) exerts more consistent and often stronger effects than the SES variables when paired up. The explanatory power of the models improves to 21% (for electoral participation in table 5.4), 17% (for elite contacting in table 5.5), and 15% (for civic participation in table 5.6) of the variance.

Model 3, which incorporates political capital, demonstrates that higher levels of political interest and attention as well as political knowledge are associated with increased electoral participation, elite contacting, and civic participation. With the more fully specified model, the SES variables (especially the previously dominant effect of education) weaken in strength, statistical significance, and consistency, while the social capital variables (most reliably organizational membership) remain strong and at times dominant effects. Adding the political variables further increases the variance explained to 28% (table 5.4), 32% (table 5.5), and 17% (table 5.6).

The most telling result is the strong and consistent civic and political effect of face-to-face deliberation in Model 4. Deliberation has statistically significant and positive effects in tables 5.4 to 5.6 after controlling for a host of potentially confounding influences. Moreover, participation in face-to-face forums had the strongest effect on elite contacting (standardized beta = .24) and civic participation (standardized beta = .27) and was among the strongest influences on electoral competition (standardized beta = .15). After controlling for a host of demographic, social, and political variables, attending even a single deliberative forum increased the number of electoral acts by .19 acts (on a two-item scale), elite contacts by .62 acts (on a four-item scale), and the number of civic acts by .43 (on a two-item scale). Finally, the addition of discursive participation improves the explanatory power of the models for electoral participation in table 5.4 (from 28% to 30%), elite contacting in table 5.5 (from 32% to 36%), and civic participation in table 5.6 (from 17% to 23%).[4]

Deliberation is thus a kind of civic and political workout. Even controlling for SES, participation in deliberative forums increases civic and electoral participation and elite contacting.

Wrestling with Causal Ambiguity: A Two-Stage Least Squares Analysis

Deliberation matters, according to the OLS analyses—it appears to serve as a pathway to other forms of civic and political engagement. If true, this finding challenges the pessimistic view that discursive participation is "just talk."

There are, however, limitations with ordinary least squares regression analyses. The most serious challenge is that they do not definitively resolve the issue of causality. In particular, we still cannot rule out the possibility that individuals inclined to engage in traditional forms of civic and political activities are also more inclined to participate in deliberative forums. The analytic challenge is intensified by our data—a survey conducted at one point in time. Establishing a causal connection from participation in face-to-face deliberative forums to other forms of engagement is difficult using a single survey.

One promising strategy is to use two-stage least squares regression analysis. Unlike ordinary least squares, this approach allows us to estimate

Table 5.4 The effects of public deliberation on electoral participation

	MODEL 1		MODEL 2		MODEL 3		MODEL 4	
	UNSTANDARDIZED	STANDARDIZED	UNSTANDARDIZED	STANDARDIZED	UNSTANDARDIZED	STANDARDIZED	UNSTANDARDIZED	STANDARDIZED
Demographic characteristics								
African American	.14 (.07)*	.06*	.08 (.07)	.03	.05 (.08)	.02	.04 (.08)	.02
Latino	-.20 (.10)*	-.06*	-.20 (.09)*	-.06*	-.14 (.11)	-.04	-.14 (.10)	-.04
Other ethnicity	-.09 (.07)	-.04	-.09 (.07)	-.04	-.13 (.08)	-.05	-.14 (.08)	-.05
Education (5 cat.)	.11 (.02)***	.19***	.10 (.02)***	.17***	.04 (.02)+	.06+	.03 (.02)	.06
Gender (F = 1)	-.01 (.04)	-.00	-.02 (.04)	-.02	.01 (.04)	.01	.01 (.04)	.00
Age (5 cat.)	.15 (.01)***	.29***	.12 (.02)***	.23***	.09 (.02)***	.19***	.10 (.02)***	.20***
Income (5 cat.)	.05 (.01)***	.12***	.05 (.01)***	.11***	.03 (.02)+	.06+	.03 (.02)+	.06+
Social capital								
Belong to organization			.15 (.04)***	.12***	.10 (.04)*	.08*	.06 (.05)	.04
Religious attendance			.04 (.01)***	.13***	.03 (.01)**	.10**	.03 (.01)**	.08**
Length of residence			.00 (.00)**	.09**	.00 (.00)***	.11***	.00 (.00)**	.11**

Political capital						
Political efficacy			.02 (.01)$^+$	.07$^+$	.01 (.01)	.05
Political trust			-.03 (.02)	-.05	-.03 (.02)	-.06
Social trust			-.01 (.02)	-.02	-.01 (.02)	-.02
Political knowledge			.04 (.02)**	.09**	.04 (.02)**	.09**
Political interest			.04 (.01)***	.17***	.04 (.01)***	.16***
Political attention			.07 (.04)$^+$	.08$^+$	.06 (.04)	.07
Ideological strength			.02 (.03)	.03	.02 (.03)	.02
Partisan strength			.11 (.04)**	.08**	.13 (.04)**	.09**
Political tolerance			.04 (.03)	.05	.04 (.03)	.04
Deliberation					.19 (.04)***	.15***
Constant	.10 (.06)	-.02 (.07)	-.46 (.11)***		-.43 (.11)***	
N	1,156	1,139	789		789	
R^2	.17	.21	.28		.30	

Source: Discursive Participation Survey. National adult sample: N = 1,501 (unweighted sample).

Notes: OLS regression method. Standard errors in parentheses. Dependent variable: Electoral participation ranges from 0 to 2 and is an additive index of the following variables: vote 2002 and volunteer for campaign.

$^+ p < .10; ^* p < .05; ^{**} p < .01; ^{***} p < .001.$

Table 5.5 The effects of public deliberation on elite contacting

	MODEL 1		MODEL 2		MODEL 3		MODEL 4	
	UNSTANDARDIZED	STANDARDIZED	UNSTANDARDIZED	STANDARDIZED	UNSTANDARDIZED	STANDARDIZED	UNSTANDARDIZED	STANDARDIZED
Demographic characteristics								
African American	-.22 (.14)	-.05	-.21 (.14)	-.04	-.29 (.16)[+]	-.06[+]	-.31 (.15)[*]	-.06[*]
Latino	-.57 (.20)[**]	-.08[**]	-.50 (.20)[**]	-.07[**]	-.27 (.21)	-.04	-.29 (.20)	-.04
Other ethnicity	-.22 (.14)	-.05	-.24 (.14)[+]	-.05[+]	-.28 (.17)[+]	-.05[+]	-.30 (.16)[+]	-.06[+]
Education (5 cat.)	.32 (.04)[***]	.27[***]	.23 (.04)[***]	.19[***]	.05 (.04)	.04	.04 (.04)	.03
Gender (F = 1)	.06 (.07)	.02	.05 (.07)	.02	.25 (.08)[**]	.09[**]	.23 (.08)[**]	.09[**]
Age (5 cat.)	.08 (.03)[**]	.08[**]	.10 (.03)[**]	.09[**]	.03 (.04)	.03	.04 (.04)	.04
Income (5 cat.)	.04 (.03)	.05	.01 (.03)	.01	.00 (.03)	.01	.01 (.03)	.01
Social capital								
Belong to organization			.66 (.08)[***]	.25[***]	.57 (.09)[***]	.22[***]	.42 (.09)[***]	.16[***]
Religious attendance			-.00 (.02)	-.00	.02 (.02)	.04	.01 (.02)	.02
Length of residence			-.01 (.00)[*]	-.07[*]	-.00 (.00)	-.03	-.00 (.00)	-.03

Political capital						
Political efficacy			.03 (.02)	.05	.01 (.02)	.02
Political trust			-.20 (.04)***	-.16***	-.20 (.04)***	-.16***
Social trust			-.04 (.04)	-.04	-.04 (.04)	-.03
Political knowledge			.16 (.04)***	.17***	.16 (.03)***	.17***
Political interest			.08 (.02)***	.17***	.07 (.02)***	.15***
Political attention			.23 (.07)**	.13**	.19 (.07)**	.11**
Ideological strength			.14 (.05)**	.09**	.13 (.05)**	.08**
Partisan strength			-.17 (.09)*	-.06*	-.13 (.08)	-.05
Political tolerance			.02 (.06)	.01	-.01 (.06)	-.00
Deliberation					.62 (.08)***	.24***
Constant	.69 (.14)***	.66 (.14)***	-.19 (.22)		-.11 (.22)	
N	1,143	1,125	785	785	785	785
R²	.11	.17	.32	.32	.36	.36

Source: Discursive Participation Survey. National adult sample: N = 1,501 (unweighted sample).

Notes: OLS regression method. Standard errors in parentheses. Dependent variable: Elite contacting ranges from 0 to 4 and is an additive index of the following variables: boycotting, signing a petition, contacting an office holder, and contacting the media.
$^+ p < .10$; $^* p < .05$; $^{**} p < .01$; $^{***} p < .001$.

Table 5.6 The effects of public deliberation on civic participation

	MODEL 1		MODEL 2		MODEL 3		MODEL 4	
	UNSTANDARDIZED	STANDARDIZED	UNSTANDARDIZED	STANDARDIZED	UNSTANDARDIZED	STANDARDIZED	UNSTANDARDIZED	STANDARDIZED
Demographic characteristics								
African American	.08 (.09)	.03	.01 (.08)	.00	.03 (.10)	.01	.01 (.10)	.00
Latino	-.08 (.13)	-.02	-.07 (.12)	-.02	.05 (.14)	.01	.03 (.13)	.01
Other ethnicity	-.15 (.09)[+]	-.05[+]	-.16 (.08)*	-.05*	-.12 (.11)	-.04	-.14 (.10)	-.04
Education (5 cat.)	.16 (.02)***	.22***	.10 (.02)***	.14***	.05 (.03)[+]	.07[+]	.04 (.03)	.06
Gender (F = 1)	.08 (.05)[+]	.05[+]	.05 (.04)	.03	.08 (.05)	.05	.07 (.05)	.04
Age (5 cat.)	.02 (.02)	.04	.01 (.02)	.01	-.01 (.02)	-.02	-.01 (.02)	-.01
Income (5 cat.)	.02 (.02)	.04	.00 (.02)	.00	.00 (.02)	.00	.00 (.02)	.00
Social capital								
Belong to organization			.38 (.05)***	.24***	.34 (.06)***	.21***	.23 (.06)***	.15***
Religious attendance			.07 (.01)***	.18***	.06 (.01)***	.15***	.05 (.01)***	.13***
Length of residence			-.00 (.00)	-.02	.00 (.00)	.04	.00 (.00)	.03

	Model 1	Model 2	Model 3		Model 4	
	b (SE)	b (SE)	b (SE)	β	b (SE)	β
Political capital						
Political efficacy			.04 (.01)**	.12**	.03 (.01)*	.08*
Political trust			-.03 (.03)	-.04	-.03 (.03)	-.04
Social trust			.04 (.03)	.06	.04 (.03)+	.06+
Political knowledge			-.01 (.02)	-.02	-.02 (.02)	-.03
Political interest			.02 (.01)	.06	.01 (.01)	.03
Political attention			.12 (.05)**	.11**	.09 (.05)*	.09*
Ideological strength			-.01 (.03)	-.01	-.02 (.03)	-.02
Partisan strength			-.09 (.06)	-.05	-.06 (.06)	-.04
Political tolerance			-.00 (.04)	-.00	-.02 (.04)	-.02
Deliberation					.43 (.06)***	.27***
Constant	.74 (.09)***	.59 (.08)***	.29 (.15)+		.34 (.14)*	
N	1,162	1,144	793		793	
R^2	.06	.15	.17		.23	

Source: Discursive Participation Survey. National adult sample: N =1,501 (unweighted sample).
Notes: OLS regression method. Standard errors in parentheses. Dependent variable: Civic participation ranges from 0 to 2 and is an additive index of the following variables: volunteer and work informally with others.
+$p < .10$; *$p < .05$; **$p < .01$; ***$p < .001$.

the causal effect of one variable (i.e., face-to-face deliberation) on others (i.e., various forms of political and civic participation) by purging two potential influences on the relationship: (1) reverse causal relationships (i.e., the possibility that participation in civic and political activities leads to participation in deliberative forums rather than or in addition to the direction of causality we posit), or (2) spuriousness (i.e., participation in *both* deliberative forums *and* other forms of civic and political engagement may be explained by some other set of factors—for example, an underlying tendency to "get involved").

The key to using two-stage least squares regression is identifying an "instrumental variable" that is arguably related causally to the independent variable in question but not to the dependent variable. This is obviously difficult when the two variables in question (face-to-face deliberation and other forms of engagement) are so closely linked theoretically.

Being invited to attend a deliberative forum, however, can serve as an instrumental variable in our analyses. Having an invitation extended to you to attend a forum should be causally related to actually attending (i.e., to the deliberation variable) but not to other forms of civic and political engagement that were not the subject of the invitation. The connection between being invited and actually attending a civic forum makes logical sense and is consistent with prior research (Verba, Schlozman, and Brady 1995; Zukin et al. 2006). Our instrumental variable is based on the following question in our national survey: "Since January 2002, have you been *invited* to attend a formal or informal meeting specifically to discuss a local, national, or international issue?"

There are two challenges with this approach. First, one could make the case that being invited to participate in a civic forum is causally linked to other forms of participation; active participants are in general more likely to be asked to participate in other ways. If this were accurate, it would violate a rule of two-stage least squares regression—namely, that the instrumental variable should be related to the independent variable (i.e., attending a deliberative forum) but not to the dependent variable (i.e., political and civic participation). This is a real concern, yet it does not appear to be a substantial risk. The key issue is the extending of an invitation. After all, the emphasis of many civic forums on attracting a broad and inclusive set of participants (as suggested in earlier chapters) makes it less likely that invitations would be limited to those who already participate in political and civic activities.

The second challenge is that only respondents who indicated that they had *not* attended a meeting in the last year were questioned whether they had been "asked to attend a meeting." Because this question was not posed to the entire sample, we created a new variable for the full sample by combining the answer to this question with a second question that was asked only of those who *had* attended a meeting:

People participate in meetings for different reasons. Using a scale from zero to ten, where 0 is "not important at all" and 10 is "very important," please tell me how important each of the following reasons were to your decision to participate in the last meeting you attended. . . . Because I was personally asked by someone to participate. (IF NECESSARY: Please tell me how important this reason was in your decision to participate in your last meeting to discuss an issue.")

Respondents who indicated that a personal invitation was "not important at all" were treated as if they had not been asked to attend. Any other response (from 1 to 10) was coded to signify that the respondent had been personally invited to participate. Our logic was that if a respondent described being personally asked to participate as an even marginally important reason for attending the forum (i.e., any response above 0), it presupposed that the respondent was invited.

We used these two questions—one asked of those who did not attend a forum in the last year and one asked of those who did—to construct a measure of whether a respondent was invited or not that could be used for our entire sample. For this composite variable, respondents were coded 0 if they either had not been asked to attend a meeting or indicated that a personal invitation was "not important at all" in their decision to attend a meeting; they scored 1 if they had been invited or if they indicated that a personal invitation was at all important in their decision to attend a meeting.

Table 5.7 presents the distribution of responses to the two questions used to create this instrumental variable, as well as the distribution of the instrumental variable itself. Panel A shows that 84% of those who did not attend a face-to-face forum in the last year had never been asked to do so. Panel B further reports that only 25% of those who did attend a face-to-face meeting ranked a personal invitation as "not at all important." Panel C draws on the results in the previous panels to create the instrumental variable for the entire sample of Americans; it indicates that 69% were not asked to participate in a face-to-face forum, and 30% were asked.

Although the instrumental variable is not ideal, there are several grounds for considering it a feasible one. First, it makes logical and theoretical sense. Second, its absolute and relative correlations with our various participation measures are reassuring. In particular, the instrumental variable is most strongly associated with face-to-face deliberation (.57) but

Table 5.7 Frequency distributions of instrumental variable and the variables used to create it

PANEL A. PERCENTAGE OF NON-FACE-TO-FACE DELIBERATORS INVITED TO A FACE-TO-FACE MEETING

	PERCENTAGE (%)
Yes	15
No	84
Don't know	0.3
Refused	0.3

Source: Discursive Participation Survey. Non-face-to-face deliberators sample: N = 745 (weighted sample).
Note: Cell entries are weighted responses to the following question: "Since January 2002, have you been INVITED to attend a formal or informal meeting to discuss a local, national, or international issue?"

PANEL B. REPORTED IMPORTANCE OF BEING INVITED TO ATTENDING A FACE-TO-FACE DELIBERATIVE FORUM

	PERCENTAGE (%)
0	25
1	6
2	6
3	5
4	3
5	10
6	3
7	6
8	8
9	4
10	24
Don't know	0.3
Refused	0.0

Source: Discursive Participation Survey. Face-to-face deliberators sample: N = 756 (weighted sample).
Note: Cell entries are responses to the following question: "People participate in meetings for different reasons. Using a scale of zero to ten, where zero is 'not important at all' and ten is 'very important,' please tell me how important the following reason was to your decision to participate in the last meeting you attended: Because I was personally asked by someone to participate."

PANEL C. NEWLY CONSTRUCTED INSTRUMENTAL VARIABLE

	PERCENTAGE (%)
Invite = 0	69
Invite = 1	30
Missing (Don't know and refusals)	0.5

Source: Discursive Participation Survey. National adult sample: N = 1,501 (weighted sample).

much more weakly related to elite contacting (.32), civic participation (.31), other forms of discursive participation (.29), and electoral participation (.18). This difference in the strength of the instrumental variable's relationship to the independent variable of interest (i.e., face-to-face deliberation) as contrasted with its weaker associations with the dependent variables is consistent with the requirement for two-stage least squares regression analyses.

Although there are potential shortcomings with using two-stage least squares regression analysis and with our instrumental variable, we are persuaded that they are outweighed by the benefits of this approach for deepening our analysis of causality. In addition, our analytic reliance on two-stage least squares regression is modest. We want to test whether the findings from two-stage least squares regression analysis fit the general pattern of deliberation affecting participation that arose from our previous two approaches (self-reports and OLS regression). Consistent evidence of deliberation effects across three divergent analytic approaches would improve our confidence that we have identified a general pattern.

Table 5.8 presents the results of the two-stage least squares regression analysis after controlling for the new instrumental variable. The findings confirm the general pattern found previously: Deliberation has statistically significant and positive effects on political capital (standardized beta = .19) and on all three forms of civic and political engagement—electoral participation (standardized beta = .12), elite contacting (standardized b=.31), and civic participation (standardized beta = .51). Participating in at least one deliberative forum in the last year increases the "amount" of political capital by 2.3 acts, the amount of electoral participation by .16 acts, and the amounts of elite contacting and civic participation by .81 acts each.

Moreover, the effects of deliberation are the dominant influences on elite contacting and civic participation, overshadowing the contributions of the usual drivers of political and civic behavior—SES and social capital. The standardized coefficient for deliberation is twice as strong as any other influence on elite contacting and more than four times larger than the strongest runner-up in influencing civic participation. In addition, the overall explanatory power of the models in table 5.8 is comparable to that of the fully specified OLS models previously presented (tables 5.4–5.6).

Overall, then, the results of the two-stage least squares analyses are consistent with our earlier findings—deliberation serves as a pathway to other forms of civic and political action. Even after purging possible confounding effects created by the impact of unmeasured influences and the causal impact of the dependent variables on face-to-face deliberation, our

Table 5.8 The effects of public deliberation on political capital and participation

	POLITICAL CAPITAL		ELECTORAL PARTICIPATION		ELITE CONTACTING		CIVIC PARTICIPATION	
	UNSTANDARDIZED	STANDARDIZED	UNSTANDARDIZED	STANDARDIZED	UNSTANDARDIZED	STANDARDIZED	UNSTANDARDIZED	STANDARDIZED
Demographic characteristics								
African American	−1.58 (.73) *	−.07 *	.05 (.08)	.02	−.32 (.15) *	−.07 *	−.00 (.10)	−.00
Latino	−3.35 (1.00) ***	−.11 ***	−.14 (.10)	−.04	−.30 (.20)	−.04	.02 (.14)	.01
Other ethnicity	−.76 (.78)	−.03	−.13 (.08)	−.05	−.31 (.16) *	−.06 *	−.16 (.11)	−.05
Education (5 cat.)	1.36 (.20) ***	.24 ***	.04 (.02) +	.06 +	.04 (.04)	.03	.04 (.03)	.06
Gender (F = 1)	−1.13 (.38) **	−.09 **	.01 (.04)	.01	.23 (.08) **	.09 **	.06 (.05)	.04
Age (5 cat.)	.12 (.17)	.02	.10 (.02) ***	.20 ***	.04 (.04)	.04	.00 (.02)	.00
Income (5 cat.)	.73 (.15) ***	.16 ***	.03 (.02) +	.06 +	.01 (.03)	.01	.00 (.02)	.01
Social capital								
Belong to organization	.53 (.46)	.04	.06 (.05)	.05	.37 (.09) ***	.14 ***	.14 (.06) *	.09 *
Religious attendance	.21 (.09) *	.07 *	.03 (.01) **	.09 **	.01 (.02)	.01	.04 (.01) **	.11 **
Length of residence	−.00 (.01)	−.01	.00 (.00) ***	.11 ***	−.00 (.00)	−.04	.00 (.00)	.02

Political capital								
Political efficacy			.05	.01 (.01)	.01	.01 (.02)	.04	.01 (.01)
Political trust			-.05	-.03 (.02)	-.16 ***	-.20 (.04) ***	-.04	-.03 (.03)
Social trust			-.02	-.01 (.02)	-.03	-.04 (.04)	.06 +	.05 (.03) +
Political knowledge			.09 *	.04 (.02) *	.17 ***	.16 (.03) ***	-.03	-.02 (.02)
Political interest			.16 ***	.04 (.01) ***	.14 ***	.07 (.02) ***	.01	.00 (.01)
Political attention			.07	.06 (.04)	.10 *	.17 (.07) *	.07	.07 (.05)
Ideological strength			.03	.02 (.02)	.08 **	.12 (.05) **	-.03	-.03 (.03)
Partisan strength			.09 **	.12 (.04) **	-.04	-.12 (.08)	-.02	-.03 (.06)
Political tolerance			.04	.03 (.03)	-.01	-.01 (.06)	-.03	-.04 (.04)
Deliberation	.19 **	2.34 (.79) **	.12 +	.16 (.09) +	.31 ***	.81 (.17) ***	.51 ***	.81 (.11) ***
Constant		18.15 (.77) ***		-.45 (.11) ***		-.08 (.22)		.38 (.15) **
N	782	782	768	768	764	764	772	772
R^2	0.231	0.231	.288	.288	.342	.342	.215	.215

Source: Discursive Participation Survey. National adult sample: $N = 1,501$ (unweighted sample).

Notes: Two-stage least squares regression method. Standard errors in parentheses. Dependent variables: See tables 5.3 through 5.6 and text.

$^+ p < .10$; $^* p < .05$; $^{**} p < .01$; $^{***} p < .001$.

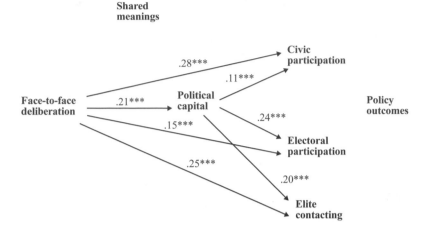

FIGURE 5.5   A REDUCED MODEL OF THE EFFECTS OF DISCURSIVE PARTICIPATION

Source: Discursive Participation Survey. National adult sample: $N = 1,501$ (unweighted sample).
Note: Path analysis presents standardized beta coefficients based on an OLS regression that is separate
from those in the previous tables. The model uses additive indexes for the social and political capital
variables and includes controls for the demographic and social capital variables that were used in our
earlier analyses. For more information on our estimation of the coefficients presented in the figure, see
page 188 of the appendix.
$^{+}p < .10; ^{*}p < .05; ^{**}p < .01; ^{***}p < .001.$

results reproduce the findings from self-reports and the OLS regression analyses. The convergence of three quite distinct bodies of evidence improves our confidence in concluding that face-to-face deliberation exerts an independent causal impact on civic and political participation. This is an impressive pattern of results that confirms the optimistic projections of democratic theorists.

Mapping the Impact of Deliberation on Engagement

Our findings regarding the political and civic effects of face-to-face deliberation may actually be overly conservative because they omit the additional indirect effects of deliberation on participation through political capital. We measure the total effects of deliberation by estimating the direct and indirect paths presented earlier in the heuristic depiction of our theoretical expectations in figure 5.3. In particular, figure 5.5 shows that deliberation has both direct effects on our three measures of participation (electoral participation, civic participation, and elite contacting), and indirect effects through political capital. The *total* effect of face-to-face deliberation on electoral participation is .20 (a direct impact of .15 plus an indirect impact through political capital of .21*.24), the total effect on elite contacting is .29, and the total effect on civic participation is .30. In general, accounting for the indirect effects of deliberation boosts its influence between about 10% and one-third.

In short, attending face-to-face deliberative forums increases other forms of political and civic participation both by directly encouraging and facilitating such engagement and by increasing resources and motivation through higher levels of political capital that in turn boost participation.

Talk Matters

The value of public talk and deliberation about issues of community concern is often dismissed. Its effects are thought to be narrowly confined to elite interactions. In terms of the mass public, deliberation is often derided as amounting to little more than idle talk that is disconnected from actual decision making (Berry, Portney, and Thomson 1993; Hibbing and Theiss-Morse 2002; Karpowitz 2003; Mendelberg and Oleske 2000; Sanders 1997; Schudson 1997; Sunstein 2001; Walsh 2003).

This chapter presents, however, the first systematic evidence that public deliberation is more than "just talk." It is an important aspect of democratic citizenship, not only in its own right, but also in its ability to stimulate and facilitate further political and civic action. The engagement of large numbers of Americans in talking about, discussing, and debating public issues is prompting them to do more to make contacts with elites (from boycotting to calling a public official or the media), to participate in civic activities (from volunteering to working with others to solve a community problem), and to engage in electoral politics (voting and working on a campaign). In addition, public talking increases citizens' store of political capital, which in turn further increases their resources and motivation to act in the political and civic world.

This conclusion is based both on self-reports of citizens who have attended deliberative forums and on our various regression analyses, which present consistent evidence of the effect of deliberation on political and civic participation. These findings challenge the pessimistic renditions of discursive participation as, at best, irrelevant to citizen engagement.

The political and civic effects of deliberation have important implications. First, they boost engagement in forms of participation that commentators have bemoaned as declining in American life (e.g., Putnam, 2000). Moreover, they provide some grounds for optimism regarding deliberation's impact on areas that we were unable to examine—notably, the formation of the discourses and socially shared meanings that underpin civil society and democratic government.

SIX

A Case Study of Deliberation in Action
Americans Discuss Social Security

In previous chapters we have examined broad patterns of deliberation among Americans. This chapter takes a closer look at one deliberative forum—entitled Americans Discuss Social Security (ADSS)—in order to study in a particular case the general questions that have motivated this book: who deliberates, how they deliberate, and to what effect. While our case study (like others) does not offer fully generalizable conclusions, it does create the opportunity to illustrate deliberation in practice and to study its nuances and complexity. Are the general patterns we find among a representative sample of Americans evident in ADSS? Conversely, does ADSS deviate from the general patterns we previously identified in ways that raise new questions and tentative hypotheses?

The Deliberative Experience: Americans Discuss Social Security

In 1998, President Clinton put Social Security at the top of the public agenda with a bold declaration in his State of the Union address:

> Now, if we balance the budget for next year, it is projected that we'll have a sizable surplus in the years that immediately follow. What should we do with this projected surplus? I have a simple four-word answer: Save Social Security first [applause]. Thank you. Tonight I propose that we reserve 100 percent of the surplus—that's every penny of any surplus—until we have taken all the necessary measures to strengthen the Social Security system for the twenty-first century. Let us say to all Americans watching tonight—whether you're 70 or 50 or whether you just started paying into the system—Social Security will be there when you need it. Let us make this commitment: Social Security first (Clinton 1998).

The Pew Charitable Trusts launched Americans Discuss Social Security (or ADSS) in order to foster an informed national discussion about Social

Security and to help Americans make sense of the debate that President Clinton sparked. In particular, Pew aimed to create "a forum for genuine learning and informed and reasoned discourse" and to "engage Americans from all walks of life in a nationwide conversation about the future of Social Security"—specifically, "How [to] . . . pay for the retirement of 76 million baby boomers."

ADSS positioned itself as a neutral and fair convener rather than as an advocate for any particular reform of Social Security. During 1998, it hosted public forums in five cities (Austin, Texas; Buffalo, New York; Seattle, Washington; Des Moines, Iowa; and Phoenix, Arizona). The forums were held on Saturdays in large convention centers to facilitate broad participation and lasted about four to five hours.

The ADSS forums were expected to engage and educate the participants in the sessions as well as Americans in the surrounding communities who learned about the forums from press coverage. Further public engagement was expected to flow from a nationally broadcast forum with President Clinton and other leading government officials. The first two sections of this chapter examine the deliberative dynamics of the five ADSS forums. Then we examine the impacts of one of the ADSS forums—the session held on May 30, 1998, with 408 residents of the Phoenix metropolitan area.[1]

Who Deliberates?

The ADSS project tried to recruit a representative cross section of the population within the five metropolitan areas where it hosted forums. It used a variety of recruiting tools, including invitations sent to large random samples of registered voters in each metropolitan area, announcements in newspapers, and outreach to members of numerous interest groups (for example, both political parties, the Chamber of Commerce, the local chapters of the AARP, and groups for disabled citizens, youth organizations, and organizations for minority groups). Most forum participants were recruited through the random selection mechanism of invitations to registered voters. Fewer than 10% of those who were invited or attended were recruited by interest groups.

How diverse were the attendees? We compared the demographic characteristics of the participants in each of the five ADSS sites to U.S. Census data. With the exception of only one site (Des Moines), respondents were fairly representative of their communities in terms of gender. The forums were not, however, representative in terms of age and income. In every site, young adults were under-represented, and adults age sixty-five and over were over-represented. In part, this was due to the topic of Social

Security, which was a bigger draw for people in retirement and near retirement than for young adults. In Phoenix, 24% of the attendees were aged eighteen to thirty-four, whereas that age group constituted 37% of the population in the metropolitan area, and 26% were senior citizens, who made up 17% of the population in the metropolitan area.

In addition, low-income people were under-represented. Thirty percent of the attendees in Phoenix had incomes of less than $30,000; 30% had incomes ranging from $30,000 to $60,000; and 40% had incomes above $60,000, while U.S. Census data showed percentages in the metropolitan area of 47% low income, 24% middle income, and 29% high income.

In short, the forums did draw diverse participants, but they were not representative of the age, income, and gender distributions within the metropolitan areas. ADSS director and moderator Carolyn Lukensmeyer tried to correct for under-representation by informing participants of the extent to which they matched the demographics of their metropolitan area. For example, she highlighted the under-representation of younger Americans and challenged the forums to give particular weight to the views of the younger participants who were attending: "The youth voice is a little bit under-represented at your tables. So what's our collective responsibility? To make sure that the young people who are at the tables have plenty of space to put out their perspectives."

ADSS's difficulty in engaging a representative group is not unique. Some of the best attempts to realize deliberative democracy have also experienced troublesome sample attrition or selection bias (Fishkin 1995; Merkle 1996). Our analyses below pursue several approaches to offset this challenge in order to examine the deliberation process and its effects.

How to Deliberate?

Our analyses of the deliberation patterns of Americans overall are evident in how ADSS structured its five forums to engage participants in a cognitive process based on evidence and reasoned argument. Three features of the ADSS forums illustrate the reason-based approach to deliberation. First, pre-registered participants received an informational packet containing Social Security background facts before the forums. This created the opportunity for participants to attend the forums with at least a minimal level of competence regarding Social Security's benefits, costs, and operations.

Second, each forum brought all participants together to hear introductory comments from the forum's main moderator, Ms. Lukensmeyer, local honorary figures, and, of particular importance, presentations by experts regarding Social Security's operations. In particular, the commissioner of the Social Security Administration, Kenneth Apfel, or one of his deputies, and a representative from the American Academy of Actuaries each made presentations about the facts of the Social Security program. Forum participants were able to ask questions of the experts and to make comments about what they had heard. (These experts were available throughout the forum, making it possible for participants to have their factual questions answered on the spot.)

A potential consequence of the cognitive approach and use of experts is that the information may be biased (perhaps inadvertently) in ways that advance or denigrate particular perspectives. Indeed, this has been a persistent concern of deliberation critics, as we noted in chapter 1. We content-analyzed the discussions during the five forums and, among our results, found that the moderators and the elites who spoke at the forum were generally neutral, though they were disproportionately critical of reforms that would privatize Social Security by allowing contributors to set up personal investment accounts (akin to an IRA), which could be put in private equities and bonds.[2] (President George W. Bush energetically promoted this kind of reform following the 2004 election.) Approximately 20% of elite statements were opposed to private accounts. As we shall see later, this did not seem to have swayed participants.

The third feature of ADSS was small-group sessions in which participants discussed their values relating to Social Security and their views about policy options to reform Social Security. These small groups gathered at round tables that accommodated 8–10 participants and a moderator who was committed and trained to facilitate balanced learning and a fair airing of views.

ADSS organizers began the small-group discussions by focusing on values, with Ms. Lukensmeyer directing participants to write down answers to two questions listed in a packet at their tables: "1. What are the most important values you and your family carry about Social Security? 2. As the country considers reforming the Social Security system, what values do you most want lawmakers to protect?" After giving people a chance to jot down answers, she asked each table to spend upwards of half an hour collectively identifying "the three or four key values that your table believes should guide policymakers as they consider the future of Social Security."

Participants in Phoenix initially expressed considerable confusion about exactly how to think about values, but eventually they identified a wide range, with the greatest attention focused on four: a safety net for those who need it, peace of mind and stability, intergenerational equity, and individualism.³ These values may reflect priming effects, as all but one of them were mentioned by Ms. Lukensmeyer or in the materials ADSS gave the table moderators.

Following the discussion of values, the focus shifted—according to our content analysis—to consideration of almost two dozen facts. Most of the discussion concentrated on the basic features of the Social Security program's benefit structures, budget, and financial solvency as well as rising life expectancy.

While the discussion of facts was straightforward and uncontentious, the small-group consideration of policy options focused on the more uncertain topic of how to "pay for the retirement of 76 million baby boomers." The information packet and Ms. Lukensmeyer challenged the participants: "Should we maintain the current system, with workers paying taxes for current retirees? Or should we change the Social Security system to allow workers to put some of their tax money into personal accounts they can invest in stocks and bonds?" Although ADSS may appear to have primed participants (three-quarters of the options that participants raised were drawn from the list of policy options presented by ADSS),⁴ the broader information environment was probably a greater influence—the nine policy options were the most widely discussed by policy makers and policy specialists in Washington and in the press. Three reform options drew particular attention according to our content analysis: (1) raising the ceiling on taxable wages above the 1998 level of $68,400, (2) reducing the cost of living adjustment (COLA), and (3) allowing individuals to invest part of their Social Security tax contributions in their own privately controlled savings accounts.

After participants discussed reform options in their small groups and then in the full forum, they used keypads to record their preferences. Seventy-four percent of attendees to the five forums either supported or were "comfortable with" raising the earning ceiling subject to payroll taxations, and 67% were opposed or "uncomfortable with" reducing the COLA. They were split on the option of establishing private accounts as a part of Social Security (39% to 41%).

Although the division over privatizing Social Security can be polarizing and provoke acrimony, the tone of the ADSS forums was varied, though dominated by a cognitive approach. More than 90% of the full forum conversations and more than 70% of the small-group deliberations were substantive and reasoned, which we defined as an attempt to provide information or advance the discussion in a nonconflictual way. Conflict and bickering were absent from the full-forum deliberation and only cropped up in less than 5% of the comments in the small-group discussions. About

12% of the small-group discussions were agreement-oriented (expressing assent with a previously expressed idea), and about 5% were questioning (politely disagreeing or expressing another point of view but not argumentative in tone).

Democratic theorists and the representative sample of Americans discussed in previous chapters suggest that the moderator is a critical organizational feature of deliberation for encouraging reason-based dialogue and tolerance of differences. In the ADSS forums, the moderator—Ms. Lukensmeyer—helped set a substantive and tolerant tone by requesting that "everyone [should be] listened to and respected." She also counseled tolerance of differences, asking participants to pay special attention to under-represented groups (e.g., youth and lower-income Americans). Indeed, ADSS decided to address values early in its program precisely in order to highlight the different sets of principles that individuals bring to civic forums.

The tilt of American deliberation toward reaching agreement also appeared to be evident in the ADSS forums in ways that may help illuminate its dynamics. Neither table moderators nor the overall moderator, Ms. Lukensmeyer, insisted that the attendees agree. Rather, a more subtle process was at work. Both the small-group discussions and the full-forum sessions involved opening the floor to airing different viewpoints, summarizing the general discussion, and, in the case of the larger forum, the use of keypads to enter votes, which were then tabulated and quickly presented. Although many attendees may well have been convinced by the evidence to converge, it is also possible that at least some participants felt socially corralled into agreeing, as the repeated summarizing of views seemed to iron out differences and create a spirit of conformity. We do not find, however, hard evidence for this more subtle form of pressuring that has concerned critics of deliberation.

Overall, then, the reason-based and substantive orientation of the ADSS forums parallels the kind of deliberative experiences reported by Americans in our representative sample.

The Effects of ADSS

The premise of ADSS was that talk matters and would affect deliberators and public policy. The program sought to have two effects. First, it promised to "create opportunities for the American people to voice their views to America's policymakers" and, indeed, it forwarded a report of forum proceedings to Congress and the Clinton Administration in June 1998. Assessing the effects of ADSS on government officials was not possible.

Even if it were possible, a variety of research studies suggest some skepticism regarding the proposition that policymakers would respond to general public opinion—especially in recent years (Bartels 2008; Jacobs and Page 2005; Jacobs and Skocpol 2005; Bartels et al. 2005) or, at best, that responsiveness is "contingent" on such factors as salience (Manza and Cook 2002, 651–53; see also Sharp 1999; Burstein 2003). As President Bush's later campaign to partially privatize Social Society in opposition to public opinion illustrates (Page and Jacobs 2009; Edwards 2007), policy initiatives by politicians on even highly salient issues like Social Security may be at odds with public opinion.

Second, ADSS set out to change the attitudes and political behavior of forum attendees in three respects. First, it sought to increase the salience of Social Security for attendees. Indeed, proponents of deliberation argue that civic dialogues should prompt citizens to think more about the issues under discussion and to become more cognizant of them (Fishkin 1991). Second, ADSS expected to increase the knowledge of participants about Social Security. This is another core assumption of the reason-based accounts of deliberation (as discussed in chapter 1); Benhabib concludes that "deliberation is a procedure for being informed" (1996, 71) and Page explains that deliberation is critical to "ensure that the public's policy preferences . . . are informed, enlightened, and authentic" (1996, 1). Third, ADSS aimed to stimulate sustained civic and political participation related to Social Security. Ms. Lukensmeyer concluded the forums by urging involvement in a range of activities from holding discussion groups to writing members of Congress. These expectations fit with the arguments of deliberation proponents who linked participation in civic dialogues with greater citizen involvement in politics (Barber 1984; Mansbridge 1983 and 1996; Pateman 1970; Fishkin 1995). If ADSS influenced its participants, we would expect individuals who attended to register statistically significant higher levels of salience, knowledge, and plans to engage in future political participation compared to the random sample of Phoenix residents and individuals who were invited to attend the forum but could not.

One test of ADSS's impact on political attitudes and participation is whether it is broadly felt or restricted to individuals with higher social and economic status. ADSS and deliberation enthusiasts emphasize the importance of including groups that are often left outside legislative politics, especially the under-represented, while critics (e.g., Sanders 1997) warn that deliberation is a process biased toward the better-off. The question is whether changes in political attitudes and behavior register equally across gender, age, income, and education subgroups, or whether they register unevenly.

We examined these potential impacts of ADSS on political attitudes and participation by using a quasi-experimental research design known as a pre-test/post-test comparison group design (Cook and Campbell 1979; Shadish, Cook, and Campbell 2001).[5] In particular, we commissioned the National Opinion Research Center (NORC) to interview a random sample of 301 respondents who were invited to attend the May 30 forum and a random sample of 236 respondents in the Phoenix metropolitan area (Maricopa County, Arizona) who were unconnected with the forum. The interviews took place May 22–29, 1998, before the forum, and June 1–21, 1998, afterward. (The survey and variables are discussed in greater detail online at http://www.press.uchicago.edu/books/jacobs.)

Our approach offers a rigorous means to study changes in opinions about Social Security. Without a careful research design, it would be difficult to identify whether changes in Social Security attitudes and behavior resulted from participating in the ADSS forums (as organizers and deliberation advocates assume) or from other extraneous factors such as unrelated press stories about Social Security, mailings from the Social Security Administration, or a public relations campaign by an interest group like the AARP. The pre-test/post-test comparison group design allows us to better isolate the effects of the forums by contrasting the change in the opinions of the participants from before and after the forum with the opinions of two comparison groups before and after the forums—those people who were invited to the forum but did not attend (nonattending "invitees") and a random sample of adults aged eighteen and over who live in the Phoenix metropolitan area. The principle advantage of the design is that if the attendees' views change significantly more than the views of the other two groups while controlling for their unequal starting points, we have some grounds to infer that the changes result from the forum rather than other factors.

Using identically worded survey questions before and after the ADSS forum in Phoenix, we generated measures for our three core areas of analytic interest—salience, knowledge, and anticipated future participation. (Exact question wordings and additional information on variable construction are available online at http://www.press.uchicago.edu/books/jacobs.) Our salience measure is based on responses to survey items that examined whether and how much time was spent thinking about, talking about, or reading about Social Security. If respondents said they spent time on any one of these activities, interviewers asked four separate questions that focused more specifically on how often they spent time thinking, talking with family members, talking with friends, or reading about Social Security. Our analyses, as discussed below, relied both on responses to some of the individual survey items as well as on an index of these items. We assessed factual knowledge related to Social Security by constructing an index based on a set of eight survey items that combined factual questions with assessments by the respondent and interviewer. Finally, we assessed plans for future participation by asking respondents about whether in the future they might possibly contact their representatives to Congress to express their views on Social Security, participate in an organization committed to discussing the future of Social Security, or talk to a family member, friend, or neighbor about Social Security. Our analysis indicates that ADSS did have an impact on forum participants but that the type of influence varied considerably.

ADSS Increased the Salience of the Social Security Issue

The salience of Social Security increased dramatically for ADSS participants. Table 6.1 shows that before the forum 68% reported that they expressed interest in Social Security in one of three distinct ways—thinking about Social Security recently, talking about it, or reading about it. Interest-based engagement in any of these three activities jumped by 18 percentage points to 86% after the ADSS forum. Among the nonattending invitees, interest slightly declined, while among respondents in the random sample, interest decreased by 17%.

We developed a salience index composed of respondents' answers to whether they had thought about Social Security recently, talked about it, or read about it. Using that index, we conducted an analysis of covariance to determine if the change from pre-forum to post-forum was significantly different for the attendees when compared first to the nonattending invitees and second to the random sample. The analysis of covariance (ANCOVA) controls for the fact that the initial interest of each group was different.[6]

The bottom portion of table 6.1 shows that the change in attendees' level of interest is statistically different from the change among both invitees and the random sample. This is true even when controlling for the samples' unequal starting points and variances. The mean score on the salience index for attendees increased by three points, from 9.5 to 12.5, while the mean salience index scores of the other two groups that did not participate in the forum actually dropped. These findings indicate that the ADSS forum had a marked effect on the salience of Social Security as an issue.

ADSS Increased Knowledge of Social Security

ADSS boosted understanding of Social Security among those who attended its forums. This is evident in three distinct sets of data. First, the self-

Table 6.1   Salience of Social Security

	ATTENDEES		INVITEES		RANDOM SAMPLE	
	PRE-FORUM	POST-FORUM	PRE-FORUM	POST-FORUM	PRE-FORUM	POST-FORUM
Thought, talked, read about SS recently						
Yes	68%	86%	60%	57%	70%	53%
No	32%	14%	41%	43%	30%	47%
Don't know	0%	0%	0%	0%	0%	0%
Salience index						
Mean (Never = 1) (3 to 24 possible)	9.5	12.5[a,b]	8.7	7.6	7.8	7.4
Standard deviation	5.5	5.2	5.6	4.7	4.8	4.8
Number of cases	157	157	84	84	148	148

Source: Americans Discuss Social Security Survey.
Notes: Column percentages do not always sum to 100% due to rounding. The salience index is composed of five items. As described in the text and in more detail online at: http://press .uchicago.edu/books/jacobs, the index includes whether respondents had thought, talked, or read about Social Security recently and *how much* they had thought about Social Security, talked about it with family, talked about it with friends, and read about it. Respondents were given a score of 3 on the index if they answered no to the initial filter question. "Don't know" responses were excluded from the index. The post-forum means of each group were compared using an analysis of covariance (ANCOVA) test to determine whether the change from pre-forum to post-forum within the attendees group was statistically different from the change in means for either the invitees or the random sample while controlling for their unequal starting points.
a The attendees' change on the index from the pre-to-post measures is statistically different from the invitees' change at the $p < .01$ level in a two-tailed test.
b The attendees' change on the index from the pre-to-post measures is statistically different from the random sample respondents' change at the $p < .001$ level in a two-tailed test.

reported level of understanding increased among forum attendees. Table 6.2 shows that the proportion of attendees who reported that they had an "excellent" or "good" understanding of the program jumped, respectively, by 16 percentage points (16% to 32%) and 11 points (46% to 57%). By contrast, the self-reported understanding of Social Security actually appeared to decline among invitees who were unable to attend the ADSS forum and respondents in the random sample.

Second, the ratings of respondent knowledge among ADSS attendees by interviewers also increased. The lower half of table 6.2 shows that interviewer scores of "very high" attendee knowledge increased by 16 percentage points after the forum, while interviewer scores for invitees and random sample respondents appeared to decline. Our analysis of mean scores confirmed the pattern: ratings of attendees' understanding of Social Security after the forums increased significantly more than did ratings of the understanding of invitees and the random sample ($p < .001$).

Third, respondents' answers to six factual questions similarly showed learning by forum attendees. Table 6.3 shows that each of the knowledge

Table 6.2   Ratings of respondents' understanding of Social Security

	ATTENDEES		INVITEES		RANDOM SAMPLE	
	PRE-FORUM	POST-FORUM	PRE-FORUM	POST-FORUM	PRE-FORUM	POST-FORUM
Respondents' self-rating						
Understanding of SS						
Excellent	16%	32%	8%	4%	18%	11%
Good	46%	57%	50%	61%	36%	40%
Fair	33%	11%	30%	31%	37%	43%
Poor	5%	1%	10%	5%	10%	6%
Don't know	0%	0%	2%	0%	0%	1%
Means (Excellent = 4)	2.7	3.2[a,b]	2.6	2.6	2.6	2.6
Interviewers' rating						
Understanding of SS						
Very high	25%	41%	23%	7%	30%	20%
Fairly high	33%	36%	30%	38%	31%	29%
Average	38%	21%	43%	48%	31%	45%
Fairly low	4%	2%	3%	7%	5%	5%
Very low	0%	0%	1%	0%	3%	2%
Not possible to tell	0%	0%	0%	0%	1%	0%
Means (Very high = 5)	3.8	4.2 [a,b]	3.7	3.5	3.8	3.6
Number of cases	157	157	84	84	148	148

Source: Americans Discuss Social Security Survey.
Note: Column percentages do not always sum to 100% due to rounding. The post-forum means of each group were compared using the nonparametric Kruskal-Wallis test because the response distributions of both variables showed extreme and noncorrectable violations of the normality and homogeneity of variance assumptions for the ANCOVA tests.
a The attendees' change from the pre-to-post means is statistically different from the pre-to-post change in the means for the invitees at the $p < .001$ level in a two-tailed test.
b The attendees' change from the pre-to-post means is statistically different from the pre-to-post change in the means for the random sample respondents at the $p < .001$ level in a two-tailed test.

items showed dramatic improvements for the attendees from the pre-forum to post-forum measures. Critical but obscure features of Social Security experienced the greatest improvements: the knowledge of attendees that program contributions were invested in U.S. Treasury bonds increased by 37 percentage points (from 59% to 96%), and their understanding that employers paid 6% of the employee payroll tax to help finance the program increased by 34 points (53% to 87%).

We used the responses to each of these six questions to develop a "Social Security information index." Respondents were given one point for each correct answer, for a possible score of 0 to 6. The last panel in table 6.3 similarly shows that attendees were more likely than the random sample and invitees to know more of the correct answers at pre-forum. These knowledge gains persist even when we control for how much respondents knew before the ADSS forums—a potentially important factor if interest in Social Security motivated participation. Specifically, attendee gains in knowledge

Table 6.3   Knowledge of Social Security facts

	ATTENDEES		INVITEES		RANDOM SAMPLE	
	PRE-FORUM	POST-FORUM	PRE-FORUM	POST-FORUM	PRE-FORUM	POST-FORUM
SS in treasury bonds						
True#	59%	96%	50%	73%	46%	55%
False	22%	0%	26%	15%	35%	27%
Don't know	19%	4%	24%	11%	19%	18%
SS has budget deficit						
True	28%	23%	57%	43%	63%	66%
False#	58%	69%	35%	42%	32%	28%
Don't know	14%	8%	7%	15%	5%	6%
Fewer workers in future						
True#	72%	84%	66%	63%	54%	64%
False	22%	13%	30%	32%	45%	32%
Don't know	6%	3%	5%	5%	1%	3%
"Pay-as-you-go" structure						
True#	78%	89%	88%	82%	80%	82%
False	15%	10%	7%	10%	16%	16%
Don't know	7%	2%	5%	8%	4%	3%
SS employee' tax rate						
About 3%	12%	1%	24%	11%	21%	18%
About 6%#	53%	87%	44%	56%	35%	48%
About 9%	14%	4%	14%	15%	20%	16%
About 15%	8%	2%	13%	11%	14%	11%
Don't know	13%	6%	5%	6%	11%	7%
SS proportion of fed. budget						
Less than 5%	37%	21%	30%	35%	38%	41%
About 10%	17%	13%	25%	20%	24%	22%
About 20%#	25%	33%	20%	23%	18%	12%
About 40%	12%	12%	8%	4%	6%	10%
50% or more	3%	3%	4%	4%	3%	2%
Don't know	7%	20%	13%	14%	11%	14%
SS information index						
Mean (0 to 6 possible; 6 = all correct)	3.4	4.6 [a,b]	3.0	3.2	2.6	2.9
Standard deviation	1.4	1.1	1.5	1.8	1.3	1.4
Number of cases	157	157	84	84	148	148

Source: Americans Discuss Social Security Survey.
Note: Figures for the six knowledge items are percentages. Column percentages do not always sum to 100% due to rounding. The # symbol denotes the correct answer. The post-forum means of each group were compared using an analysis of covariance (ANCOVA) test to determine whether the change from pre-forum to post-forum within the attendees group was statistically different from the change in means for either the invitees or the random sample while controlling for their unequal starting points.
a The attendees' change on the index from the pre-to-post measures is statistically different from the invitees' change at the $p < .001$ level in a two-tailed test.
b The attendees' change on the index from the pre-to-post measures is statistically different from the random sample respondents' change at the $p < .001$ level in a two-tailed test.

Table 6.4   Future participation in politics and Social Security

	ATTENDEES		INVITEES		RANDOM SAMPLE	
	PRE-FORUM	POST-FORUM	PRE-FORUM	POST-FORUM	PRE-FORUM	POST-FORUM
Contact Congress						
Very likely	47%	49%	32%	37%	20%	19%
Somewhat likely	33%	35%	38%	36%	36%	33%
Somewhat unlikely	12%	12%	18%	12%	22%	27%
Very unlikely	8%	5%	12%	15%	22%	21%
Don't know	0%	0%	0%	0%	0%	0%
Participate in organization						
Very likely	47%	40%	32%	23%	18%	17%
Somewhat likely	37%	43%	41%	46%	38%	33%
Somewhat unlikely	14%	7%	17%	17%	22%	28%
Very unlikely	3%	10%	10%	14%	22%	22%
Don't know	0%	1%	1%	0%	1%	0%
Talk to family or friends						
Very likely	83%	83%	71%	65%	63%	55%
Somewhat likely	13%	14%	18%	30%	22%	30%
Somewhat unlikely	1%	3%	2%	4%	5%	7%
Very unlikely	2%	1%	8%	1%	10%	7%
Don't know	0%	0%	0%	0%	1%	0%
Future participation index						
Mean (Very likely = 4) (3 to 12 possible)	10.2	10.2	9.6	9.3	8.4	8.3
Standard deviation	1.7	1.8	2	2.1	2.3	2.2
Number of cases	157	157	78	78	148	148

Source: Americans Discuss Social Security Survey.
Note: Column percentages do not always sum to 100% due to rounding. The "don't know" responses were excluded in the computation of the means. Two nonparametric Kruskal-Wallis tests showed insignificant differences between the attendees' change in the index scores and each of the other two groups.

were significantly greater than the gains in knowledge for invitees and respondents in the random sample ($p < .001$).

ADSS EXERTED LITTLE IMPACT ON FUTURE PARTICIPATION

Going to the ADSS forum did little to affect political participation, mostly because of the already high level of engagement of the attendees. Table 6.4 shows that forum participants indicated little change from their pre- to post-forum interviews in whether they were "very" or "somewhat" likely to contact Congress (80% to 84%), participate in organizations to address Social Security (84% to 83%), and talk to family or friends about the program (96% to 97%). In addition, interviews with invitees and respondents in the random sample did not generally register much change either. Similarly, the mean index score for the attendees remained at 10.2, and the scores for the other two groups were also largely unchanged.

In short, the ADSS forums did not seem to increase participation among attendees as expected by organizers and by deliberation advocates more generally. These results differ, however, from those in chapter 5, which suggested that participation in deliberative forums led to future civic and political engagement. The case of ADSS may not be representative of many deliberative forums. Deliberation effects may vary, for instance, by level of government; forums devoted to local or state issues—a large proportion of the civic dialogues that Americans generally participate in—may produce the higher levels of involvement in the political process that we found in chapter 5.

SUBGROUP DIFFERENCES IN EFFECTS

Our findings that ADSS increased salience and knowledge but not future participation appeared to be consistent across subgroups. To investigate the potential that some subgroups (such as seniors) changed significantly more than other demographic groups between the pre- and post-forum surveys, we conducted an analysis of covariance that controlled not only for selection effects but also for statistical interactions. In particular, we examined whether men and women and respondents with different levels of education, income, and age changed in similar or significantly different ways from pre-forum to post-forum surveys.

We found no statistically significant interaction effects. This means that each of the subgroups we examined changed in more or less similar ways from the time period before the forum to the time period after the forum. In other words, the changes we found cut across traditional demographic groups—young, middle-aged, and old; rich and poor; men and women; and well educated and the not-so-well-educated. Of particular importance, these findings do not support the suspicion that ADSS might especially prompt seniors compared to other demographic groups to become more interested, knowledgeable, and active.

These results ease our initial concern that the over-representation of older, better-educated, and higher-income respondents at the ADSS forums might compromise our ability to generalize. Evidence that the effects of ADSS are homogeneous and do not differentially affect some groups more than others gives us greater confidence to generalize from our findings about ADSS forums to other similar types of deliberative forums.

DELIBERATION IN ACTION IN AMERICANS DISCUSS SOCIAL SECURITY

This chapter's close study of organized forums on Social Security breaks into the "black box" of deliberation. ADSS displays the dynamics and effects that confirm the expectations of both the advocates and critics of deliberation. Forum organizers were effective organizers—they convened large- and small-group sessions and created a final segment with the entire group that conveyed the views of the different tables. ADSS followed many of the organizing principles identified in chapter 4, including the fostering of deliberation based on reason, tolerance for differing perspectives, and the search for agreement.

Even more important, we have shown that the ADSS forum in Phoenix had important effects. At a time when critics bemoan the lack of citizen competence and the decline of citizen involvement, participants in the ADSS deliberative forum did in fact attach greater importance to Social Security and learn more about the program compared to those who did not attend the forum. The impacts of ADSS imply that deliberation can play a critical role in bolstering the competence of citizens in a democratic process of decision making.

Some findings, however, may support the concerns of critics. The disproportionate turnout of the better-educated, higher-income earners, and older Americans echoes a consistent criticism of deliberation as reinforcing existing structural inequalities in civic and political life. In addition, our pre-test/post-test quasi-experimental design revealed the difficulty in prompting participants to become *more* actively involved with the issue in the future than they were in the past. Moreover, ADSS had limited "ripple effects" within the Phoenix metropolitan area. Only 10% of the Phoenix-area residents in our random sample reported hearing about any meetings or forums about Social Security in the Phoenix area.

The previous chapter's findings that deliberation *does* prompt increases in civic and political participation among Americans in general might lead some to dismiss our findings of ADSS's lack of effects on participation. We would counsel against such hasty conclusions. The impact of deliberation is probably contingent on a number of factors, including the role of the moderator, the kind of information that participants receive, the issue under discussion, and who attends and actually participates in the dialogue.

Part 2

WHY DISCURSIVE
PARTICIPATION?

SEVEN

Organizing Deliberation

As previous chapters have made clear, discursive participation about issues of public concern can take many forms—from an exchange over the
phone or via e-mail to an informal conversation at work or home to participation in more public or semipublic forums. While any form of political
talk requires some degree of individual interest, ability, and opportunity,
participation in public forums can be particularly costly, requiring individuals who are willing and able to talk collectively with each other in
public and to devote time and effort to interacting with others who may
not understand their views or who might even oppose them.

Several trends, documented most comprehensively by Putnam (2000),
suggest that citizens may be unwilling or unable to participate in such
deliberative forums. For one, generational change is removing the cohort
raised during the Second World War, a cohort that was intensely mobi-
lized and civic-minded. In their place are more recent generations that
may have less time and reason to form and sustain the social networks and
organizational memberships necessary for collective action, in large part
because they are more mobile, more likely to live in disconnected, subur-
ban neighborhoods, and thus less rooted in particular, socially integrated
communities. In addition, contemporary families—especially younger
families—have less time to invest in their communities because both
adults (when two adults are present) often work outside the home, pursue careers, spend considerable time commuting, and are overwhelmed
by the responsibilities of parenting and other functions. Moreover, technology such as television, the Internet, and video and on-line games may
encourage people to pull back from activities that encourage local community connectedness in favor of more individualized pursuits or more
ephemeral communities of interest. Finally, the basic building blocks of
public deliberation—political and social or interpersonal trust—are also
in decline in recent decades (see also, Brehm and Rahn 1997). Put simply,

participation in deliberative forums may run against the grain of contemporary life for most citizens.

In addition to these individual-level barriers to participating, there are often significant costs associated with organizing deliberative forums. While some of these costs are borne by public-spirited individuals who devote their personal time and resources to organizing informal gatherings of citizens, traditionally this role has been played by community organizations of various stripes. But driven by some of the same trends discussed above, locally embedded, membership-driven organizations that have historically been a staple of American civil society appear to be on the decline (Putnam 2000; Skocpol 2003). How then do we explain our (and others') findings that, despite these individual and organizational constraints, a substantial percentage of Americans regularly engage in some form of face-to-face, group deliberation?

The answer, we believe, lies in part in a growing movement spearheaded by a loose network of government agencies, businesses, civic groups, nongovernmental organizations and foundations that is designed to reconstitute the discursive, deliberative aspects of civil society. This movement is motivated by a belief in the importance of citizen's discursive involvement in the pressing issues of the day, both as a means to achieve other goals (i.e., to promote a policy change) and as an end in itself (i.e., a component of the broader community's fabric). Indeed, a veritable revolution has occurred over the past two decades in the formation of organizations and a "profession" devoted to the participation of ordinary citizens in discussions of issues affecting their communities. The effect of this organizational infrastructure for public deliberation is to subsidize the costs and increase the benefits to individuals talking together. This chapter first provides a brief overview of the history, purpose, and membership of this evolving public deliberation movement and then uses our own survey of local and national organizations that conduct deliberative forums to examine these organizations in more careful detail.

The Structure of the Public Deliberation Movement

Several disparate forms of deliberative organizations have developed. These organizations can be differentiated by whether they are temporary or permanent, by who initiates them, and by who participates in them (Leighninger 2006; Button and Ryfe 2005; Ryfe 2002).

An important variation among new deliberative organizations—the focus of this chapter—is their degree of coordination (independent or linked) and whether they are local or national. The last two decades have seen the emergence of a loosely affiliated network of organizations dedicated to encouraging public deliberation. Simplifying somewhat, this network consists of three layers (see fig. 7.1). At the base are local organizations such as church groups, civic associations, businesses, schools, libraries and the like (Leighninger 2006). In some cases these are free-standing entities with no formal affiliations to more regional or national organizations (for example, a local reading group); in others they are local chapters of larger organizations (for example, a local chapter of a union or club). Some have a long-standing presence in their communities and engage in a wide range of activities, of which forums are only one part (for example, the Parent Teacher Association), while others are created on a more ad hoc basis and focus on more specific issues (for example, a group organized around concerns over a recent racial incident or a community development plan). Despite this variation, they do share a common feature—they all have the local social capital and grassroots connections to bring members (of the organization or the larger community) together to discuss an issue in public.

One step removed from these local organizations are national organizations created explicitly to encourage local dialogue and deliberation (for an excellent overview and categorizing of sixteen such organizations, see Ryfe 2002). These more recent organizations tend to be supported by foundations, are steeped in various and often competing theories and practices of dialogue and deliberation, and are centrally committed to the processes of public participation rather than to particular issues or communities. Examples of such organizations include the National Issues Forums, Everyday Democracy, and America*Speaks*. The National Issues Forums began in 1981 and is supported by the Kettering Foundation. It describes itself as "a nonpartisan, nationwide network of locally sponsored public forums for the consideration of public policy issues [that brings people] . . . together to reason and talk—to deliberate about common problems." The forums "focus on an issue such as health care, immigration, Social Security, or ethnic and racial tensions . . . [to] provide a way for people of diverse views and experiences to seek a shared understanding of the problem and to search for common ground for action" (http://www.nifi.org/forums). Everyday Democracy, which was previously known as the Study Circles Resource Center, is a national organization that harbors a similar mission of "help[ing] local communities find ways for all kinds of people to think, talk and work together to solve problems." Founded in 1989 with the support of philanthropist Paul Aicher, Everyday Democracy has worked with more than 550 communities to "hel[p] people connect public dialogue to real solutions" (http://www.everyday-democracy.org/en/Index.aspx).

FIGURE 7.1   THE STRUCTURE OF THE PUBLIC DELIBERATION MOVEMENT

America*Speaks* is a third illustration of a nonpartisan organization that is committed to "democratic deliberation . . . [to] access the collective wisdom of the American people" (http://www.americaspeaks.org). America*Speaks*, which was founded in 1995 by Dr. Carolyn J. Lukensmeyer, has run large-scale forums in all fifty states and the District of Columbia. For example, in 2005, it partnered with Maine Governor John Baldacci to convene Maine Tough Choices, a twenty-first-century town meeting on health care policy. In 2006, it partnered with Shaping America's Youth (SAY) and hosted town meetings in Memphis, Tennessee, and Dallas, Texas (America*Speaks* 2006).

While the goals, methods, and even the definitions of "deliberation" and "dialogue" advocated by these organizations and the dozens of others like them vary in subtle but important ways, many serve as instigators of collective, facilitated public talk and as professional consultants to more local groups interested in conducting deliberative forums. (For a more detailed discussion of both the various conceptualizations of deliberation and dialogue, and specific examples of how these models have been applied in local settings, see Gastil 2008 and Gastil and Levine 2005).

The third and final layer in the organizational structure of the public deliberation movement consists of umbrella groups or professional associations. These include the International Association for Public Participation, the National Coalition for Deliberative Democracy, and the Deliberative Democracy Consortium. The International Association for

Public Participation (IAPP) was founded in 1990 "to respond to the rising global interest in public participation."[1] The association serves, according to its 2006 *Annual Report*, the "growing group of people who design, implement, use and participate in public participation processes." The IAPP has grown from three hundred members in 1992 to more than one thousand members in 2007. The IAPP has organizational members from twenty-six different countries and sixteen worldwide chapters that provide professional training and other services. Conferences have been held every year since 1992, alternating between Canada and the United States.

The IAPP has two main purposes—promoting wide participation as a value in itself and as an indispensable input for decision makers, and training a large pool of professionals to create and sustain processes of public participation. The association broadly seeks to "promote and improve the practice of public participation" in several ways. First, one of its "core values" is to "see[k] out and facilitate the involvement of those potentially affected by or interested in a decision." The association's assumption is that "those who are affected by a decision have a right to be involved in the decision making process" and to "influence the decision." In "advocat[ing] for the public participation process," the association emphasizes the importance of "respect[ing] and amplify[ing] voices that often go unheard"—a theme of its spring 2004 conference in Madison, Wisconsin.

The association links its efforts to stimulate public participation in community decisions with a commitment to "educat[ing] decision makers about the value of public participation." Its devotion to helping the public to "play an effective role in public participation processes" is reflected in the association's awards to local and city governments for seeking out the "community's shared views" and in its efforts, as demonstrated in a collaboration with the Kettering Foundation, to "bridge the gap between the public and formal institutions of government."

The IAPP's second contribution to fostering deliberative forums is—as its 2005 *Annual Report* explains—to "encourage and enhance the professional development of people working in public participation." The primary service of the association is to offer technical assistance and to "mentor new practitioners." It sponsors certified training programs in the tools and skills needed to organize and facilitate the process of public participation.

Another umbrella association within the public deliberation movement is the National Coalition for Deliberative Democracy (NCDD). The NCDD resulted from the Hewlett-funded National Conference on Dialogue and Deliberation in 2002.[2] Starting from the premise that "dialogue and deliberation are powerful group processes that help people bridge gaps, make better decisions, take collective action, resolve conflict and become more active citizens," the initial purpose of the coalition was to address what many practitioners felt was a growing, vibrant, but inchoate field:

> Although they are by no means new processes, dialogue and deliberation have enjoyed a tremendous growth in popularity in recent years. This growth has been so grassroots that numerous streams of practice (deliberative democracy, conflict transformation, intergroup dialogue, etc.) developed without much awareness of one other. The result of this was the emergence of an important but disjointed field whose practitioners are versed in completely different terminology, techniques and resources, and emphasize different outcomes—despite the similarity of their basic values and principles.

The NCDD describes its mission as "bring[ing] together and support[ing] people, organizations, and resources in ways that expand the power of discussion to benefit society." Its aspirations and underlying values are typical of many such associations and their member organizations:

> NCDD envisions a future in which all people—regardless of income, position, background or education—are able to engage regularly in lively, thoughtful, and challenging conversations about what really matters to them, in ways that have a positive impact on their lives and their world. We envision a society in which systems and structures support and advance inclusive, constructive dialogue and deliberation. NCDD embraces and demonstrates the following values and principles: collaboration and active participation, openness and transparency, inclusivity, balance, curiosity and commitment to learning, action, and service to others.

To translate these aspirations and values into practice, the NCDD "brings together people and groups who actively practice, promote and study inclusive, high quality conversations." The coalition works to develop "a common knowledge base in the dialogue and deliberation community [through efforts] to create a shared language, a sense of mutual respect and an openness to collaboration among the various streams of practice that center around the processes of dialogue and deliberation, [and build] knowledge and foster connections and a sense of unity in the field." The NCDD also provides practitioners and researchers with "important resources, information, news and tools," initiates and runs "collaborative projects with other dialogue and deliberation programs to build knowledge in the field," and provides "members of the dialogue and deliberation community with the means to collaborate on projects."

One of the most important tools used by the NCDD (and other umbrella associations) is its Web site, which as of 2008 had approximately twenty-five hundred visitors and more than twelve thousand page views each day. The Web site contains a "comprehensive and up-to-date collection of resources, news, events and opportunities related to dialogue and deliberation," including "a feature that categorizes and describes high-tech tools, products and programs that can enhance online and face-to-face dialogue and deliberation programs [and] a glossary defining over 100 key terms used throughout the field."

As of 2008 the NCDD had nearly eight hundred members and a monthly e-mail newsletter sent to more than ten thousand individuals working in the area of public "dialogue and deliberation." Member organizations include America*Speaks* and Everyday Democracy as well as other public deliberation organizations such as the Open Space Institute, the Jewish-Palestinian Living Room Dialogue Project, Search for Common Ground, The Public Conversations Project, the Center for Nonviolent Communication, Web Lab, and Campus Compact. Individual members include "public officials, students, artists, practitioners, scholars and others."

Our third and final example of an umbrella association is the Deliberative Democracy Consortium (DDC). The DDC was founded in 2002 with funding from the Hewlett Foundation. Its mission is "to bring together practitioners and researchers to support and foster the nascent, broad-based movement to promote and institutionalize deliberative democracy at all levels of governance in the United States and around the world."[3] Composed of more than thirty member organizations, DDC's goals include "help[ing] public leaders find the examples and resources they need to engage citizens," "integrat[ing] research and practice in the field," "integrat[ing] online and face-to-face approaches [to deliberation]," "articulat[ing] how democracy is changing," and "help[ing] to build a permanent infrastructure for deliberative democracy." To achieve these goals, the DDC engages in activities such as the "design of, and experimentation with, innovative deliberative practices," the development of "evaluation models and tools," "relationship building, collaboration and convening within the field," the creation of "connections between the field of deliberation and other related fields," the dissemination of "results to the public, decision-makers, academics," the promotion of "the philosophy and methods of deliberative democracy to all levels of government," and increasing "the credibility and visibility of the deliberative democracy movement in the United States and around the world."

Members of these associations include the Center for Deliberative Democracy, the Information Commons, and the Citizens Participation

Partnership Project as well as organizations we discussed above—the National Issues Forums, Everyday Democracy, America*Speaks,* Web Lab, and the Public Conversations Project. Members also include numerous organizations and firms that specialize in facilitating public deliberation projects, individual consultants, mid-level government employees who are legally mandated to include citizen participation in the development and/or implementation of public policy initiatives, and, to a lesser degree, researchers interested in the issue of public deliberation from a more scholarly perspective.

A Closer Look at the Origins and Makeup of the Public Deliberation Movement

The emergence of a movement and network devoted to fostering public participation reflects and contributes to community interest in deliberation and to the formation of an organizational infrastructure that helps to foster public talk. In addition to understanding the professionalization of public deliberation, we need to know more about the organizations that do the actual work of public participation in schools, libraries, and government offices. By whom and how is public deliberation organized? Are these organizations new or well-established? To what extent are they independent or part of a large national organization or initiative? Are they for-profit or nonprofit operations? What motivates them? Also, do their operations reflect the active, professional model promoted by organizations such as the IAPP, or do they resemble a more ad hoc set of arrangements indicative of a decentralized field? These are important questions that reveal the values of these organizations and their capacity to offset the costs to individuals of participating in public deliberations.

To begin to answer these questions, we conducted a mail survey of 396 local and national organizations that plan and run public forums. While our survey is not entirely representative of these organizations, it offers, to the best of our knowledge, the first large-scale examination of the organizational infrastructure of public deliberation. It was conducted at the moment at which this infrastructure was first emerging, which may offer particular insights into the founding goals and objectives of these organizations. Put in perspective, we mainly surveyed organizations from the base of the public deliberation movement charted in figure 7.1—namely, local organizations or national organizations with local chapters.

The survey, funded by the Pew Charitable Trusts, designed by the authors, and conducted by the Survey and Evaluation Research Laboratory of

Virginia Commonwealth University, was mailed to 1,678 organizations in 1998. As no comprehensive list of such organizations existed at the time of the survey (and to our knowledge still does not exist), this mailing list was compiled from a variety of sources, including searches of the Nexis database of media coverage for references to organizations that had conducted forums, the Internet, foundation lists of deliberative organizations they have funded, and membership in the International Association of Public Participation.[4] To guard against the risk of systematic bias that can arise with low response rates, organizations that did not return the original survey were recontacted by mail at least three times.

In the end, just over 10% (170) of the organizations we contacted informed us that they were not involved in citizen deliberations or that we had already contacted someone else in their organization who had completed the survey. An additional 5% of the surveys (92) were returned unopened because the organizations no longer existed. Of the remaining 1,416 surveys, 396 were returned completed (28%). Given the absence of an authoritative and current directory of deliberative associations, the highly decentralized and sometimes fleeting nature of many of these organizations, and their lack of time and staffing to complete the survey, a better than one-in-four response rate is not surprising. We also supplemented the survey with information gathered from telephone interviews, e-mail exchanges, media accounts, Web sites, printed material provided by organizations, and direct observation of several forums.

The 396 organizations that completed the survey all worked with citizens to facilitate deliberative forums. They were a diverse set of associations—from locally based organizations such as a Nebraska library, a Wisconsin community organization called We the People, and local branches of the League of Women Voters to government bodies such as a national environmental agency and the Department of Transportation. Completed questionnaires were coded on the basis of specified rules designed to provide a portrait of the public deliberation community at a crucial moment in its development. An independent coder was briefed on the coding rules and then independently coded a randomly selected set of 10% of all questionnaires. The overall intercoder reliability was 87%.

The survey of deliberative organizations revealed two important findings; one concerns the grassroots and nonprofit origins of the public deliberation movement, and the second is the degree to which the deliberative organizations collectively reflect the values, processes, and goals articulated by more national organizations and umbrella associations.

The Local and Nonprofit Roots of the Public Deliberation Movement

Analysis of our data reveals that organizing public deliberations was (in 1998) a relatively new activity. As table 7.1 shows, only 34% of these organizations existed prior to 1990, with 66% emerging after this date. This growth in organizations devoted to public deliberation is consistent with more impressionistic narratives regarding the history of the field, as well as with the emergence of the national organizations and umbrella associations discussed earlier in this chapter.

The data also suggest that the organization of deliberative forums was largely a local activity rather than a campaign launched at the national level and "imposed" on communities. Table 7.2 shows that 35% of the organizations that conducted citizen dialogues were locally run and had no affiliations with state, regional or national associations; another 35% were affiliated with state, regional, or national associations but run by local organizations; only a quarter were run and organized directly by state, regional, or national organizations. The large number of local deliberative organizations that were unaffiliated or only loosely affiliated (70%) suggests that the deliberative turn in American politics was a genuine grassroots phenomenon, though the fact that half were at least affiliated with larger state, regional, or national associations indicates that even in 1998 a nascent deliberative network was underway. In short, although national organizations have played a role in fostering public deliberation, the engines of public forums are local and rooted in communities.

Despite the professionalization of the field of public deliberation, these community efforts were run largely by nonprofit organizations. For example, while 92% of the organizations we surveyed had partnerships to assist them with organizing and running their forums, 61% of these organizations partnered with other local, nonprofit associations (data not presented in the tables). Overall, then, as the public deliberation movement was emerging, local communities were investing in it as a contribution to their civic life rather than as a for-profit venture. One likely effect of this

Table 7.1　Founding of deliberative organizations interviewed

	PERCENTAGE (%)
Founded before 1990	34
Founded between 1990 and 1995	36
Founded after 1995	30

Source: Survey of deliberative organizations commissioned by authors, N = 396.

Table 7.2   Affiliations of organizations conducting public deliberations

	PERCENTAGE (%)
Local affiliations only	35
Local organizations with some affiliation with state, regional, or national associations	35
State affiliations	16
National affiliations	11
Other	3

Source: Survey of deliberative organizations commissioned by authors, N = 396.

approach was to reduce the financial and logistical costs of participation that would otherwise be borne by individual citizens.

DELIBERATIVE VALUES AND PROFESSIONAL PROCESSES

Despite the grassroots and only loosely networked character of the organizations participating in our survey, they tended to share three features articulated by more national deliberative organizations such as NIF and umbrella associations such as the IAPP.

One central tendency of the local organizations we interviewed was to embrace the mission of associations such as the IAPP to promote public participation. Table 7.3 indicates that the primary purpose of the deliberative forums organized by our respondents was to provide information, solicit input from the community, and develop and implement plans to solve problems. Six out of ten associations reported that they selected topics based on community concerns (at times with staff input). The topics addressed by forum organizers included not only specific policy concerns such as cleaning up the environment or improving the transportation infrastructure, but also broader topics such as citizenship and diversity. In general, deliberative organizations worked to foster public forums in order to provide policy specific benefits and also to build broader community bonds—core values of umbrella and national organizations.

The orientation of deliberative organizations toward fostering public participation is also evident in types of participants they recruited. The data provided in table 7.4 shows that the most common types of recruits were broad groupings of Americans—the general public, particular demographic groups, or community leaders and activists. Twice as many associations attributed their strategies of recruitment to the pursuit of general and diverse input (46%) as opposed to identifying the narrow concerns of stakeholders (24%). Not surprisingly, the organizations tended to use public outreach to recruit participants (66%) rather than targeting their invitations (27%).

Table 7.3   Purpose and topics of forums hosted by deliberative organizations

	PERCENTAGE (%)
Purposes of citizen forums	
Civic education	
Provide information	45
Citizen engagement	
Solicit citizen input	39
Develop relationships	29
Involve citizens	19
Instrumental	
Develop plan; solve problem	24
Develop consensus	14
Garner citizen support	8
Topics that forums address	
Broad	
Citizenship, elections, values	34
Diversity (race, orientation, tolerance)	25
Specific	
Environment (cleanup)	33
Infrastructure (roads)	33
Education	20
Economic	18
Health	14
International (immigration)	10
Family (youth)	8
Crime (violence)	6
Welfare and poverty	5
Method for selecting topics	
Broad	
Community issue or need	35
Staff and community together select topic	23
Narrow	
Staff chooses topic	19
Topic preselected from existing program or plan	21

Source: Survey of deliberative organizations commissioned by authors, N = 396.
Note: Percentage does not add to 100 because respondents chose more than one response.

The collective commitment to the values and goals of the larger public deliberation movement is also evident in the types of organizations engaged in public deliberation, the sources of their financial support, and the way in which information produced by deliberative forums was used. Table 7.5 shows that eight out of ten organizations engaged in deliberative forums were nonprofits, government entities, educational groups, or libraries, while only 19% were businesses. Most financial support for deliberative forums was provided by third parties (government entities, foundations, and individuals) committed to the public-interest contributions

Table 7.4 The participants that deliberative organizations recruit

	PERCENTAGE (%)
Types of participants recruited	
General public	82
Demographic groups (age, race, income)	52
Community leaders and activists	44
Stakeholders	24
Elected officials	15
Others	11
Reason participants are recruited	
Seek general or diverse input	46
Seek input of stakeholders	24
Require support of participants	13
Mandated to invite participants	7
Require knowledge of participants	4
Other	6
Method for recruiting participants	
Public outreach	66
Targeted invitees	27
Recommendations	4
Other	2

Source: Survey of deliberative organizations commissioned by authors, N = 396.
Note: Percentage does not add to 100 because respondents chose more than one response.

Table 7.5 Types of organizations that conduct public deliberations

		PERCENTAGE (%)
Type of deliberative organization		
Non profits		35
Citizen	11	
Diversity	9	
Environmental	3	
Health	2	
Other	10	
Government		22
Local	11	
State	7	
National	4	
Business		19
General business	4	
Consulting firm	6	
Independent consultant	9	
Education		11
Library		10
Media		2
Other		3

Source: Survey of deliberative organizations commissioned by authors, N = 396.
Note: Percentage does not add to 100 because respondents chose more than one response.

of these forums and to reducing the costs to individuals of engaging in public talking. Sources of funding such as fees and membership dues that could limit access to participation were generally less common (table 7.6). Moreover, two-thirds of the organizations publicly disseminated their results through press releases, official testimony, newsletters, and web postings, compared to only 19% that restricted the use of their deliberations to producing internal reports and 13% that made no organized effort to disseminate the results of their forum's discussions (table 7.7).

A second striking feature of local organizers is their commitment to follow "best practices" in their administration, positioning them to offset some of the demands on and barriers to the participation of individuals in civic forums. Table 7.8 shows that 88% of the organizations surveyed reported that discussion facilitators were formally trained; forums were rarely run by people without experience and qualifications in conducting public discussions. Three-quarters of the organizations running the forums used staff or hired outside professional facilitators. Respondents'

Table 7.6 Sources of funding for deliberative organizations

	PERCENTAGE (%)
Government	34
Grants	31
Contributions	29
Fees	26
Foundations	24
Dues	8
In-kind contributions/volunteer	8
Other	8

Source: Survey of deliberative organizations commissioned by authors, N = 396.
Note: Percentage does not add to 100 because respondents chose more than one response.

Table 7.7 Dissemination of public comments at forums by deliberative organizations

	PERCENTAGE (%)
Internal use of public comments	
Internal report	19
No dissemination beyond participants or observers	7
Informal use of public comments	6
External dissemination of public comments	
Press release	31
Testimony	15
Newsletter	12
Web site or Internet	7

Source: Survey of deliberative organizations commissioned by authors, N = 396.
Note: Percentage does not add to 100 because respondents chose more than one response.

Table 7.8   Training, identity, and style of facilitators

	PERCENTAGE (%)
Extent of training	
Trained	88
Not trained	12
Who facilitators are	
Staff member	38
Outside professional facilitator	34
Citizen volunteer	14
Board/executive member	12
Other	2
Reason for particular approach to facilitation	
Logistical reasons (ease)	19
Enhance dialogue	19
Dictated by outside format	14
Maintain neutrality	13
Varies or group decides	8
Combination of reasons	28

Source: Survey of deliberative organizations commissioned by authors, $N = 396$.
Note: Percentage does not add to 100 because respondents chose more than one response.

explanations for their approach to facilitation seem to reflect a thoughtful mix of pragmatic and aspirational reasons from logistics (19%) and format (14%) to enhancing dialogue (19%) and maintaining neutrality (13%).

A third theme was the commitment of many of the local organizations we surveyed to making deliberation a routine and active part of community life (see table 7.9), echoing the focus of national organizations on encouraging extensive small-group discussion of complicated or thorny issues. Two-thirds of the organizations reported conducting six or more deliberative forums a year, with 25% conducting more than twenty a year. About half of the organizations also reported that the groups they organized met four or more times a year and that each meeting ran three hours or more. Finally, more than half the forums had thirty or fewer participants, and only 15% had more than one hundred participants.

In sum, our data suggests that even in this relatively early period in the emergence of the contemporary public deliberation movement, local organizations were loosely networked, aware of the broader democratic purposes of their efforts, and committed to many of the best procedures advocated by the larger field of which they were a part. While addressing issues of local concern and building local social capital, they were simultaneously reinvigorating and reinventing democratic practice in the United States.

Table 7.9   Extent of activity by organizers of deliberative organizations

	PERCENTAGE (%)
Number of dialogues held in past year	
1–5 forums	32
6–20 forums	38
21 or more forums	25
Average number of participants	
15 or fewer participants	26
16–30 participants	28
31–60 participants	21
61–100 participants	10
101 or more participants	15
Number of times forums meet to discuss issue	
1–3 meetings	46
4–5 meetings	29
6 or more meetings	25
Duration of typical forum	
2 hours	47
3 hours	24
4 hours or more	26

Source: Survey of deliberative organizations commissioned by authors, N = 396.
Note: Percentage does not add to 100 because respondents chose more than one response.

Enabling Public Deliberation

Engaging in public talking is an individual decision influenced by a large number of personal resources and characteristics. Individual choices to participate in public forums are shaped, however, by the broader organizational context of discursive practice, and the opportunities and roadblocks this context provides. On the one hand, the factors that led to the decline in social capital documented by Putnam (2000) and others undoubtedly has worked to diminish citizens' interest in and ability and opportunity to participate in collective activities such as deliberative forums. On the other hand, this breakdown in the traditional institutions of civil society has been at least partially counteracted by the emergence of individuals, organizations, and associations committed to promoting the value and practice of public participation in deliberative forums and to boosting the capacity of communities to organize and conduct public dialogues. This chapter situates our earlier findings in the context of the evolving deliberative movement in American communities and provides a glimpse into the motivations and practices of the groups engaged in the day-to-day facilitation of democratic deliberation.

Our review suggests a complex, interactive mix of independent and coordinated activities, loose networks of like-minded organizations, and bottom-up and top-down leadership, synthesis, facilitation, and coordination—in short a movement. This movement is being led by a coalition of local, regional, and national foundations, civic groups, nongovernmental organizations, mid-level civil servants, academics, and professional associations. And it shares a set of underlying values, goals, and practices that hearken back to many of the central themes of American politics and public life. It is "progressive" in the sense that it depends in part on the theories and actions of reform-minded elites. It is "populist" in the sense that grassroots organizations are playing a significant role in conceiving, planning, and conducting discursive dialogues, and its organization, funding, and operation are restricted neither to governmental nor business sectors. It is "communitarian" in its emphasis on local civil society. It is "republican" in its simultaneous awareness of citizens' civic duties and of the representative nature of many aspects of the political process. It is "democratic" in its belief in the ultimate authority of citizens to govern themselves. And it is "deliberative" in its fundamental commitment to the importance and efficacy of inclusive, equitable public dialogue that is tied to actual decision making.

We have no wish to romanticize this movement, and we do not claim that it has succeeded in mixing these often inconsistent strands of American political thought and practice, that it has taken enough root to remain a stable feature of American political life, that it is immune from abuse, or that by itself it can counteract the more pernicious effects of a deteriorating public sphere. We believe, however, that driven at least in part by this movement, discursive participation in general and participation in deliberative forums more specifically are genuine and significant features of contemporary American democracy worthy of careful study and, perhaps, nurturing.

EIGHT

The Practice of Deliberation and the Hope for Democratic Renewal

Aleksandr Solzhenitsyn rose into the Pantheon of human rights activists through his blood-chilling accounts of the Soviet Union's labor camp system known as the Gulag. His reward was the Nobel Prize for Literature in 1970 along with deportation from the Soviet Union in 1974. Solzhenitsyn retreated from the world stage by moving to a tiny town in the United States (Cavendish, Vermont) where he lived for nearly two decades. Like other visitors to the United States before him, Solzhenitsyn came to marvel at American democracy and its striking departures from the political system of his native country, as he explained in his 1994 farewell address to the town: "I have observed here in Cavendish, and in the surrounding towns the sensible and sure process of grassroots democracy where the local population decides most of its problems on its own, not waiting for the decisions of higher authorities. Alas, this we still do not have in Russia, and that is our greatest shortcoming" (quoted in Bryan 2004, xvi).

The spirit of Solzhenitsyn's testimonial to the democratic practice of Americans has been amplified by advocates of an invigorated citizenry within the United States. Observers of America's towns and local cities report that they are seeing a "transformative shift" from expert rule to shared governance, from "elite-directed modes of participation and toward . . . publics . . . more active than ever in a wide range of elite-challenging forms of political participation" (Leighninger 2006, 18–19; Sirianni and Friedland 2001, 9). These observers report that "communities are moving beyond the traditional assumptions that the role of government is provid[ing] services and the role of citizens is to pay taxes for those services" (Leighninger 2006, 21–22).

But assessments of the health of American democracy divide—like so much else about American politics—into extremes. While the vitality of American democracy and civil life have been extolled, some observers also portray American citizens as driven from public life by political distrust and a sense that government does not care about them (Putnam 2000; Patterson 2002; Erikson and Tedin 2001; Zukin et al. 2006).

We have amassed a veritable warehouse of data to assess these dueling accounts of American democracy and conclude with the kind of measured assessment that befits a complicated topic. Public deliberation falls short of meeting the lofty hopes of democratic theorists who imagined it would become the salvation of democracy and resurrect the citizen-ruler of ancient Athens. But deliberation does not need to achieve these idealized standards to justify a correction to its one-sided rejection both by critics who worry that it is a haven of intolerance subjugating the already disadvantaged and by scholars of political and civic participation who consider it a marginal element of public life in America. Our in-depth and wide-ranging analyses of public deliberation warrant, in our view, both appreciation of the mass public's substantial participation in public talking and candor in acknowledging that deliberation falls short of the lofty goals set for it.

Our measured conclusions about street-level deliberation significantly revise previous assumptions and characterizations of deliberation. Deliberation in America is not only extensive today, but it also presents opportunities for the future expansion and rejuvenation of democracy.

A Measured Resurrection of Public Deliberation

Our analyses revise past theorizing and research on five critical dimensions of deliberation.

AN AMERICA OF PUBLIC TALKERS

Our findings demonstrate that discursive politics generally and public deliberation more specifically are not infrequent and isolated phenomena as some have previously assumed. Chapter 2 showed that discursive participation is extensive. More than 80% of Americans engage in some form of public talk; this includes 68% who participated in informal conversations about public issues in person or on the phone ("traditional talking") and 25% who attended face-to-face forums. Current research on political and civic participation that fails to mention public deliberation is clearly presenting an incomplete and unbalanced portrayal of American citizens. Although Americans' discursive participation exceeds the assumptions of many previous researchers, it falls short of the expectations of universal engagement suggested by some democratic theorists. Moreover, the archetypal deliberative forum—face-to-face interactions—is not attended by three-quarters of Americans. If it is expected to be a fountain of life for today's Athenian citizens, the water pressure appears to be low.

A reasonable appraisal of the extent of public deliberation requires an appreciation of the context of American civic and political participation and institutions. Deliberation takes time, effort, and skill. Deliberators are often expected to collect and process information on a policy area, formulate positions on it, and then articulate that position publicly. These demands on citizens represent a kind of "entry fee" for deliberation and make discursive participation more of a personal challenge than other political actions such as pulling a lever in the privacy of a voting booth.

The particular burdens of face-to-face deliberation—its cognitive costs and its demand for skillful and, for some, embarrassing efforts at public persuasion—have given rise to the conclusion that it was impractical. Some have declared that face-to-face deliberation has been replaced by "mediated" deliberation through professional communicators and the mass media (Page 1996). Given the fact that public talking is taxing and, as we discovered, rarely delivers significant tangible rewards like the election of a favored candidate or passage of a supported policy, why is deliberation as extensive as it is?

Engagement with deliberation and signs of democratic revival result, in part, from the disjuncture between growing citizen capacity and perceptions of weak or declining government capacity to function as an effective and responsive representative institution. Higher levels of education and the shift to a service economy have equipped more citizens with the skills and confidence to take the initiative in attending and participating in democratic life and, specifically, civic dialogues. The increasing capacity of citizens contrasts with historic levels of polarization among the political parties at the elite level, and, at the mass level, it coincides with persistent political distrust, weak political efficacy, and impatience with rigid ideological approaches, which are amplified by the mass media (Cappella and Jamieson 1997; Jamieson 1992). Where citizens are capable and are acting as independent, resourceful, and self-initiating agents, government often continues to treat them as "targets" rather than coproducers of common goods. While government service delivery remains indispensable in certain respects, the emergent mismatch in citizen and government capacities has generated sharp exchanges between government officials and citizens who are angry and have the information, skills, and confidence to address their discontent. The resulting sparks have been on display in such high-profile episodes as the responses to the government's bungled handling of the Katrina hurricane and its aftermath, the financial crises starting in 2008, government responses to the 9/11 terrorists attacks (as the families of 9/11 victims publicly remind the nation), and local government fumbling in addressing issues ranging from public safety to race relations. Put simply, government too often seems broken, and informed citizens want to be part of the solution. In this environment, some government officials have responded by sharing governance through deliberative processes in order "to help their communities function more democratically *and* more effectively" (Leighninger 2006, 2, emphasis added; Bryan 2004; Sirianni and Friedland 2001).

Although the costs of deliberation are higher than those of many other forms of political participation (namely, voting), the benefits are also greater. Frank Bryan points to the social and political payoffs of New England town meetings to explain why "ordinary citizens are far more willing to expend the energy to practice real democracy in their towns than the ordinary American is to expend the energy to vote in representative democracy" (2004, 286). Although small-town democracy may be limited to certain geographic areas, the practice of deliberation also appears to be gratifying to participants and therefore "worthwhile." Walsh (2004) found that public talkers *enjoyed* their interchanges about politics in her qualitative study, and 73% of a national sample of participants in deliberative polling rated their experience with the highest score, "extremely valuable" (Fishkin 1995, 187). As electoral politics and the legislative arena have fallen in public esteem, Americans may value discursive participation as an alternative pathway to public education (i.e., it delivers information and improves understanding), moral development (i.e., it fulfills a sense of responsibility to the community), and social gratification (i.e., it offers a format for interactions and building personal networks; see Button and Mattson 1999, 631–37).

In addition to generating significant payoffs to citizens, the costs of participating may not be as significant or be borne as directly by individuals as has been assumed. The emergence of interconnected networks and community organizations committed to convening public forums—a development examined in chapter 7—diminishes the direct burdens on individuals of convening civic forums. In addition to this organizational infrastructure for public forums, technological changes have widened access to the Internet and instilled the requisite skills in using the Web among a broad (but not uniform) swath of Americans, especially the young (Iyengar, Luskin, and Fishkin 2003; Cappella, Price, and Nir 2002; Price and Cappella 2002; Price et al. 2003). The development of a deliberation infrastructure as well as breakthroughs in communication and familiarity with them serve to mitigate the costs previously associated with public talking.

Public deliberation falls short of the expectations of its most enthusiastic promoters. Nonetheless, there is substantial discursive participation in a variety of forms and at a level that is impressive, given the notable costs and limited tangible benefits.

REPRESENTATION AND INDIRECT INFLUENCES

Deliberation has been sharply criticized for creating another facet of "gated democracy"—an enclave reserved for the same group of affluent, better-educated, and already engaged Americans who disproportionately vote, write checks, and engage in other ways (Sanders 1997; Mansbridge 1983). The more "costly" forms of deliberation—namely, face-to-face meetings—are especially prone to being unrepresentative of the diversity of the entire community. The risk, observers warn, is that critical voices and interests are ignored or neglected.

Our analyses of deliberation in chapter 3 found that income, education, and other dimensions of social and economic status (SES) were an inconsistent, weak, and, at times, nonexistent *direct* influence on public talking. We found that organizational membership and political capital were the most consistent and strongest indicators of which individuals were discursively active. Deliberation is not—according to the survey data in chapters 3 and 4 and our case study of ADSS in chapter 6—"owned" or dominated by the better-off; participation extends beyond personal networks. Organizers of larger face-to-face forums reach out to a wide array of neighbors, often independently of government.

Nonetheless, there is evidence that SES plays an indirect role. The more highly educated, for instance, tend to join organizations at higher rates, which in turn may disproportionately bias public talking. In addition, deliberators did not perceive their discursive interactions as particularly diverse. The absence of consistent direct effects of SES on deliberation does not mean, then, that public talking is fully representative or inclusive of the general population.

Our findings suggest a measured conclusion: deliberation fails to meet the most optimistic expectations of representativeness, but it is not subject to the takeover by the "ruling class" and its cronies that the harshest critics of deliberation suspected.

REASONED TALK

Benjamin Barber (1984) criticized representative government as "thin democracy." It reduces citizens to mere voters and remains content to aggregate demands of contending interests. Instead of narrowly equating democracy with elections and a method for selecting government officials (Schumpeter 1950), Barber and other democratic theorists called for a new type of democracy—an "authentic democracy" based on reasoned public deliberation that shapes the preferences of citizens and infuses them with new energy and participatory zeal (Dryzek 2000; Benhabib 1996; Gutmann and Thompson 1996).

Deliberation, then, is not simply about quantity—how many people engage in public talk, for instance—but also about the character of the interactions among citizens. The findings presented in chapter 4 show that the vast majority of face-to-face deliberators reported participating in forums that were anchored in reason, neutral or balanced information, and a search for collective benefits and consensual decisions. These findings are consistent, to some degree, with Barber's call for "authentic democracy" (1984).

Public Talking and Individual Autonomy

The development of public deliberation into a mass phenomenon offers the potential for a reasoned search for the common good among a wide spectrum of Americans (Sandel 1996). But how tolerant are civic forums to diverse perspectives? The search for agreement (even when mediators welcome individuals to air differences) may discourage or fail to actively welcome disagreement and thereby pose a risk to fundamental individual rights to dissent from the majority's perspective (Dworkin 1978). The heated clash of the "rights movement" and public deliberation could conceivably emerge in particularly stark terms in face-to-face forums.

Our analyses (especially in chapter 4) do not appear to support the concern about the possibility of significant intolerance and coercion. Only about 5% of deliberators strongly complained that they disagreed with the forum's decisions, that facilitators did not give priority to making sure everyone's opinions were heard, that the forum did not make airing differences an important goal, or that they felt anger during the last meeting. Our case study of ADSS in chapter 6 showed how a moderator can play an important role in encouraging tolerance by stating, as the ADSS moderator did, that everyone should be "listened to and respected."

After weighing the normative questions about whether deliberation threatens or encumbers individual liberty or agency, we could not identify persistent evidence of intolerance. The complaints that were reported could be accounted for with less ominous explanations. The small numbers may reflect statistical "noise" in the survey. Moreover, individual ease and skill with public talking varies. Rather than reflecting coercive or intolerant procedures or practices, the complaints of some deliberators may reflect their personal unease about engaging in discursive activities or insecurity about their communicative skills, especially in face-to-face forums. Our evidence fits with previous studies, including Katherine

Cramer Walsh's (2007) examination of racial dialogue, which report a balancing of the search for unity with respect for difference.

DELIBERATION'S IMPACT

Discursive politics alone is unlikely to have the direct and dramatic impact of a critical election or major protest. Nonetheless, deliberation can achieve important effects that have the potential to form the basis for democratic renewal. For example, the case study of ADSS in chapter 6 showed that deliberation can result in significant gains in knowledge, thus increasing citizen competence. In addition, chapter 5 showed that attending deliberative forums can prompt participants to increase their subsequent engagement in civic activities, contacting influential elites, and voting. In short, political talk is not only valuable in and of itself; it can act as a pathway to more informed, reasoned, and active engagement in public life.

Deliberation and the Rejuvenation of Democratic Life

There have been a number of efforts to reengage citizens in public life. Reform movements ranging from efforts to enact campaign finance legislation to efforts to reinstill a civic mission among journalists have aimed at reincorporating citizens in public life. Public deliberation appears to be another component of today's democratic rejuvenation. "Our most compelling enterprise," Bryan declares, is to "save the American republic by showing its leaders how to repair its underpinning, a citizenry acquainted with democracy" (2004, 279).

Public deliberation is a social and political phenomenon characterized by a distinctive combination of four features. First, it is a complex mix of uncoordinated talk, discrete organizations and associations, and loosely networked national umbrella groups. Second, it is focused more on *how* one addresses public issues than on any particular issue such as the environment or campaign finance reform. Third, while the specific issues being discussed vary from the very local to the international, it is fundamentally a local, community-based movement (Sirianni and Friedland, 2001; Leighninger, 2006; Bryan, 2004). Fourth, it is a broadly inclusive movement. The organizations that convene deliberative forums indicate that they recruit broadly; the deliberators themselves overwhelmingly reported that their forums were organized to air differences of opinion and different points of view. The implication of these and other findings is that public deliberation is generally motivated not by ideology or partisanship but by a conception of a new and more active medium of citizen engagement that seeks to incorporate diverse perspectives and elements of the community.

Deliberation is already an important (though largely ignored) form of political engagement. The critical question is whether it offers still greater potential for contributing to democratic rejuvenation in America. Unfortunately, attention to deliberation has "tended to focus on how to run the meetings rather than how to recruit participants" (Leighninger 2006, 8). Evaluating the potential of deliberation raises two critical challenges—what is required to make it more available and widely practiced and what unique contributions it can make to public life in America today.

THE CONDITIONS FOR EXPANDED DELIBERATION

The quality of democracy rests on institutions and information (Dewey 1954; Dahl 1989). Widening deliberation will require strengthening the organizational infrastructure of civic dialogue in ways that diminish the burden on individuals alone, instilling a deliberative habit, and establishing deliberation as an influential compliment to an exclusive focus on electoral and legislative politics (Fung 2004; Bryan 2004).

Building Infrastructure and Diffusing Skills

Chapter 7 demonstrated that a network of local and national organizers has emerged to enable community deliberation. Further expansion of this network and the number of forum organizers, which seems likely, would widen the capacity and therefore the potential for increasing the number of Americans who deliberate. One of the critical contributions of expanding the discursive infrastructure is to help recruit deliberators, especially Americans who have refrained from public talking. Chapter 4 demonstrates that personal contacts from familiar individuals as well as organizational and media efforts are critical factors in encouraging discursive participation.

Although the organizational infrastructure of the public participation profession is essential, the proliferation of citizen deliberation can also be advanced through the training of face-to-face deliberators. This would diffuse the expertise for running deliberative sessions. An important motivation for the deliberation movement is to avoid repeating the unfortunate history of large, mass membership voluntary associations; professional managers during the latter quarter of the twentieth century disconnected these associations from their community roots and eroded their earlier success in drawing members from across economic and social lines (Skocpol 2003).

Instilling Deliberation

A second way to widen discursive participation is to instill the habits, skills, and motivation to deliberate among all age groups, starting with elementary and high school students. Although public talking was once a critical habit and skill taught to students as part of training in "rhetoric," this element of the school curriculum has faded.

Moving forward, the training of Americans (starting with students) for public deliberation should focus on at least three dimensions. First, the tools of public speaking should be taught. Today, these tools are the by-product of occupation or membership in an organization. Teaching public speaking would expand this skill set and diminish its tie to occupational success, an indirect (and limiting) effect of social and economic advantage. Second, public speaking should be instilled as a habit rather than as an occasional and extraordinary activity that elicits personal anxiety and trepidation. Third, publicly speaking up for one's interests and values should be revalued as normatively appropriate. Although today's deliberation helpfully focuses on collective considerations, these conversations should be based—as many democratic theorists insist—on an appreciation of interests and values rather than on assumptions that values and interests should not be present in problem-solving discussions.

A Public Space for Independent Community Talking

A third ingredient for expanding public deliberation is explicit encouragement of its status as both a forum independent of government and a source of policy proposals. Public deliberation today continues a tradition of citizens gathering to formulate community responses to pressing challenges that is independent of and at some distance from government. This independence from legislative politics may be a particular and growing draw, given Americans' low regard for lawmaking bodies and their process of producing policy (Hibbing and Theiss-Morse 2002). Deliberation offers an outlet for political expression and for reacting to community challenges that are not sullied by the adversarial and seemingly corrupt ways of politicians. In short, opportunities to deliberate can be expanded in several ways. Widening the already impressive level of discursive participation is certainly possible.

THE CONTRIBUTION OF DELIBERATION TO DEMOCRATIC REJUVENATION

Robust and expanded deliberation can contribute to mitigating three challenges facing contemporary American public life.

Finding the Common Good and Respecting Individuals

Public deliberation can contribute to the search for and embrace of the common good. The search for joint gains has, unfortunately, been stymied in part because it is starkly contrasted with individual interests. In reality, public talking about interests and values offers a means for identifying and finding areas of joint gains.

Democratic theorists have been justifiably concerned that efforts at building consensus may come at the expense of recognizing genuine individual interests (Sanders 1997). The reality is that all people are motivated to some extent by economic and other forms of personal interests, a drive to improve their sense of well-being, and moral and ethical concerns.

Deliberation based on reason and balanced information, which is fairly common according to our analyses, offers the possibility to focus public talking on interests, values, and facts instead of on positions, which can be polarizing. Public deliberation, as it is developing, offers three valuable contributions. First, the general reliance (especially in face-to-face forums) on neutral and fact-based information creates the opportunity for discussion to proceed independently of positions. In a situation where political parties have adopted polarized positions, for instance, deliberative forums can start on a foundation of information and evidence that is objective and balanced. This is what the ADSS forums tried to do, as we reported in chapter 6. Second, once the discussion begins, it can focus on identifying interests that are shared or compatible (they do exist). Third, forums of public talking create arenas for recognizing options and proposals where divergent interests can jointly gain. Where options do not exist, public deliberation can help formulate options that do present mutually advantageous outcomes or to facilitate reasoned acceptance of differences, as suggested by previous research (Walsh 2007) and by the evidence presented in chapters 4, 5, and 6.

Deliberation, then, creates the potential for circumventing divisiveness over publicly established positions in favor of independent information and evidence, the identification of shared interests, and the recognition of mutually beneficial options. In today's context of hyper-adversarialism over entrenched public positions, public deliberation offers a rare opportunity to foster community expression and collective problem solving.

Carving Out a Public Sphere Independent of Government Manipulation

Government and prominent stakeholders expend enormous organizational and financial resources on shaping public thinking (Habermas 1989; West and Loomis 1998; Jacobs and Burns 2004; Jacobs and Shapiro 2000; and Druckman and Jacobs 2006). The number and types of pressure groups in Washington and around the country have expanded since the 1960s. Although groups representing consumers and the disadvantaged have also grown (from product safety to environmental concerns and the poor), the number and dominance of business and professional groups expanded and solidified in the face of policy changes that threatened them during the 1960s and 1970s (Berry 1999; Schlozman et al. 2005). The competition among interest groups and the perception of greater uncertainty prodded them to shift strategies; they used paid advertisements, studies, and press coverage to redefine conditions harmful to them as broader public problems, to raise the visibility of their problems, and to define the "solution" (West and Loomis 1998).

Government leaders similarly developed the capacity to move public opinion by first crafting messages that resonated with the mass public and then saturating the country with those messages. Modern presidents, for instance, developed a "public opinion apparatus" for the purpose of changing public preferences to support the policies that the White House and its allies favored (Jacobs and Shapiro 2000; Jacobs 1993).

The result of government and stakeholder strategies and capacity-building is that the deliberation and discourse among everyday Americans is at serious risk of being contaminated by crafted presentations aimed with great skill at manipulating citizens to adopt evaluations and preferences that they would not otherwise embrace. The potential effect is to deflect and stifle the emergence of some issues before they can emerge onto the government agenda or, if they do emerge, to defeat them in the relatively narrow and more contained arenas of government decision making.

A vibrant and decentralized movement of public deliberators could create a haven for citizens to talk publicly and reach conclusions independent of the manipulative strategies of government and stakeholders. Indeed, the remarkable extent of participation that we have documented may in part stem from the search by citizens for an arena for public discussion that is authentic and free of sophisticated and concerted efforts at manipulation.

Feelings and Public Talk

Public talking (especially in larger groups) has long been tarnished by the suspicion that it may activate emotions that truncate thinking. Dispassionate reasoning has long been favored over emotion as a basis for public talking (Young 2000). Indeed, our study finds that the reason-based approach to deliberation dominates civic dialogues.

The widespread and not unfounded fear is that public appeals aimed at sparking anger and the perception of threat can lead to false or misleading conclusions, intolerance, and support for violations of individual liberties (Walton 1992; Gallois 1993; Theis-Morse, Marcus, and Sullivan 1993). Rallies by Hitler and Stalin are credited with igniting passionate responses and orgies of violence and intolerance; this reputation has cast an ominous cloud over public meetings that appeal to emotion. Emotion, it is assumed, is the enemy of reasoned and tolerant deliberation.

The distrust of emotion as an element of public deliberation rests on a critical, untested assumption regarding the way in which people process information and reach judgments. The assumption is that the information distributed to deliberators is stored in memory, which then determines an individual's evaluation of the issue under discussion. The quality of citizen evaluation can be improved, it follows, by enhancing the evidence that is stored in memory.

Research by social psychologists has demonstrated, however, that rather than storing facts in memory and drawing on them when reaching judgments, individuals rely on the cognitively less-taxing process of reaching judgments "online"—integrating new information into a "running tally" of their current impression (Hastie and Park 1986; Lodge and McGraw 1995; Lodge, McGraw, and Stroh 1989 and 1990; Lodge and Stroh 1993; McConnell, Sherman, and Hamilton 1994).

Emotion may make a positive contribution to "online" thinking, the processing of information, and the reaching of judgments. Social psychology research reports that tapping people's emotions may provide a critical lever to increasing their willingness to absorb the costs of participating in deliberative forums and modifying their existing views. Anger, fear, and other emotions can heighten attention, prompting people to work through complex issues that lack clear solutions, and boosting their commitment to the deliberation process (Glaser and Salovey 1998; Showers and Cantor 1985; Walton 1992; Gallois 1993; Theiss-Morse, Marcus, and Sullivan 1993).

Future efforts to study and encourage deliberation should consider that allowing affective responses into deliberative settings may be constructive. In particular, it may increase the motivation of citizens to absorb the costs of discursive participation, leading in turn to still wider involvement, and to collecting, processing, and storing new information. Serious thought should be devoted, then, to experimenting with deliberative forums that allow emotion as an element. Responsible public appeals to emotion may be a way to trigger deeply felt values and commitments and to increase people's willingness to devote themselves to public deliberation.

Permitting appropriate emotions to enter into deliberation may require different modalities of communication. Iris Young points to the "exclusionary bias" of civic forums—such as those organized by Americans Discuss Social Security—that rely upon expert testimony, reports, and other "styles of expression [that are] . . . dispassionate, orderly or articulate" (2000, 6–7). Although the reason-based approach remains critical, Young challenges deliberators to accept that "inclusion specifically requires openness to a plurality of modes of communication" (12). National Issues Forums, for instance, use storytelling and narrative modes of communication, which are more inclusive than modes based on technical knowledge, discursive skills, and personal comfort with open conflict (Ryfe 2002, 360, 367; Ryfe 2006, 72).

DELIBERATION AND GOVERNMENT POLICYMAKING

Fervent advocates of deliberation distance civic dialogue from government, treating it as a superior and indeed more valuable form of citizenship. Some leaders of civic dialogues pose deliberation and political representation as contending alternatives, worrying that focusing on citizen influence on government will "reduce deliberation to an instrumental process" (Button and Ryfe 2005, 25; Ryfe 2002; Leighninger 2006).

Separating deliberation's civic mission from its government policymaking role is unnecessary and indeed harmful to democratic revival. Just as stifling "expert rule" and excessive government can be damaging, conceptions of "citizen rule" are naive. Authority is essential for sustaining order and protecting individual liberties. Expertise is indispensable on most policy matters. Posing citizen empowerment as a separate and stark alternative to government policymaking and expertise sets up a false choice. A more constructive path forward is to develop approaches for incorporating deliberation into representative government, combining vigorous citizens and appropriate schemes of representation and expert judgment (Warren 1996; Fung 2004). For example, highly technical fields such as biotechnology and the genetic modification of living organisms require both analyses by scientific experts and broader public conversations regarding risks and benefits (Kapuscinski et al. 2003; Dahl 1989). Indeed, numerous areas require both expertise and deliberation, from Social Security and the allocation of government funding for medical research to decisions about the storage of materials harmful to humans and the environment (Dresser 2001; McAvoy 1999).

No doubt, some efforts to promote policy decisions by experts or insiders have been presented by government agencies and special interests in the guise of engaging citizens when in fact these forums were unrepresentative and biased. Phony deliberation was displayed, for example, by the Federal Communication Commission's 2003 meetings on its proposals to loosen media ownership rules: they were presented as engaging citizens, but in fact they were poorly publicized, largely staged, and ultimately ignored. Efforts at phony deliberation depart from the core traits of democratic discursive participation that we have identified—representativeness, inclusion, reason-based arguments, and supportive of democratic engagement. Expanding discursive participation requires a simultaneous commitment to the democratic principles of deliberation, government policymaking, and appropriate incorporation of expertise.

In truth, citizen life and government are inextricably linked: An active and informed citizenry is a requirement for a healthy democracy (Dewey 1954), and vibrant democracy fosters capable and engaged citizens (Page and Shapiro 1992; Popkin 1991). A growing body of research shows that demonstrable political influence fosters not only wise policy but also a citizenry that is motivated to engage in civic and political life (Skocpol 2003) and defines its interests in and through community deliberation (Mettler and Soss 2004). Andrea Campbell demonstrates, for instance, that civic and political engagement by seniors increased, exceeding levels found among other subgroups of citizens, as Social Security developed and fostered a rationale for engagement. Theda Skocpol's (2003) analyses of mass-membership voluntary associations during the nineteenth century document that the meshing of local groups with policymakers at the state and national levels similarly generated a participatory ethos. In addition, government sponsorship may actually mitigate some of the inequalities that concern critics of deliberation and contribute to broader access.

The challenge facing deliberation is not to elude the seductive embrace of becoming too influential but to avoid irrelevance to government as part of an effort to foster widespread and enduring citizen life. A growing body of research documents the government's unresponsiveness and perhaps declining responsiveness to citizens (Bartels 2008; Gilens 2005; Jacobs and Page 2005; Jacobs and Shapiro 2000). Larry Bartels' *Unequal Democracy* (2008) finds that the U.S. Senate has been attentive to the preferences of high-income earners but far less responsive (if at all) to middle- and lower-income Americans. An official task force of the American Political Science Association concludes that "politicians are disconnected from citizens" and acutely attentive to the "loud and consistent chorus of the few" (Bartels et al., 2005, 117 and 137).

A growing number of democratic theorists and deliberationists stress the importance of linking public talking to government agendas and decisions. Young criticizes "theorists and activists [who] have wrongly assumed that representative institutions are incompatible with deep democracy" (2000, 7–8). John Gastil similarly insists that "public deliberation must ultimately connect the community with its government" (2000, 7). Bryan cautions against fixating on "participation in groups that practice real democracy rather than on governments that do" (2004, 14). The reality, as three leading deliberationists argue, is that "most public deliberations do not directly alter public decisions and actions"; the challenge is to make the "deliberative process . . . count . . . [which will require that] powerful actors . . . be encouraged, persuaded, or obliged to heed [citizens]" (Levine, Fung, and Gastil 2005, 276).

Deliberation has important and increasingly valuable roles in putting issues on the government agenda, developing broad proposals for lawmakers to consider, and creating incentives for policymakers to respond to the broad public. In a time when the halls of government are dominated by well-paid lobbyists with privileged access and dictated by unified political parties, deliberative forums may offer a pathway for citizen voices. Some or even many of the issues and proposals that are presented by citizen deliberators will—after proper consideration—not deserve further consideration, but it is important that they be heard. (A similar weeding-out process scrutinizes the recommendations of many legislators, helping to account for the 95% or more of legislation that is introduced into Congress but fails to be enacted into law [Manning 2004].)

Better connecting citizen deliberation to government could give broad publics the persistent and loud presence that special interests currently enjoy. Widening the presence and perhaps influence of ordinary citizen deliberators may also feed back into the community, encouraging more citizen participation by showing that the effort is "worthwhile."

Getting serious about genuinely fostering government responsiveness to deliberative forums will require institutional and political sophistication. We doubt that simply sending reports to the U.S. Congress (as we saw in the case of ADSS) will have results. Even well-designed deliberative polls are unlikely to have "recommending effects" without attention to political institutions and the political incentives that they foster (Fishkin 1995).

The future of genuinely democratic deliberation lies in a reformed political process. The key challenge is to increase the benefit to government officials of responding to citizens and to heighten their perception of certain costs for discounting public preferences in order to pursue narrow policy goals favored by party activists, contributors, and other insiders. "Scaling up" deliberation to connect to policymaking—as Levine, Fung, and Gastil (2005) recommend—is cultivated by the broad agenda of reforms aimed at opening up the American representative process. These reforms include accelerated campaign finance reform to control who contributes, how, and when to elections, and reform of the redistricting process to counteract the ability of the elected to choose their voters instead of the reverse.

In addition to changing the broad institutional incentives to reward responsiveness to citizens, there are certain institutional reforms that can empower deliberation within government agenda-setting and policymaking processes. Future efforts to promote public talking need to focus in particular on redesigning government to authorize genuinely democratic deliberative forums with decision-making power. Reconstituting the institutions of the Chicago Police Department and Chicago public schools developed participatory democracy by "incorporating empowered participation and deliberation into their governance structures" (Fung 2004, 4). The key is that formal channels were established for citizens to exercise their voice and influence over agendas and government action. Efforts to "embed" deliberation into government institutions in Bridgeport, Connecticut, and San Jose, California, are other examples of efforts to join public talking and political representation (Fagotto 2006).

Further democratizing American political representation is a key to the continued revitalizing of citizen agency and the restoration of self-governance. Accomplishing this ambitious agenda will require sustained inventiveness in how deliberation is conducted as well as hard-headed determination in reshaping government institutions to create environments that are responsive and provide citizens with some significant measure of self-governance.

The 2008 presidential campaign of Barack Obama capitalized on the Internet and the kind of online public talking that we have studied. It is an open question, though, whether these and other forms of public deliberation lead to a more open style of governing or to another generation of strategic crafted talk to manipulate public thinking (Jacobs and Shapiro 2000). What is clear is that an era of public deliberation has arrived; the battle now focuses on how it is used and to what purpose.

APPENDIX

Coding of Variables from Discursive Participation Survey of the General Public

The following appendix contains the actual question wording for the variables used in this analysis. It also contains descriptions of constructed variables. In addition, the appendix contains discussions of the decisions made in constructing variables. Actual question wordings are in italics.

DEMOGRAPHICS

Age (in years)
D1. What year were you born?
VARIABLE: AGE

    1 = 18–29
    2 = 30–39
    3 = 40–49
    4 = 50–64
    5 = 65+
    Excludes = Don't Know; Refused

Racial Category
D2. What racial or ethnic group or groups best describe you? (READ TOP 7 CHOICES)
VARIABLE: RACE

    1 = African American
    2 = Hispanic
    3 = White
    4 = Other race (Asian, Native American, Multiracial, Some other group)
    Excludes = Don't Know; Refused

Dummy variables were also created (all exclude Don't Know; Refused):
VARIABLE: AFRICAN

    1 = African American
    0 = Other (Hispanic, White, Asian, Native American, Multiracial, Some other group)

VARIABLE: HISP

    1 = Hispanic
    0 = Other (African American, White, Asian, Native American, Multiracial, Some other group)

VARIABLE: <u>WHITE</u>

    1 = White

    0 = Other (African American, Hispanic, Asian, Native American, Multira-
cial, Some other group)

VARIABLE: <u>OTHERRACE</u>

    1 = Other race (Asian, Native American, Multiracial, Some other group)

    0 = Other (African American, Hispanic, White)

Income

D3. *About how much was your TOTAL FAMILY INCOME last year before taxes? Was it . . .*

VARIABLE: <u>INCOME</u>

    1 = Less than $30,000 (less than $10,000, $10,000 to less than $15,000, $15,000 to less than $20,000, $20,000 to less than $30,000)

    2 = $30,000 to less than $50,000

    3 = $50,000 to less than $75,000

    4 = $75,000 to less than $100,000

    5 = $100,000 or more

    Excludes = Don't Know; Refused

Education

D6. *What is the highest grade of school, or year of college, you have completed and gotten credit for? (READ CHOICES 1–6)*

VARIABLE: <u>EDUCATION</u>

    0 = Less than high school (Grade school or less, Some high school)

    1 = High School

    2 = Some College

    3 = College Graduate

    4 = Postgraduate (Masters or Doctorate)

    Excludes = Don't Know; Refused

Gender

VARIABLE: <u>GENDER</u>

    0 = Male

    1 = Female

    Excludes = Don't Know; Refused

POLITICAL CHARACTERISTICS

Ideology

Q160. *Ideology: In politics today, do you consider yourself a liberal, moderate or conservative? (PROBE: If conservative or liberal, ask "and would that be strong or not so strong?")*

VARIABLE: <u>IDEO</u>

    1 = Strong Liberal

    2 = Somewhat Liberal

3 = Moderate
4 = Somewhat Conservative
5 = Strong Conservative
Excludes: Don't Know; Refused

Party Identification

Q161. *Generally speaking, do you consider yourself a Democrat, Republican, Independent or something else?*

VARIABLE: PID

1 = Democrat
2 = Non-Identifier (includes Independent; Other; Don't Know)
3 = Republican
Excludes = Refused

Dummy variables were also created (all exclude Refused):

VARIABLE: DEM

1 = Democrat
0 = Other (Non-Identifier; Republican)

VARIABLE: REP

1 = Republican
0 = Other (Democrat; Non-Identifier)

VARIABLE: NONIDEN

1 = Non-Identifier
0 = Other (Democrat; Republican)

SOCIAL CAPITAL

Length of Residence

Recorded in whole numbers and rounded up for one-half year or more.

D4. *How long have you lived in the town where you reside?*

VARIABLE: RESIDE

0 = Less than a year
Excludes: Don't Know; Refused

Religious Attendance

D8. *Besides weddings and funerals, how often do you attend religious services? (READ CHOICES 1–7)*

VARIABLE: RELATT

0 = Never
1 = A few times a year
2 = Once every few months
3 = Once a month
4 = A few times a month
5 = Once a week
6 = More than once a week
Excludes: Don't Know; Refused

Belong to Organization

Q162. *Are you currently a member of any organization—for example, unions or professional associations, fraternal groups, recreational organizations, political issue organizations, community or school groups, or religious organizations?*

VARIABLE: BELONG

1 = Yes, belong
0 = No, do not belong
Excludes: Don't Know; Refused

POLITICAL CAPITAL

Political Trust

Political trust was the sum of responses to the following two questions; the index ranges from 0 to 4:

Q125. *How much of the time do you think you can trust government officials to do what's right—just about always, most of the time, only some of the time, or never?*

VARIABLE: PTRUST1

0 = Never
1 = Some of the time
2 = Most of the time
3 = Just about always

Q126. *Would you say that government is pretty much run by a few big interests looking out for themselves or that it is run for the benefit of all the people?*

VARIABLE: PTRUST2

0 = Pretty much run by a few big interests looking out for themselves
1 = It is run for the benefit of all the people

VARIABLE: PTRUST

\# = SUM of PTRUST1 and PTRUST2
0 = Low
1 = Medium
2 = High
3 = Very High
4 = Extremely High
All exclude: Don't Know; Refused

Political Efficacy

Political efficacy was the sum of responses to the following three questions; the index ranges from 0 to 9.

Next, I am going to read you several statements about government officials. For each one tell me whether you agree or disagree with it.

Q127. *I don't think public officials care much about what people like me think. (PROBE: "Do you strongly or somewhat agree/disagree.")*

VARIABLE: EFFIC1

0 = Strongly Agree
1 = Somewhat Agree

2 = Somewhat Disagree

3 = Strongly Disagree

Q128. People like me don't have any say about what the government does. (PROBE: "Do you strongly or somewhat agree/disagree.")

VARIABLE: EFFIC2

0 = Strongly Agree

1 = Somewhat Agree

2 = Somewhat Disagree

3 = Strongly Disagree

Q129. Sometimes politics and the government seem so complicated that a person like me can't really understand what's going on. (PROBE: "Do you strongly or somewhat agree/disagree.")

VARIABLE: EFFIC3

0 = Strongly Agree

1 = Somewhat Agree

2 = Somewhat Disagree

3 = Strongly Disagree

VARIABLE: POLEFF

= SUM of EFFIC1 and EFFIC2 and EFFIC3

All exclude: Don't Know; Refused

Social Trust

Social trust is a summary of the responses to the following questions; the index of social trust ranges from 0 to 3.

Q130. Do you think most people would try to take advantage of you if they got a chance, or would they try to be fair?

VARIABLE: STRUST1

0 = Try to take advantage of you

1 = Try to be fair

Q131. Would you say that most of the time people try to be helpful, or that they are mostly looking out for themselves?

VARIABLE: STRUST2

1 = People try to be helpful

0 = People are looking out for themselves

Q132. Generally speaking, would you say that most people can be trusted or that you can't be too careful in dealing with people?

VARIABLE: STRUST3

1 = Most people can be trusted

0 = Can't be too careful in dealing with people

VARIABLE: STRUST

= SUM of STRUST1 and STRUST2 and STRUST3

0 = Low
1 = Medium
2 = High
3 = Very High
All exclude: Don't Know; Refused

Political Knowledge

Political knowledge is a summary of correct responses to the following questions, where questions Q159 and Q159a are counted as one question. "Don't know" and refusals are counted as incorrect answers. The index of political knowledge ranges of 0 to 5:

Q155. What job or political office is held by Dick Cheney?

Q156. Whose responsibility is it to determine if a law is constitutional or not? Is it the president, the Congress or the Supreme Court?

Q157. How much of a majority is required for the U.S. Senate and House to override a presidential veto?

Q158. Which party has the most members in the House of Representatives in Washington?

Q159. Would you say that one of the parties is more conservative than the other at the national level?

IF YES: Q159a. Which party is more conservative?

VARIABLES: KNOW1; KNOW2; KNOW3; KNOW4; KNOW5

1 = Correct
0 = Incorrect (Other response; Don't Know; Refuse)

VARIABLE: PKNOW

\# = SUM of KNOW1 and KNOW2 and KNOW3 and KNOW4 and KNOW5

Political Interest

Q135. On a scale of 0 to 10, with 0 being "a total lack of interest" and 10 being "a great deal of interest," how interested are you in politics?

VARIABLE: POLINT

0–10 = 0–10
Excludes: Don't Know; Refused

Political Attention

Q136. How much attention would you say you pay to politics and government—a lot, a fair amount, not much, none at all?

VARIABLE: POLATT

0 = None at all
1 = Not much
2 = A fair amount
3 = A lot

Excludes: Don't Know; Refused

Ideological Strength

Q160. In politics today, do you consider yourself a liberal, moderate, or conservative? (PROBE: If conservative or liberal, ask "And would that be strong or not so strong?")

VARIABLE: IDSTR

0 = Moderate
1 = Not so strong
2 = Strong
Excludes: Don't Know; Refused

Partisan Strength

Q161. Generally speaking, do you consider yourself a Democrat, Republican, Independent, or something else?

VARIABLE: PIDSTR

0 = No Party Attachment (includes Independent; Other; Don't Know)
1 = Party Attachment (includes Republican; Democrat)
Excludes: Refused

Political Tolerance

Political Tolerance is sum of responses to the following three questions; the index ranges from 0 to 2. The higher the number, the higher the political tolerance.

Q133. Some people believe that because of 9/11 we should take away from radical Islamic Fundamentalist groups the freedom of speech and the right to organize. Others believe that the Bill of Rights guarantees these rights to all groups, including radical Islamic Fundamentalists. Which is closer to your view?

Q134. Some people believe that because of hate crimes we need to take away from radical racist groups like the Ku Klux Klan the freedom of speech and the right to organize. Others believe that the Bill of Rights guarantees these rights to all groups, including the Klan. Which is closer to your view?

VARIABLE: PTOL1; PTOL2

0 = Take away
1 = Protect

VARIABLE: POLTOL

\# = SUM of PTOL1 and PTOL2
0 = Low
1 = Medium
2 = High
All exclude: Don't Know; Refused

Political Capital Summary Measure (Additive Index)

VARIABLE: POLCAP

\# = POLEFF + PTRUST + STRUST + PKNOW + POLINT + POLATT + IDSTR + PIDSTR + POLTOL
Excludes: Don't Know: Refused

Dichotomized Political Capital Variables (used for table 6.1)

PC1 = POLITICAL EFFICACY 2 POINT

  0 = 0, 1, 2, 3, 4
  1 = 5, 6, 7, 8, 9

PC2 = POLITICAL TRUST 2 POINT

  0 = Low, Medium
  1 = High, Very High, Extremely High

PC3 = SOCIAL TRUST 2 POINT

  0 = Low, Medium
  1 = High, Very High

PC4 = POLITICAL KNOWLEDGE 2 POINT

  0 = 0, 1, 2, 3
  1 = 4, 5

PC5 = POLITICAL INTEREST 2 POINT

  0 = 0, 1, 2, 3, 4, 5
  1 = 6, 7, 8, 9, 10

PC6 = POLITICAL ATTENTION 2 POINT

  0 = Not at all, Not much
  1 = A fair amount, A lot

PC7 = IDEOLOGICAL STRENGTH 2 POINT

  0 = Moderate, Not so strong
  1 = Strong

PC8 = POLITICAL TOLERANCE 2 POINT

  0 = Low, Medium
  1 = High

PC9 = PARTISAN STRENGTH 2 POINT

  0 = None
  1 = High

DISCURSIVE PARTICIPATION

Face-to-Face Deliberation

Q1. *Since the beginning of LAST YEAR—that is since January of 2002—have you at-tended a formal or informal meeting organized by yourself, by someone else you know personally, or by a religious, social, civic, governmental or political group to specifi-cally discuss a local, national, or international issue—for example, neighborhood crime, housing, schools, social security, election reform, terrorism, global warming, or any other public issue that affects people?*

VARIABLE: DIS1

  0 = No (includes Don't Know and Refused)
  1 = Yes

Internet Deliberation

Q62. *Just thinking about the time since the beginning of last year—that is, since Janu-ary 2002—have you participated in any INETERNET chat rooms, message boards, or*

other online discussion groups organized to SPECIFICALLY discuss a local, national or international issue?
VARIABLE: <u>DIS2</u>

> 0 = No (includes Don't Know and Refused)
> 1 = Yes

Internet Talker

Q106. How often do you use e-mail or instant messaging to talk INFORMALLY with people you know about public issues that are local, national, or international concerns. Would you say you do this every day, a few times a week, once a week, a few times a month, or less often than this?
VARIABLE: <u>DIS3</u>

0 = Less often, Never (includes Don't Know and Refused)
1 = Every day, A few times a week, Once a week, A few times a month

Traditional Talker

Q115. How often do you have informal face-to-face or phone conversations or exchanges with people you know about public issues that are local, national, or international concerns? I'm talking about exchanges or conversations of any length. Would you say you do this every day, a few times a week, once a week, a few times a month, or less often than this?
VARIABLE: <u>DIS4</u>

> 0 = Less often, Never (includes Don't Know and Refused)
> 1 = Every day, A few times a week, Once a week, A few times a month

Persuade Issue

People are active in their community and express their beliefs in many ways. I will now list some activities that people sometimes take part to stay active and to express their beliefs. For each, please tell me if you have done it in the last year—that is since January of 2002.
Q152. Tried to persuade someone about your view on a public issue.
VARIABLE: <u>DIS5</u>

> 0 = No (includes Don't Know and Refused)
> 1 = Yes

Persuade Vote

Q153. Tried to persuade someone else about whom to vote for in a local, state or national election.
VARIABLE: <u>DIS6</u>

> 0 = No (includes Don't Know and Refused)
> 1 = Yes

Nondiscursive Measure

VARIABLE: <u>DIS7</u>

> 0 = No (MDIS1 + MDIS2 + MDIS3 + MDIS4 + MDIS5 + MDIS6 = 0)
> 1 = Yes (MDIS1 + MDIS2 + MDIS3 + MDIS4 + MDIS5 + MDIS6 $\geq$ 1)

Discursive Participation Summary Measure
VARIABLE: DIS8

$$# = MDIS1 + MDIS2 + MDIS3 + MDIS4 + MDIS5 + MDIS6$$

Discursive Participation Summary Measure—Dichotomized
VARIABLE: DIS9

    0 = 0, 1, 2
    1 = 3, 4, 5, 6

POLITICAL BEHAVIOR

The following variables are dummy variables coded 1 if the respondent said "yes" to the behavior in question and 0 if the respondent said "no."
People are active in their community and express their beliefs in many ways. I will now list some activities that people sometimes take part to stay active and to express their beliefs. For each, please tell me if you have done it in the last year—that is since January of 2002.

Boycott
Q143. Refused to buy something because of conditions under which the product is made, or because you dislike the conduct of the company that produces it.
VARIABLE: BOYCOTT

Petition
Q142. Signed an e-mail or written petition about a political or social issue.
VARIABLE: PETITION

Contact Official
Q139. Contacted or visited a candidate for office or public official at any level of government to express your opinion.
VARIABLE: CONTOFF

Contact Media
Q140. Wrote, called or e-mailed a newspaper, magazine or television news show to express your opinion on an issue.
VARIABLE: CONTMED

Community Service
Q147. Volunteered or participated in some kind of community service.
VARIABLE: COMMUNITY

Work Informally
Q150. Worked informally with others to solve a problem in the community where you live.
VARIABLE: WORKINF

Vote 2000

Q137. *Did you vote in the 2000 presidential election between Al Gore and George Bush?*
VARIABLE: VOTE00

Vote 2002

Q138. *And did you vote in the congressional elections that occurred in November 2002?*
VARIABLE: VOTE02

Volunteer for Campaign

Q151. *Volunteered to work for a political candidate or party.*
VARIABLE: VOLCAMP

Elite contacting is an index summing Boycott, Petition, Contact Official and Contact Media. The scale ranges from 0 to 4.

Civic participation is an index summing Community Service and Work Informally. The index ranges from 0 to 2.

Electoral participation is an index summing Vote 2002 and Volunteer for Campaign. The index ranges from 0 to 2.

Political and civic participation is an index summing the scales for elite contacting, civic participation and electoral participation. The index ranges from 0 to 8.

All exclude: Don't Know; Refused

MEETING CHARACTERISTICS

Q6. *Thinking about the LAST meeting you participated in, what public issue did you discuss?*
VARIABLE: ISSUE

> 1 = War / Terrorism / Iraq / Middle East
> 2 = Local Issues
> 3 = Children's Issues
> 4 = Social Policy
> 5 = Other Issues
> 6 = Social Welfare and Economic Policy
> 7 = Economic Development

Organization

Q7. *Still thinking about the last meeting you participated in to discuss a public issue, did you or someone you know personally such as a family member, friend, neighbor, or co-worker help to organize it?*
VARIABLE: ORGANIZE1

0 = No
1 = Yes
Excludes: Don't Know; Refused

Q8. Who helped organize the meeting?
VARIABLE: <u>ORGANIZE2</u>

1 = Respondent
2 = Family Member
3 = Friend
4 = Neighbor
5 = Co-Worker / Employer
6 = Committee or Organization / Group / Association / Community
7 = City Council / Government Official or Agency / Political Group
8 = School / Teachers
9 = Church / Religious Group
10 = Police or Fire Department
80 = Other
Excludes: Don't Know; Refused

Q9. And was the last meeting you attended sponsored or organized by a religious, social, civic, governmental, political, or other any organized group?
VARIABLE: <u>ORGANIZE3</u>

0 = No
1 = Yes
Excludes: Don't Know; Refused

Q10. Can you tell me what kind of organization or group that was?
VARIABLE: <u>ORGANIZE4</u>

1 = Church or religious group
2 = Civic or community organization, association, or club
3 = Business or business organization
4 = Labor union
5 = Government official or agency
6 = School or college
7 = Political candidate or party
8 = Social club or organization
9 = Sports club or organization
80 = Someone else
Excludes: Don't Know; Refused

Location

Q11. Still thinking about the last meeting you attended this year to discuss a public issue, please tell me where it was held. (ASK OPEN-ENDED AND CODE INTO CATEGORIES. PROBE IF NECESSARY: "Did it occur in a school, a library, the offices or space of a community group, someone's home, or somewhere else?")
VARIABLE: <u>LOCATION</u>

1 = Own home

2 = Someone else's home
3 = Church, synagogue, or other place of worship
4 = Library
5 = School or college
6 = Government building or office
7 = Offices or space of a community or civic group
8 = Some other public building or community center
9 = Offices or space of a local business
10 = Restaurant
11 = Outdoors
12 = Hotel / Convention center
80 = Someplace else
Excludes: Don't Know; Refused

Meeting Size

Q12. Approximately how many people attended this meeting? (PROBE IF UNCERTAIN: "Just want your best guess.")

VARIABLE: SIZE1

= Number of people

VARIABLE: SIZE2

1 = 0–19
2 = 20–39
3 = 40–99
4 = 100+

VARIABLE: SIZE3

1 = Small
2 = Large
All exclude: Don't Know; Refused

People Respondent Knew at Meeting

Q13. Generally speaking, how many of the people at the last meeting you attended would you say you already knew or were acquainted with—All of the people, most of them, some of them, only a few of them, or none of them? (PROBE IF UNCERTAIN: "What is your best sense?")

VARIABLE: PPLKNEW

0 = None of them
1 = Only a few of them
2 = Some of them
3 = Most of them
4 = All of them
Excludes: Don't Know; Refused

Diversity

The following variables are continuous variables, coded 0 for "not diverse at all" to 10 for "very diverse". Don't Know; Refused excluded.

Q14. Different meetings attract different mixes of people. Using a scale from 0 to 10, where 0 is "not diverse at all" and 10 is "very diverse," how racially or ethnically diverse would you say the people at the last meeting you attended were? (PROBE: "What's your best sense?" By "not diverse at all," we mean everyone had exactly the same racial or ethnic characteristic, and by "very diverse" we mean there was a fairly equal mix of all examples of that racial or ethnic characteristic.)

Q15. Using the same scale from zero to ten, where zero is "not diverse at all" and ten is "very diverse," how diverse were the people attending this meeting by income? (PROBE IF UNCERTAIN: "What is your best sense?")

Q16. How diverse were the people attending this meeting by age?

Q17. How diverse were the people attending the meeting by gender?

Q18. And, using the same scale, how diverse were the points of view expressed during the meeting?

Find Out about Meeting

Q19. How did you find out about the last meeting you attended?
VARIABLE: FINDOUT

    1 = Friend / Neighbor / Family Member
    2 = E-mail
    3 = Mail
    4 = Flyer / Poster / Leaflet / Memo
    5 = Religious organization (church)
    6 = Club or organization
    7 = Work / School
    8 = Newspaper
    9 = Radio
    10 = Television
    11 = Internet
    12 = Respondent helped organize it
    13 = Regular meetings that respondent already attended
    14 = Solicited phone call
    15 = By word of mouth
    80 = Other
    Excludes: Don't Know; Refused

Reading Material

Q29. Were you given any reading materials before, during, or after the last meeting you attended to help you better understand or think about the issue?
VARIABLE: READING1

    0 = No
    1 = Yes
    Excludes: Don't Know; Refused

Q30. When were you given this material—before the meeting, during the meeting, or after the meeting?

VARIABLE: <u>READING2</u>

   1 = Before

   2 = During

   3 = After

   Excludes: Don't Know; Refused

Q31. Which of the following best describes this material? Would you say it was generally neutral and objective, generally balanced between different points of view, or generally biased in favor of a particular point of view?

VARIABLE: <u>READING3</u>

   1 = Neutral / Objective

   2 = Balanced

   3 = Biased

   Excludes: Don't Know; Refused

Meeting Purpose

The following variables are continuous variables, coded 0 for "not important at all" to 10 for "very important." Don't Know; Refused excluded.

Q32i. Meetings to discuss public issues serve different purposes. Using a scale from zero to ten, where zero is "not important at all" and ten is "very important," please tell me how important each of the following goals were to the last meeting you attended this year.

Q32. To teach people about the issue in a neutral, factual way.

Q33. To allow people to air differences of opinion and discuss different points of view.

Q34. To allow people to come to agreement about the importance of the issue being discussed, its causes, and/or how it might be addressed.

Q35. To give people an opportunity to decide on concrete actions to take to address the issue.

Meeting Participation

The following variables are continuous variables, coded 0 for "not often at all" to 10 for "very often." Don't Know; Refused excluded.

Q36. Using a scale from zero to ten, where zero is "not often at all "and ten is "very often," how often would you say you personally participated in the discussion during the last meeting you attended?

Q37. What about others at the meeting? Using the same scale, where zero is "not often at all" and ten is "very often," how often would you say most other people participated in the discussion?

Reason for Attending Meeting

The following variables are continuous variables, coded 0 for "not important at all" to 10 for "very important." Don't Know; Refused excluded.

IQ38. People participate in meetings for different reasons. Using a scale from zero to ten, where zero is "not important at all" and ten is "very important," please tell me how important each of the following reasons were to your decision to participate in the last meeting you attended.

Q38. I felt it was my duty as a citizen or member of the community.

Q39. The issue under discussion directly affected me and my family.

Q40. The issue under discussion directly affected other people who live in my community.

Q42. The issue being discussed just sounded interesting to me.

Q43. It was a chance to meet or talk to other people who share my interests.

Q44. Because I was personally asked by someone to participate.

Other Reason for Attending Meeting

Q45. Are there any other reasons why you participated in your last meeting to discuss a public issue? (IF YES, ASK: "What were they?" AND RECORD VERBATIM.)
VARIABLE: <u>OTHERREASON</u>

1 = No
2 = Interested / Curious about the issue
3 = Was asked or required to participate
4 = The issue affects family or career
5 = The issue affects children
6 = To voice his or her concerns
7 = To socialize
8 = Sense of civic duty / responsibility
80 = Other
Excludes: Don't Know; Refused

Feelings

The following variables are continuous variables, coded 0 for "not often at all" to 10 for "very often." Don't Know; Refused excluded.
IQ46. Now I'd like to ask you a few questions about your experiences in the last meeting you attended this year. I am going to read you a list of words or statements. On a scale from zero to ten, where zero is "not often at all" and ten is "very often," please tell me how often you felt the following ways during the last meeting you attended.

Q46. Enthusiastic

Q49. Anxious

Q50. Angry

Q54. More understanding of different points of view.

Decision Making

Q55. *Was any decision made at the last meeting you attended regarding what specifically should be done to address the issue that was being discussed?*
VARIABLE: DECISION1

0 = No
1 = Yes
Excludes: Don't Know; Refused

Q56. *Did you agree with this decision?*
VARIABLE: DECISION2

0 = No
1 = Yes
Excludes: Don't Know; Refused

Q56A. *Did the majority of the other participants agree with the decision, or did the majority of them disagree?*
VARIABLE: DECISION3

1 = Majority Agreed
2 = Majority Disagreed
Excludes: Don't Know; Refused

Follow-up Actions

Q57. *Using a scale from zero to ten, where zero is "not likely at all" and ten is "very likely," please tell me how likely you are to attend another meeting to discuss a public issue in the next six months.*
VARIABLE: FOLLOW1

0–10 = 0–10
Excludes: Don't Know; Refused

Q58. *People sometimes follow up their participation in public meetings with other kinds of activities intended to address the problem that was discussed. Have you engaged in any charitable, civic or political activities AS A DIRECT RESULT of the last meeting you attended about a public issue?*
VARIABLE: FOLLOW2

0 = No
1 = Yes
Excludes: Don't Know; Refused

Q59. *What activity or activities did you do?*
VARIABLE: FOLLOW3

1 = Contacted or visited a candidate for office or public official
2 = Wrote, called or e-mailed a newspaper, magazine, or television news show
4 = Signed an e-mail or written petition
5 = Refused to buy something because of conditions under which it was made

7 = Purchased a certain product or service because you like the conduct of the company that produces it
8 = Walked, ran, or bicycled for a charitable cause
9 = Voted in an election for local, state, or national office
10 = Volunteered or participated in some kind of community service
11 = Joined a political or civic organization
12 = Discussed public issues with others
14 = Gave money to a charitable or political cause
15 = Volunteered to work for a political candidate or party
16 = Tried to persuade someone about your view on a public issue
17 = Tried to persuade someone else about whom to vote for in a local, state, or national election
18 = Fund-raising
19 = Distributed information
20 = Protest / Rally
80 = Other
Excludes: Don't Know; Refused

MEETING FACILITATOR

Facilitator

Q20. *Was there someone at the last meeting you attended who was responsible for leading or facilitating the discussion?*
VARIABLE: FACILITATOR

0 = No
1 = Yes
Excludes: Don't Know; Refused

Q27. *Was there any one else at the last meeting you attended whose role was to serve as a neutral expert on the issue being discussed and to help educate participants in other ways?*
VARIABLE: EXPERT

0 = No
1 = Yes
Excludes: Don't Know; Refused

Q28. *Did the meeting include any people whose roles were to formally advocate for or debate different points of view on the issue being discussed?*
VARIABLE: ADVOCATE

0 = No
1 = Yes
Excludes: Don't Know; Refused

Role of Facilitator

The following variables are continuous variables, coded 0 for "not often at all" to 10 for "very often." Don't Know; Refused excluded.

IQ21. *Discussion leaders often play different roles during the course of a meeting. Using a scale from zero to ten, where zero is "not often at all" and 10 is "very often," please tell me how often the leader or facilitator of the last meeting you attended played any of the following roles.*

Q22. *Trying to educate the meeting's participants about the issue being discussed in a neutral, balanced way.*

Q23. *Making sure that everyone's opinions were heard.*

Q24. *Attempting to convince people of a particular point of view.*

Q25. *Helping the group come to agreement on the issue.*

Q26. *Trying to convince people to do something about the issue.*

INSTRUMENTAL VARIABLES

Invite

The text describes the instrumental variable used in 2SLS regression involving face-to-face deliberation. The variable combines responses to Q2, asked of non–face-to-face deliberators, and Q44, asked of face-to-face deliberators. "No" responses to Q2 and responses of 0 to Q44 are coded as 0; responses of "yes" to question 2 and responses of greater than 0 to Q44 are coded as 1.

Q2. *Since January 2002, have you been INVITED to attend a formal or informal meeting to specifically discuss a local, national or international issue?*

People participate in meetings for different reasons. Using a scale from zero to ten, where zero is "not important at all" and ten is "very important," please tell me how important each of the following reasons were to your decision to participate in the last meeting you attended.

Q44. *Because I was personally asked by a person to participate.*

VARIABLE: INVITE

Excludes: Don't Know; Refused

Hours on Internet

For the 2SLS equations involving Internet deliberation and Internet talk, the following questions were combined to create an instrumental variable. Responses of "No" to question 1 were coded as 0 (for zero hours on average per day on the Internet), and remaining responses to Q61 were coded from 1 to 6 to create an index with values from 0 to 6.

Q60. *Do you currently use the World Wide Web, e-mail, or some other feature of the Internet from home, work, somewhere else, or do you not currently use the Internet?*

Q61. *How many hours a day on average do you use the World Wide Web, e-mail, or some other feature of the Internet from home, work, or somewhere else?*

Less than 1 hour

1 to less than 4 hours
4 to less than 7 hours
7 to less than 14 hours
14 to less than 21 hours
21 or more hours

PATH ANALYSIS

To obtain the coefficients for the path analysis in figure 5.5, we ran a series of regressions. The dependent variable for each regression is located on the right of the path analysis and has arrows directed at it. For each dependent variable, the independent variables are those from which the arrows originate. See below for a detailed list of the regressions (listed as they appear from top to bottom in the path analysis). In addition, each regression included as control variables all of the demographic characteristics and social capital measures: race, education, gender, age, income, belong to organization, religious attendance, and length of residence.

Regression 1: DV = Civic Participation; IV = Face-to-Face Deliberation, Political Capital Summary Measure
Regression 2: DV = Political Capital Summary Measure; IV = Face-to-Face Deliberation
Regression 3: DV = Electoral Participation; IV = Face-to-Face Deliberation, Political Capital Summary Measure
Regression 4: DV = Elite Contacting; IV = Face-to-Face Deliberation, Political Capital Summary Measure

NOTES

CHAPTER ONE

1. For some exceptions, see Mansbridge 1983; Fishkin 1991; Fishkin and Luskin 1999a; and Fung 2004.

CHAPTER TWO

1. The response rate is 43.4% for the general population survey and 45.8% for the over-sample based on the RR3 calculation recommended by the American Association for Public Opinion Research (AAPOR 2008).

2. More than 69% of the respondents who indicated that they had attended a meeting in the last year answered each of the forty-eight follow-up questions, which generally were open-ended and asked detailed questions about their experiences. Moreover, for the great majority of these extensive and detailed questions, only 1% answered "Don't know" or "No answer" to any single question; no more than 7.5% did not answer, and this was quite uncommon. Only 0.4% of respondents did not answer the last question in the battery. This pattern suggests that respondents were answering based on generally clear recollections and were not responding out of a sense of social desirability.

3. We treated respondents as "face-to-face deliberators" if they answered yes to the following question: "Since the beginning of last year—that is since January of 2002—have you attended a formal or informal meeting organized by yourself, by someone else you know personally, or by a religious, social, civic, governmental, or political group specifically to discuss a local, national, or international issue—for example, neighborhood crime, housing, schools, social security, election reform, terrorism, global warming, or any other public issue that affects people?"

4. This group of discursive participants is derived from responses to the following question: "How often do you use e-mail or instant messaging to talk INFORMALLY with people you know about public issues that are local, national, or international concerns? Would you say you do this every day, a few times a week, once a week, a few times a month, or less often than this?" Respondents were treated as "Internet talkers" if they indicated "Every day," "A few times a week," "Once a week," or "A few times a month."

5. The question was "How often do you have informal face-to-face or phone conversations or exchanges with people you know about public issues that are local, national, or international concerns? I'm talking about exchanges or conversations of any length. Would you say you do this every day, a few times a week, once a week, a few times a month, or less often than this?" Respondents were considered "traditional talkers" if they answered "Every day," "A few times a week," "Once a week," or "A few times a month."

6. The question was "People are active in their community and express their beliefs in many ways. I will now list some activities that people sometimes take part in to stay active and to express their beliefs. For each, please tell me if you have done it in the last

year—that is, since January of 2002. Have you tried to persuade someone about your view on a public issue?"

7. The question on vote persuasion had the same stem as the question on issue persuasion. Specifically, the question was "People are active in their community and express their beliefs in many ways. I will now list some activities that people sometimes take part in to stay active and to express their beliefs. For each, please tell me if you have done it in the last year—that is, since January of 2002. Have you tried to persuade someone else about who to vote for in a local, state, or national election?"

8. The specific questions (aside from voting) asked if respondents had engaged in any of these activities in the last year. The voting questions asked if they had voted in 2000 and 2002.

CHAPTER THREE

1. The ratings have a standard deviation of approximately 3, which is large relative to the mean scores. The distribution of the racial and income diversity responses tends to cluster at 5 or below on the 11-point scale; age diversity clusters more in the upper half of the scale; the distributions of responses regarding diversity of viewpoints, especially gender, tended to be bell-shaped, with a spike a 5. It appears that some meetings are extremely homogenous, while others are quite diverse.

2. Americans did perceive greater diversity in chat rooms regarding both point of view and race and ethnicity—the former was rated 6.4 (s.d. of 2.9), while the latter was scored 5.9 (s.d. of 3.0).

3. We explored a number of different measures for meeting size, including a log of the meeting size, a dummy variable of it, and a dichotomous measure for large meetings. The results were largely similar.

4. Although the ratings varied (standard deviations of 3.0 for personal participation and 2.3 for participation by others), ratings of personal participation tended to cluster toward the bottom half of the scale, with peaks at 5 (18%), 0 (12%), and 7 (11%), while ratings of participation by others were distributed higher up the scale—5 (24%), 8 (16%), and 6 and 7 (13% each).

CHAPTER FOUR

1. The wording of the root question on forum purpose that initiated a series of probes was the following: "Meetings to discuss public issues serve different purposes. Using a scale from zero to ten, where zero is 'not important at all' and ten is 'very important,' please tell me how important each of the following goals were to the last meeting you attended this year."

2. Respondents were asked several sets of questions that focused on their personal experiences and evaluations. The most in-depth series of probes was initiated by the following question: "People participate in meetings for different reasons. Using a scale from zero to ten, where zero is 'not important at all' and ten is 'very important,' please tell me how important each of the following reasons were to your decision to participate in the last meeting you attended."

CHAPTER FIVE

1. Verba, Schlozman, and Brady (1995) do provide data on attending meetings and discussing politics, but they treat "talk" as something different from civic and political engagement.

2. Note that there is no path from "civic participation" to policy outcomes because our definition of civic participation involves citizen action that is intended to deal directly with an issue rather than to pressure government to act.

3. To the extent that collinearity is a concern, there is little evidence of it. Deliberation and belonging to an organization are only modestly correlated at the .01 level. The diagnos-

tics for detecting collinearity (variance inflation factor, or VIF) for all three models scored quite low—from 1 (the minimum, which means no collinearity) to 1.3 (the maximum score can exceed 10). As we suggest in the next paragraph, the lack of collinearity fits with the substantive interpretation of our findings—namely, that deliberation (and not SES directly) boosts political capital.

4. There is little evidence of collinearity among deliberation and the non-SES variables. The correlations are weak, and the VIF scores are weak. As we suggest in the next paragraph in the text, this is consistent with our substantive finding.

CHAPTER SIX

1. This chapter is based on an evaluation of the ADSS project, which was conducted for the Pew Charitable Trusts (Cook and Jacobs 1998).

2. We content-analyzed transcripts from the five forums to determine the directionality of statements regarding particular policy reforms (i.e., whether the statements were for, against, or neutral), the frequency with which distinct values are mentioned, the facts that were discussed, and other aspects of the forum deliberations. Over all, we coded 10,351 statements, with 3,507 from the full forums and 6,844 from the small-group discussions. The content analysis of our two trained coders was assessed in terms of intercoder reliability; an independent coder found that our two coders agreed on their coding decisions regarding different dimensions of our content analysis on between 80% to more than 90% of the cases, which gives us confidence in the accuracy of the content analysis.

3. Other values they discussed included the assurance of human dignity, accountability, solidarity/community, universality, status quo/maintaining the original purpose of Social Security, equality between men and women, poverty reduction, needs-based, anti-government, pro-government, and equality of outcome/egalitarianism.

4. The nine options can be clumped into three patterns: (A) Restructure Social Security: (1) Allow individual accounts (in any form: instead of, in addition to, or as part of Social Security). (B) Reduce benefits: (1) Reduce cost-of-living adjustments (COLAs); (2) increase retirement age; (3) reduce benefits across the board for everyone; (4) reduce benefits for high-income beneficiaries. (C) Raise taxes: (1) Raise the ceiling on amount of earnings subject to payroll taxation; (2) increase Social Security payroll tax; (3) tax Social Security like a private pension (increase percentage of benefits that are taxable).

5. This section is based on Cook and Jacobs 1998 and Cook, Barabas, and Jacobs 2003.

6. The ANCOVA analysis controls for selection effects (i.e., that some groups may have different starting points at time one in regard to such things as knowledge, salience, or participation levels). In some circumstances we were not able to use the ANCOVA test due to violations of the normality and homogeneity of variance assumptions underlying the model. Consequently, we used a nonparametric test, the Kruskal-Wallis test, in situations noted in the text and tables when the data showed statistically significant and noncorrectable deviations from the assumptions underlying the ANCOVA models. The two methods nearly always produced similar findings, but we deferred to the more conservative nonparametric test whenever the assumptions were not met and we had to choose between the two methods.

CHAPTER SEVEN

1. The discussion of the IAPP is based on its Web site: www.iap2.org.

2. All quotations and general descriptions of the NCDD are from or based on its Web site: http://www.thataway.org/.

3. Descriptions and quotations are drawn from the DDC Web site: http://www.deliberative-democracy.net/.

4. At the time of the survey, neither the NCDD nor the DDC existed.

REFERENCES

Aaken, Anne van, Christian List, and Christoph Luetge, eds. 2004. *Deliberation and Decision: Economics, Constitutional Theory and Deliberative Democracy*. Aldershot, UK: Ashgate.

Abramson, Paul R. 1983. *Political Attitudes in America: Formation and Change*. San Francisco: W. H. Freeman.

Almond, Gabriel. 1960. *The American People and Foreign Policy*. New York: Praeger.

Almond, Gabriel, and Sidney Verba. 1963. *The Civic Culture*. Princeton, NJ: Princeton University Press.

American Association for Public Opinion Research. 2008. "Standard Definitions: Final Dispositions of Case Codes and Outcome Rates for Surveys." Available online at the association's Web site: http://www.aapor.org/uploads/Standard_Definitions_04_08_Final.pdf.

American Political Science Association Task Force. 2004. "Inequalities of Political Voice." Online at the association's Web site: www.apsanet.org

America*Speaks*. 2006. *AmericaSpeaks News* 3, no. 1, April.

Barabas, Jason. 2004. "How Deliberation Affects Policy Opinions." *American Political Science Review* 98 (November): 687–701.

Barber, Benjamin. 1984. *Strong Democracy*. Berkeley and Los Angeles: University of California Press.

Barnes, Samuel, Max Kaase, Klaus Allerbeck, Barbara G. Farah, Felix Heunks, Ronald Inglehart, M. Kent Jennings, Hans D. Klingemann, Allan Marsh, and Leopold Rosenmayr. 1979. *Political Action: Mass Participation in Five Western Democracies*. Beverly Hills, CA: Sage.

Bartels, Larry. 2008. *Unequal Democracy: The Political Economy of the New Gilded Age*. Princeton, NJ: Princeton University Press.

Bartels, Larry, Hugh Heclo, Rodney Hero, and Lawrence Jacobs. 2005. "Inequality and American Governance." In Jacobs and Skocpol, *Inequality and American Democracy*, 88–155.

Benhabib, Seyla. 2002. *The Claims of Culture: Equality and Diversity in the Global Era*. Princeton, NJ: Princeton University Press.

———. 1996. "Toward a Deliberative Model of Democratic Legitimacy." In *Democracy and Difference: Contesting the Boundaries of the Political*, ed. S. Benhabib, 67–94. Princeton, NJ: Princeton University Press.

———. 1992a. "Models of Public Space: Hannah Arendt, the Liberal Tradition, and Jürgen Habermas." In *Habermas and the Public Sphere*, ed. Craig Calhoun, 73–98. Cambridge, MA: MIT Press.

———. 1992b. *Situating the Self: Gender, Community and Modernism in Contemporary Ethics*. New York: Routledge.

———. 1989. "Liberal Dialogue vs. a Critical Theory of Discursive Legitimation." In *Liberalism and the Moral Life*, ed. Nancy Rosenblum, 143–56. Cambridge, MA: Harvard University Press.

————. 1985. "The Utopian Dimension in Communicative Ethics." *New German Critique* no. 35:83–96.

Bennett, Stephen E., Bonnie S. Fisher, and David Resnick. 1995. "Political Conversations in the United States: Who Talks to Whom, Why, and Why Not." *American Review of Politics* 16:277–98.

Berelson, Bernard, Paul Lazarsfeld, and William McPhee. 1954. *Voting: A Study of Opinion Formation in a Presidential Campaign*. Chicago: University of Chicago Press.

Berry, Jeffrey M. 1999. *The New Liberalism: The Rising Power of Citizen Groups*. Washington, DC: Brookings Institution Press.

Berry, Jeffrey M., Kent E. Portney, and Ken Thomson. 1993. *The Rebirth of Urban Democracy*. Washington, DC: Brookings Institution Press.

Bessette, Joseph. 1980. "Deliberative Democracy: The Majoritarian Principle in Republican Government." In *How Democratic Is the Constitution?* ed. Robert Goldwin and William Shambra, 102–16. Washington, DC: American Enterprise Institute.

Bettencourt, B. Ann, and Nancy Dorr. 1998. "Cooperative Interaction and Intergroup Bias: Effects of numerical Representation and Cross-Cut Role Assignment." *Personality and Social Psychology Bulletin* 24, no. 12:1276–93.

Bohman, James. 1996. *Public Deliberation: Pluralism, Complexity, and Democracy*. Cambridge, MA: MIT Press

Bohman, James, and William Rehg. 1997. *Deliberative Democracy*. Cambridge, MA: MIT Press

Bornstein, Gary. 1992. "The Free-Rider Problem in Intergroup Conflicts over Step-Level and Continuous Public Goods." *Journal of Personality and Social Psychology* 62, no. 4:597–606.

Bornstein, Gary, and Amnon Rapoport. 1988. "Intergroup Competition for the Provision of Step-Level Public Goods: Effects of Preplay Communication." *European Journal of Social Psychology* 18:125–42.

Bottger, Preston C. 1984. "Expertise and Air Time as Bases of Actual and Perceived Influence in Problem-Solving Groups." *Journal of Applied Psychology* 69:214–21.

Bouas, Kelly S., and S. S. Komorita. 1996. "Group Discussion and Cooperation in Social Dilemmas." *Personality and Social Psychology Bulletin* 22:1144–50.

Bowers, William J., Benjamin D. Steiner, and Marla Sandys. 2001. "Race, Crime and the Constitution: Death Sentencing in Black and White: An Empirical Analysis of the Role of Jurors' Race and Jury Racial Composition." *University of Pennsylvania Journal of Constitutional Law* 3:171–274.

Brady, Henry E. 1999. "Political Participation." In *Measures of Political Attitudes*, ed. John P. Robinson, Phillip R. Shaver, and Lawrence S. Wrightsman, 737–801. San Diego, CA: Academic Press.

Brady, Henry E., Sidney Verba, and Kay Schlozman. 1995. "Beyond SES: A Resource Model of Political Participation." *American Political Science Review* (June): 271–94.

Brehm, John, and Wendy Rahn. 1997. "Individual-Level Evidence for the Causes and Consequences of Social Capital." *American Journal of Political Science* 41 (July): 999–1023.

Brooks, Clem, and Jeff Manza. 1997. "Class Politics and Political Change in the United States, 1952–1992." *Social Forces* no. 76 (December): 379–409.

Bryan, Frank. 2004. *Real Democracy: The New England Town Meeting and How It Works*. Chicago: University of Chicago Press.

Burke, Edmund. 1949. *Burke's Politics: Selected Writings and Speeches of Edmund Burke on Reform, Revolution, and War*. Ed. Ross J. S. Hoffmann and Paul Levack. New York: A. A. Knopf

Burnstein, Eugene, and Amiram Vinokur. 1977. "Persuasive Argumentation and Social Comparison as Determinants of Attitude Polarization." *Journal of Experimental Social Psychology* 13:315–32.

Burnstein, Eugene, Amiram Vinokur, and Yaacov Trope. 1973. "Interpersonal Comparison versus Persuasive Argumentation: A More Direct Test of Alternative Explanations for Group-Induced Shifts in Individual Choice." *Journal of Experimental Social Psychology* 9, no. 3:236–45.

Burstein, Paul. 2003. "The Impact of Public Policy: A Review and an Agenda." *Political Research Quarterly* 56 (March): 29–40.

Button, Mark, and Kevin Mattson. 1999. "Deliberative Democracy in Practice: Challenge and Prospects for Civic Deliberation." *Polity* 31 (Summer): 609–37.

Button, Mark, and David Michael Ryfe. 2005. "What Can We Learn from the Practice of Deliberative Democracy." In Gastil and Levine, *Deliberative Democracy Handbook*, 20–33.

Campbell, Andrea Louise. 2003. *How Policies Make Citizens: Senior Political Activism and the American Welfare State*. Princeton, NJ: Princeton University Press.

Cappella, Joseph, and Kathleen Hall Jamieson. 1997. *Spiral of Cynicism: The Press and the Public Good*. New York: Oxford University Press.

Cappella, Joseph, Vincent Price, and Lilach Nir. 2002. "Argument Repertoire as a Reliable and Valid Measure of Opinion Quality: Electronic Dialogue During Campaign 2000." *Political Communication* 19:73–93.

Chambers, Simone. 2003. "Deliberative Democratic Theory." *Annual Review of Political Science* 6:307–26.

———. 1996. *Reasonable Democracy: Jürgen Habermas and the Politics of Discourse*. Ithaca, NY: Cornell University Press.

CIRCLE (Center for Information and Research on Civic Learning and Education). 2002. "Youth Voter Turnout Has Declined By Any Measure." Online at http://civicyouth.org/research/products/fact_sheets_outside.htm.

Clinton, William J. 1998. "Address before a Joint Session of Congress on the State of the Union." Washington, DC, January 27.

Cobb, Michael, and James H. Kuklinski. 1997. "Changing Minds: Political Arguments and Political Persuasion." *American Journal of Political Science* 41 (January): 88–121.

Cohen, Joshua. 1998. "Democracy and Liberty." In Elster, *Deliberative Democracy*, 185–231.

———. 1989. "Deliberation and Democratic Legitimacy." In *The Good Polity: Normative Analysis of the State*, ed. Alan Hamlin and Phillip Petit, 17–34. Cambridge: Basil Blackwell.

Comstock, George, and Erica Scharrer. 2005. *The Psychology of Media and Politics*. New York: Elsevier Academic Press.

Conover, Pamela Johnston, Donald D. Searing, and Ivor Crewe. 2004. "The Elusive Ideal of Equal Citizenship: Political Theory and Political Psychology in the United States and Great Britain." *Journal of Politics* 66, no. 4:1036–68.

Cook, Fay Lomax, Jason Barabas, and Lawrence Jacobs. 2003. "Deliberative Democracy in Action: An Analysis of the Effects of Public Deliberation." Unpublished ms., Northwestern University and University of Minnesota.

Cook, Fay Lomax, Michael X. Delli Carpini, and Lawrence R. Jacobs. 2007. "Who Deliberates? Discursive Participation in America." In Rosenberg, *Deliberation, Participation, and Democracy: Can the People Govern?* 25–44.

Cook, Fay Lomax, and Lawrence R. Jacobs. 1998. "Deliberative Democracy in Action: Evaluation of *Americans Discuss Social Security*." Report to the Pew Charitable Trusts.

Cook, Thomas D., and Donald T. Campbell. 1979. *Quasi-Experimentation: Design and Analysis Issues for Field Settings*. Chicago: Rand McNally.

Cooke, Jacob, ed. 1961. *The Federalist*. Middletown, CT: Wesleyan University Press.

Dahl, Robert. 1989. *Democracy and Its Critics*. New Haven, CT: Yale University Press.

———. 1985. *A Preface to Economic Democracy*. Berkeley and Los Angeles: University of California Press

———. 1956. *A Preface to Democratic Theory*. Chicago: University of Chicago Press

Davis, James H., Robert M. Bray, and Robert W. Holt. 1977. "The Empirical Study of Decision Processes in Juries: A Critical Review." In *Law, Justice and the Individual in Society*, ed. J. L. Tapp and F. J. Levine, 326–61. New York: Holt, Rinehart and Winston.

Davis, James H., Tatsuya Kameda, Craig Parks, Mark Stasson, and Suzi Zimmerman. 1989. "Some Social Mechanics of Group Decision Making: The Distribution of Opinions,

Polling Sequence, and Implications for Consensus." *Journal of Personality and Social Psychology* 57:1000–12.

Davis, James H., Mark Stasson, Kaoru Ono, and Suzi Zimmerman. 1988. "Effects of Straw Polls on Group Decision-Making: Sequential Voting Patterns, Timing, and Local Majorities." *Journal of Personality and Social Psychology* 55:918–26.

Dawes, Robyn M., Alphons J. C. van de Kragt, and John M. Orbell. 1990. "Cooperation for the Benefit of Us: Not Me, or My Conscience." In *Beyond Self-Interest*, ed. Jane Mansbridge, 97–110. Chicago: University of Chicago Press.

Delli Carpini, Michael X. 1997. "The Impact of the 'Money + Politics' Citizen Assemblies on Assembly Participants." Report to the Pew Charitable Trusts, Philadelphia.

Delli Carpini, Michael X., Fay Lomax Cook, and Lawrence R. Jacobs. 2004. "Public Deliberation, Discursive Participation, and Citizen Engagement: A Review of the Empirical Literature." *Annual Review of Political Science* 7:315–44.

Delli Carpini, Michael X., and Scott Keeter. 1996. *What Americans Know About Politics and Why It Matters*. New Haven, CT: Yale University Press.

Denver, David, Gordon Hands, and Bill Jones. 1995. "Fishkin and the Deliberative Opinion: Lessons from a Study of the Granada 500 Television Program." *Political Communication* 12:147–56.

Dewey, John. 1954. *The Public and Its Problems*. Athens, OH: Swallow Press. Originally published in 1927.

Doble, John, and Amy Richardson. 1991. *A Report on the 1990–1991 NIF Research Forums Results*. New York: Public Agenda Foundation.

Dresser, Rebecca. 2001. *When Science Offers Salvation: Patient Advocacy and Research Ethics*. New York: Oxford University Press.

Druckman, James N., and Lawrence R. Jacobs. 2006. "Lumpers and Splitters: The Public Opinion Information That Politicians Collect and Use." *Public Opinion Quarterly* 70 (December): 453–76.

Dryzek, John. 2000. *Deliberative Democracy and Beyond: Liberals, Critics, Contestations*. New York: Oxford University Press.

———. 1990. *Discursive Democracy: Politics, Policy, and Political Science*. Cambridge: Cambridge University Press.

Dworkin, Ronald. 1978. *Taking Rights Seriously*. Cambridge, MA: Harvard University Press.

Edwards III, George C., 2007. *Governing by Campaigning*. New York: Pearson & Longman.

Eliasoph, Nina. 1998. *Avoiding Politics: How Americans Produce Apathy in Everyday Life*. Cambridge: Cambridge University Press.

Elster, Jon. 1998. *Deliberative Democracy*. New York: Cambridge University Press.

Erikson, Robert, and Kent Tedin. 2001. *American Public Opinion*. 6th ed. New York: Longman.

Etzioni, Amitai. 1997. *The New Golden Rule: Community and Morality in a Democratic Society*. New York: Basic Books.

Fagotto, Elena. 2006. "Embedded Deliberation: Moving from Deliberation to Action." Paper presented at the National Conference on Dialogue and Deliberation, San Francisco, August 3–6.

Fisher, Roger, and William Ury. 1981. *Getting to Yes: Negotiating Agreement without Giving In*. New York: Penguin Books.

Fishkin, James. 1999. "Toward a Deliberative Democracy: Experimenting with an Ideal." In *Citizen Competence and Democratic Institutions*, ed. S. Elkin, and K. E. Soltan, 279–90. State College: Pennsylvania State University Press.

———. 1995. *The Voice of the People: Public Opinion and Democracy*. New Haven, CT: Yale University Press.

———. 1991. *Democracy and Deliberation: New Directions for Democratic Reform*. New Haven, CT: Yale University Press.

Fishkin, James, and Peter Laslett. 2003. *Debating Deliberative Democracy*. Malden, MA: Blackwell.

Fishkin, James, and Robert Luskin. 1999a. "Bringing Deliberation to the Democratic Dialogue." In *A Poll with a Human Face: The National Issues Convention Experiment in Political Communication*, ed. M. McCombs and A. Reynolds, 3–38. Mahwah, NJ: Lawrence Erlbaum.

———. 1999b. "The Quest For Deliberative Democracy." *Good Society* 9:1–8.

———. 1999c. "Making Deliberative Democracy Work." *Good Society* 9:22–29.

Forester, John. 1999. *The Deliberative Practitioner: Encouraging Participatory Planning Processes.* Cambridge, MA: MIT Press.

———. 1989. *Planning in the Face of Power.* Berkeley and Los Angeles: University of California Press.

Frank, Thomas. 2004. *What's the Matter with Kansas?* New York: Metropolitan Books.

Fraser, Nancy. 1997. "Communication, Transformation, and Consciousness-Raising." In *Hannah Arendt and the Meaning of Politics*, ed. Craig Calhoun and John McGowan, 166–78. Minneapolis: University of Minnesota Press.

———. 1992. "Rethinking the Public Sphere: A Contribution to the Critique of Actually Existing Democracy." In *Habermas and the Public Sphere*, ed. Craig Calhoun, 109–42. Cambridge, MA: MIT Press.

Fung, Archon. 2004. *Empowered Participation: Reinventing Urban Democracy.* Princeton, NJ: University of Princeton Press.

Gaertner, Samuel, L., John F. Dovidio, Mary C. Rust, Jason A. Nier, Brenda S. Banker, Christine M. Ward, Gary R. Mottola, and Missy Houlette. 1999. "Reducing Intergroup Bias: Elements of Intergroup Cooperation." *Journal of Personality and Social Psychology* 76:388–402.

Gallois, Cynthia. 1993. "The Language and Communication of Emotion." *American Behavioral Scientist* 36, no. 3:309–38.

Gamson, William. 1992. *Talking Politics.* New York: Cambridge University Press.

Gans, Curtis. 2002. "Report on Trends in U.S. Voter Turnout." Washington, DC: Center for the Study of the American Electorate.

Gastil, John. 2008. *Political Communication and Deliberation.* Thousand Oaks, CA: Sage.

———. 2000. *By Popular Demand.* Berkeley and Los Angeles: University of California Press.

———. 1993. Democracy in Small Groups: Participation, Decision Making, and Communication. Philadelphia, PA: New Society Publishers.

Gastil, John, E. Pierre Dees, and Phil Weiser. 2002. "Civic Awakening in the Jury Room: A Test of the Connection between Jury Deliberation and Political Participation." *Journal of Politics* 64, no. 2:585–95.

Gastil, John, and James Dillard. 1999a. "The Aims, Methods, and Effects of Deliberative Civic Education Through the National Issues Forums." *Communication Education* 48, no. 3:179–82.

———. 1999b. "Increasing Political Sophistication Through Public Deliberation." *Political Communication* 16, no. 1:3–23.

Gastil, John, and William Keith. 2005. "A Nation That (Sometimes) Likes to Talk." In Gastil and Levine, *Deliberative Democracy Handbook*, 3–19.

Gastil, John, and Peter Levine, eds. 2005. *The Deliberative Democracy Handbook: Strategies for Effective Civic Engagement in the Twenty-First Century.* San Francisco: Josey-Bass.

Gilens, Martin. 2005. "Inequality and Democratic Responsiveness." *Public Opinion Quarterly* 69 (December): 778–96.

Glaser, Jack, and Peter Salovey. 1998. "Affect in Electoral Politics." *Personality and Social Psychological Review* 2:156–72.

Graber, Doris A. 2001. *Processing Politics: Learning from Television in the Internet Age.* Chicago: University of Chicago Press.

Gunderson, Adolph. 1995. *The Environmental Promise of Democratic Deliberation.* Madison: University of Wisconsin Press.

Gutmann, Amy, and Dennis Thompson. 2004. *Why Deliberative Democracy?* Princeton: Princeton University Press.

————.1996. *Democracy and Disagreement: Why Moral Conflict Cannot be Avoided in Politics and What Can Be Done About It.* Cambridge, MA: Harvard University Press.

Habermas, Jürgen. 1989. *The Structural Transformation of the Public Sphere.* Cambridge, MA: MIT Press. Originally published in 1962.

Hastie, Reid, and Bernadette Park. 1986. "The Relationship between Memory and Judgment Depends on Whether the Judgment Task Is Memory-Based or On-Line." *Psychological Review* 93:258–68.

Hastie, Reid, Steven D. Penrod, and Nancy Pennington. 1983. *Inside the Jury.* Cambridge, MA: Harvard University Press.

Held, David. 1987. *Models of Democracy.* Stanford, CA: Stanford University Press.

Hibbing, John, and Elizabeth Theiss-Morse. 2002. *Stealth Democracy: Americans' Beliefs about How Government Should Work.* New York: Cambridge University Press.

Holbrook, Thomas. 1999. "Political Learning from Presidential Debates." *Political Behavior* 21:67–89.

Honig, Bonnie. 1996. "Difference, Dilemmas, and the Politics of Home." In *Democracy and Difference: Contesting the Boundaries of the Political,* ed. S. Benhabib, 257–77. Princeton, NJ: Princeton University Press.

Huckfeldt, Robert, and John Sprague. 1995. *Citizens, Politics, and Social Communication: Information and Influence in an Election Campaign.* Cambridge: Cambridge University Press.

International Association for Public Participation. 2007. Online at http://www.iap2.org/.

Insko, Chester A., John Schopler, Stephen M. Drigotas, Kenneth A. Graetz, James Kennedy, Chante Cox, and Garry Bornstein. 1993. "The Role of Communication in Interindividual-Intergroup Discontinuity." *Journal of Conflict Resolution* 37, no. 1:108–38.

Iyengar, Shanto, Robert Luskin, and James Fishkin. 2003. "Facilitating Informed Public Opinion: Evidence from Face-to-Face and On-Line Deliberative Polls." Paper presented at the annual meeting of the American Political Science Association, Philadelphia.

Jacobs, Lawrence. 1993. *The Health of Nations: Public Opinion and the Making of U.S. and British Health Policy.* Ithaca, NY: Cornell University Press.

Jacobs, Lawrence, and Melanie Burns. 2004. "The Second Face of the Public Presidency: Presidential Polling and the Shift from Policy to Personality Polling." *Presidential Studies Quarterly* 34, no. 3:536–56.

Jacobs, Lawrence R., Fay Lomax Cook, and Michael Delli Carpini. 2000. "Talking Together: Public Deliberation and Discursive Capital." Report to the Pew Charitable Trusts, September.

Jacobs, Lawrence, and Benjamin I. Page. 2005. "Who Influences U.S. Foreign Policy?" *American Political Science Review* 99 (February): 107–24.

Jacobs, Lawrence, and Robert Shapiro. 2000. *Politicians Don't Pander: Public Manipulation and the Loss of Democratic Responsiveness.* Chicago: University of Chicago

Jacobs, Lawrence, and Theda Skocpol, eds. 2005. *Inequality and American Democracy: What We Know and What We Need to Learn.* New York: Russell Sage Foundation.

James, Rita M. 1959. "Status and Competence of Jurors." *American Journal of Sociology* 64, no. 5:563–70

Jamieson, Kathleen H. 1992. *Dirty Politics.* New York: Oxford University Press.

Kameda, Tatsuya. 1991. "Procedural Influence in Small Group Decision Making: Deliberation Style and Assigned Decision Rule. *Journal of Personality and Social Psychology* 61, no. 2:245–56.

Kaplan, Martin F., and Charles E. Miller. 1987. "Group Decision Making and Normative versus Informational Influence: Effects of Type of Issue and Assigned Decision Rule." *Journal of Personality and Social Psychology* 53 (August): 306–13.

Kapuscinski, Anne, Robert Goodman, Stuart Hahn, Lawrence R. Jacobs, Emily Pullins, Charles Johnson, Jean Kinsey, Ronald Krall, Antonio La Viña, Margaret Mellon, and Vernon Ruttan. 2003. "Making 'Safety First' a Reality for Biotechnology Products." *Nature Biotechnology* 21 (June): 599–601.

Karpowitz, Christopher. 2003. "Public Hearings and the Dynamics of Deliberative Democracy: A Case Study." Paper presented at the annual meeting of the Midwest Political Science Association, Chicago.

Karpowitz, Christopher, and Jane Mansbridge. 2005. "Disagreement and Consensus: The Importance of Dynamic Updating in Public Deliberation." In Gastil and Levine, *Deliberative Democracy Handbook*, 237–53.

Kennan, George. 1951. *American Diplomacy, 1900–1950*. Chicago: University of Chicago Press.

Kernell, Samuel. 2007. *Going Public: New Strategies of Presidential Leadership*. Washington, DC: CQ Press.

Kerr, Norbert L., and Cynthia M. Kaufman-Gilland. 1994. "Communication, Commitment, and Cooperation in Social Dilemmas." *Journal of Personality and Social Psychology* 66, no. 3:513–29.

Kim, Joohan, Robert Wyatt, and Elihu Katz. 1999. "News, Talk, Opinion, Participation: The Part Played by Conversation in Deliberative Democracy." *Political Communication* 16, no. 4:361–85.

Kirchler, Erich, and James H. Davis. 1986. "The Influence of Member Status Differences and Task Type on Group Consensus and Member Position Change." *Journal of Personality and Social Psychology* 51, no. 1:83–91.

Knoke, David. 1990. "Networks of Political Action: Toward Theory Construction." *Social Forces* 68, no. 4:1041–63.

Ladd, Carl Everett. 2000. *The Ladd Report: Startling New Research Shows How an Explosion of Voluntary Groups, Activities, and Charitable Donations Is Transforming Our Towns and Cities*. New York: Free Press.

Lazarsfeld, Paul, Bernard Berelson, and Hazel Gaudet. 1944. *The People's Choice: How the Voter Makes Up His Mind in a Presidential Campaign*. 2nd ed. New York: Columbia University Press.

Leighninger, Matt. 2006. *The Next Form of Democracy: How Expert Rule Is Giving Way to Shared Governance*. Nashville, TN: Vanderbilt University Press.

Levine, John M., and Eileen Russo. 1995. "Impact of Anticipated Interaction on Information Acquisition." *Social Cognition* 13, no. 3:293–317.

Levine, Peter, Archon Fung, and John Gastil. 2005. "Future Directions for Public Deliberation." In Gastil and Levine, *Deliberative Democracy Handbook*, 271–88.

Lind, E. Allan, and Tom R. Tyler. 1988. *The Social Psychology of Procedural Justice*. New York: Plenum.

Lindblom, Charles. 1977. *Politics and Markets: The World's Political Economic Systems*. New York: Basic Books.

Lindeman, Mark. 2002. "Opinion Quality and Policy Preferences in Deliberative Research." In *Research in Micropolitics: Political Decision Making, Deliberation and Participation*, ed. Michael X. Delli Carpini, Leonie Huddy, and Robert Shapiro, 6:195–221. Greenwich, CT: JAI Press.

Lippmann, Walter. 1955. *Essays in the Public Philosophy*. Boston: Little, Brown.

Lodge, Milton, and Kathleen McGraw, eds. 1995. *Political Judgment: Structure and Process*. Ann Arbor: University of Michigan Press.

Lodge, Milton, Kathleen McGraw, and Patrick Stroh. 1990. "On-Line Processing in Candidate Evaluation: The Effects of Issue Order, Issue Importance, and Sophistication." *Political Behavior* 12: 41–58.

———. 1989. "An Impression-Driven Model of Candidate Evaluation." *American Political Science Review* 83:399–419.

Lodge, Milton, and Patrick Stroh. 1993. "Inside the Mental Voting Booth: An Impression-Driven Process Model of Candidate Evaluation." In *Explorations in Political Psychology*, ed. Shanto Iyengar and William McGuire, 225–63. Durham, NC: Duke University Press.

Lowi, Theodore. 1989. *The Personal President: Power Invested, Promise Unfulfilled*. Ithaca, NY: Cornell University Press.

————. 1979. *The End of Liberalism.* 2nd ed. New York: W. W. Norton.

Loyacano, Marjorie E. 1992. *National Issues Forums Literacy Program: Linking Literacy and Citizenship, 1988–1991.* Dayton, OH: Kettering Foundation.

Luskin, Robert, and James Fishkin, eds. 1999. "Symposium on Deliberative Democracy." *Good Society* 9, no. 1 (entire issue).

————. 1998. "Deliberative Polling, Public Opinion, and Representative Democracy: The Case of the National Issues Convention." Paper presented at the annual meeting of the American Association for Public Opinion Research, St. Louis.

Luskin, Robert, James Fishkin, and Roger Jowell. 2002. "Considered Opinions: Deliberative Polling in Britain." *British Journal of Political Science* 32:455–87.

Luskin, Robert, James Fishkin, Roger Jowell, and Alison Park. 1999. "Learning and Voting in Britain: Insights from the Deliberative Poll." Paper presented at the annual meeting of the American Political Science Association, Atlanta, GA.

Luskin, Robert, James Fishkin, Ian McAllister, John Higley, and Pamela Ryan. 2000. "Information Effects in Referendum Voting: Evidence from the Australian Deliberative Poll." Paper presented at the annual meeting of the American Political Science Association, Washington, DC.

Luskin, Robert, James Fishkin, and Dennis Plane. 1999. "Deliberative Polling and Policy Outcomes: Electric Utility Issues in Texas." Paper presented at the annual meeting of the Association of Public Policy, Analysis, and Management, Washington, DC.

Maass, Anne, and Russell D. Clark. 1984. "Hidden Impact of Minorities: Fifteen Years of Minority Influence Research." *Psychological Bulletin* 95, no. 3:428–50.

Macedo, Stephen. 1999. *Deliberative Politics: Essays on Democracy and Disagreement.* New York: Oxford University Press.

Manning, Jennifer E. 2004. "Congressional Statistics: Bills Introduced and Laws Enacted, 1947–2003." CRS Report for Congress.

Mansbridge, Jane. 1996. "Reconstructing Democracy." In *Revisioning the Political: Feminist Reconstructions of Traditional Concepts in Western Political Theory*, ed. Nancy J. Hirschmann and Christine Di Stefano, 117–38. Boulder, CO: Westview Press.

————. 1983. *Beyond Adversary Democracy.* Chicago: University of Chicago Press.

Manza, Jeff, and Fay Lomax Cook. 2002. "A Democratic Polity? Three Views of Policy Responsiveness to Public Opinion in the United States." *American Politics Research* 30, no. 6:630–67.

McAvoy, Gregory. 1999. *Controlling Technocracy: Citizen Rationality and the NIMBY Syndrome.* Washington, DC: Georgetown University Press.

McConnell, Grant. 1966. *Private Power and American Democracy.* New York: Knopf.

McConnell, Allen, Steven Sherman, and David Hamilton. 1994. "On-Line and Memory-Based Aspects of Individual and Group Target Judgments." *Journal of Personality and Social Psychology* 67:173–185.

McDonald, Michael, and Samuel Popkin. 2001. "The Myth of the Vanishing Voter." *American Political Science Review* 95, no. 4: 963–74.

McLeod, Jack, Dietram Scheufele, and Patricia Moy. 1999. "Community, Communication, and Participation: The Role of Mass Media and Interpersonal Discussion in Local Political Participation." *Communication Research* 23:179–209.

Mendelberg, Tali. 2002. "The Deliberative Citizen: Theory and Evidence." In *Research in Micropolitics: Political Decision Making, Deliberation and Participation*, ed. Michael X. Delli Carpini, Leonie Huddy, and Robert Shapiro, 6:151–93. Greenwich, CT: JAI Press.

Mendelberg, Tali, and Christopher Karpowitz. 2000. "Deliberating About Justice." Paper presented at the annual meeting of the American Political Science Association, Washington, DC, September.

Mendelberg, Tali, and John Oleske. 2000. "Race and Public Deliberation." *Political Communication* 17, no. 2:169–91.

Merkle, Daniel M. 1996. "The National Issues Convention Deliberative Poll." *Public Opinion Quarterly* 60:588–619.

Mettler, Suzanne. 2002. "Bringing the State Back into Civic Engagement: Policy Feedback Effects of the G.I. Bill for World War II Veterans." *American Political Science Review* 96 (June): 351–65.

Mettler, Suzanne, and Joe Soss. 2004. "The Consequences of Public Policy for Democratic Citizenship: Bridging Policy Studies and Mass Politics." *Perspectives on Politics* 2, no. 1: 55–73.

Michelman, Frank. 1988. "Law's Republic." *Yale Law Journal* 97, no. 8:1493–1537.

Miller, Norman, and Gaye Davidson-Podgorny. 1987. "Theoretical Models of Intergroup Relations and the Use of Cooperative Teams as an Intervention for Desegregated Settings." *Annual Review of Personality and Social Psychology: Group Processes and Intergroup Relations* 9:23–39.

Morgenthau, Hans. 1973. *Politics Among Nations*. New York: Knopf.

Morrell, Michael. 1999. "Citizens' Evaluations of Participatory Democratic Procedures." *Political Research Quarterly* 52, no. 2:293–322.

Moscovici, Serge. 1980. "Toward a Theory of Conversion Behavior." In *Advances in Experimental Social Psychology*, ed. L. Berkowitz, 13:209–39. New York: Academic Press.

Moscovici, Serge, and Marisa Zavalloni. 1969. "The Group as a Polarizer of Attitudes." *Journal of Personality and Social Psychology* 12, no. 2:125–35.

Mouffe, Chantal. 1996. "Democracy, Power, and the 'Political.'" In *Democracy and Difference: Contesting the Boundaries of the Political*, ed. S. Benhabib, 245–56. Princeton, NJ: Princeton University Press.

Mutz, Diana. 2006. *Hearing the Other Side: Deliberative versus Participatory Democracy*. New York: Cambridge University Press.

Myers, David G., and Helmut Lamm. 1976. "The Group Polarization Phenomenon." *Psychological Bulletin* 83, no. 4:602–27.

Nemeth, Charlan J. 1986. "Differential Contributions of Majority and Minority Influence." *Psychological Review* 93, no. 1:23–32.

Nemeth Charlan J., Jeffrey Endicott, and Joel Wachtler. 1976. "From the '50s to the '70s: Women in Jury Deliberations." *Sociometry* 39, no. 4:293–304.

Nemeth, Charlan J., and Julianne Kwan. 1985. "Originality of Word Associations as a Function of Majority and Minority Influence." *Social Psychology Quarterly* 48, no. 3: 277–82.

Nemeth, Charlan J., and Ofra Mayseless. 1987. *Enhancing Recall: The Contributions of Conflict, Minorities and Consistency*. Berkeley and Los Angeles: University of California Press.

Nemeth, Charlan J., and John Rogers. 1996. "Dissent and the Search for Information." *British Journal of Social Psychology* 25:67–76.

Nemeth, Charlan J., and Joel Wachtler. 1983. "Creative Problem Solving as a Result of Majority vs. Minority Influence." *European Journal of Social Psychology* 13, no. 1:45–55.

Nie, Norman, Jane Junn, and Kenneth Stehlik-Barry. 1996. *Education and Democratic Citizenship in America* Chicago: University of Chicago Press.

Orbell, John M., Alphons J. van de Kragt, and Robyn M. Dawes. 1988. "Explaining Discussion-Induced Cooperation." *Journal of Personality and Social Psychology* 54, no. 5:811–19.

Ostrom, Elinor. 1998. "A Behavioral Approach to the Rational Choice Theory of Collective Action." *American Political Science Review* 92:1–22.

Page, Benjamin. 1996. *Who Deliberates? Mass Media in Modern Democracy*. Chicago: University of Chicago Press.

Page, Benjamin, and Lawrence Jacobs. 2009. *Class War?* Chicago: University of Chicago Press.

Page, Benjamin I., and Robert Y. Shapiro. 1992. *The Rational Public: Fifty Years of Trends in Americans' Policy Preferences*. Chicago: University of Chicago Press.

Pateman, Carole. 1970. *Participation and Democratic Theory*. Cambridge: Cambridge University Press.

Patterson, Thomas. 2002. *The Vanishing Voter*. New York: Knopf.

Penrod, Steven, and Reid Hastie. 1980. "A Computer Simulation of Jury Decision Making." *Psychological Review* 87, no. 2:133–59.

Pierson, Paul. 1993. "When Effect Becomes Cause: Policy Feedback and Political Change." *World Politics* 45: 595–628.

Popkin, Samuel. 1991. *The Reasoning Voter: Communications and Persuasion in Presidential Campaigns*. Chicago: University of Chicago Press.

Price, Vincent, and Joseph N. Cappella. 2001. "Online Deliberation and Its Influence: The Electronic Dialogue Project in Campaign 2000." Paper presented at the annual meeting of the American Association for Public Opinion Research, Montreal, Canada.

———. 2002. "Online Deliberation and Its Influence: The Electronic Dialogue Project in Campaign 2000." *IT and Society* 1:303–28.

Price, Vincent, D. Goldthwaite, Joseph Cappella, and A. Romantan. 2003. "Online Discussion, Civic Engagement, and Social Trust." Working Paper. University of Pennsylvania, Philadelphia.

Price, Vincent, L. Nir, and Joseph Cappella. 2002. "Does Disagreement Contribute to More Deliberative Opinion?" *Political Communication* 19:95–112.

Putnam, Robert. 2000. *Bowling Alone: The Collapse and Revival of American Community*. New York: Simon and Shuster.

Rahn, Wendy, and John Transue. 1998. "Social Trust and Value Change: The Decline of Social Capital in American Youth." *Political Psychology* 19, no. 3:545–65.

Ridgeway, Cecilia L. 1987. "Nonverbal Behavior, Dominance, and the Basis of Status in Task Groups." *American Sociological Review* 52 (October):683–94.

———. 1981. "Nonconformity, Competence, and Influence in Groups: A Test of Two Theories." *American Sociological Review* 46:333–47.

Rosenau, James N. 1961. *Public Opinion and Foreign Policy: An Operational Formulation*. New York: Random House.

Rosenberg, Shawn, ed. 2007. *Deliberation, Participation and Democracy: Can the People Govern?* New York: Palgrave Macmillan.

Ryfe, David Michael. 2006. "Narrative and Deliberation in Small Group Forums." *Journal of Applied Communications Research* 34 (February): 72–93.

———. 2005. "Does Deliberative Democracy Work?" *Annual Review of Political Science* 8:49–71.

———. 2002. "The Practice of Deliberative Democracy: A Study of Sixteen Deliberative Organizations." *Political Communications* 19:359–77.

Sally, David. 1995. "Conversation and Cooperation in Social Dilemmas: A Meta-Analysis of Experiments from 1958 to 1992." *Rationality and Society* 7:58–92.

Sandel, Michael. 1996. *Democracy's Discontent: America in Search of a Public Philosophy*. Cambridge, MA: Harvard University Press.

Sanders, Lynn. 1997. "Against Deliberation." *Political Theory* 25 (June): 347–76.

Sartori, Giovanni. 1987. *The Theory of Democracy Revised: Part 1, The Contemporary Debate*. Chatham, NJ: Chatham House.

Schattschneider, E. E. 1960. *The Semisovereign People: A Realist's View of Democracy in America*. New York: Holt, Rinehart and Winston.

Schkade, David, Cass R. Sunstein, and Daniel Kahneman. 2000. "Deliberating about Dollars: The Severity Shift." *Columbia Law Review* 100:1139–75.

Schlozman, Kay, Benjamin Page, Sidney Verba, and Morris Fiorina. 2005. "Inequalities of Political Voice." In Jacobs and Skocpol, *Inequality and American Democracy*, 19–87.

Schudson, Michael. 1997. "Why Conversation Is Not the Soul of Democracy." *Critical Studies in Mass Communication* 14, no. 4:297–309.

Schumpeter, Joseph. 1976. *Capitalism, Socialism, and Democracy*. 5th ed. London: Allen and Unwin.

————. 1950. *Capitalism, Socialism, and Democracy*. New York: Harper.

Shadish, William R., Thomas D. Cook, and Donald T. Campbell. 2001. *Experimental and Quasi-Experimental Designs for Generalized Causal Inference*. Boston: Houghton Mifflin.

Sharp, Elaine B. 1999. *The Sometime Connection: Public Opinion and Social Policy*. Albany, NY: State University of New York Press.

Showers, Carolin, and Nancy Cantor. 1985. "Social Cognition: A Look at Motivated Strategies." *Annual Review of Psychology* 36:275–305.

Sirianni, Carmen, and Lewis Friedland. 2001. *Civic Innovation in America: Community Empowerment, Public Policy and the Movement for Civic Renewal*. Berkeley and Los Angeles: University of California Press.

Skocpol, Theda. 2003. *Diminished Democracy: From Membership to Management in American Civic Life*. Norman: University of Oklahoma Press.

Skocpol, Theda, and Morris Fiorina, eds. 1999. *Civic Engagement in American Democracy*. Washington, DC: Brookings Institution Press.

Skocpol, Theda, Marshall Ganz, and Ziad Munson. 2000. "A Nation of Organizers: The Institutional Origins of Civic Voluntarism in the United States." *American Political Science Review* 94, no. 3:527–46.

Smith, Eric R. A. N. 1989. *The Unchanging American Voter*. Berkeley and Los Angeles: University of California Press.

Smith, Graham, and Corinne Wales. 2000. "Citizens' Juries and Deliberative Democracy." *Political Studies* 48:51–65.

Sokoloff, Harris, Harris M. Steinberg, and Steven N. Pyser. 2005. "Deliberative City Planning on the Philadelphia Waterfront." In Gastil and Levine, *Deliberative Democracy Handbook*, 185–96.

Soss, Joe. 1999. "Lessons of Welfare: Policy Design, Political Learning, and Political Action." *American Political Science Review* 93:363–80.

Strodtbeck, Fred L., Rita M. James, and Charles Hawkins. 1957. "Social Status in Jury Deliberations." *American Sociological Review* 22, no. 6:713–19.

Strodtbeck, Fred L., and Richard D. Mann. 1956. "Sex Role Differentiation in Jury Deliberations." *Sociometry*. 19, no. 1:3–11.

Sulkin, Tracy, and Adam Simon. 2001. "Habermas in the Lab: A Study of Deliberation in an Experimental Setting." *Political Psychology* 22: 809–826.

Sullivan, John, James Piereson, and George Marcus. 1989. *Political Tolerance and American Democracy*. Chicago: University of Chicago Press.

Sunstein, Cass. 2002. "On a Danger of Deliberative Democracy." *Daedalus* 131 (Fall): 120–24.

————. 2001. *Republic.com*. Princeton, NJ: Princeton University Press.

————. 1993. *Democracy and the Problem of Free Speech*. New York: Free Press.

————. 1988. "Beyond the Republican Revival." *Yale Law Journal* 97:1539–90.

Susskind, Lawrence, and Connie Ozawa. 1984. "Mediated Negotiation in the Public Sector: The Planner as Mediator." *Journal of Planning Education and Research* 4:5–15.

Teixeira, Ruy. 1992. *The Disappearing American Voter*. Washington, DC: Brookings Institution Press.

Theiss-Morse, Elizabeth, George Marcus, and John Sullivan. 1993. "Passion and Reason in Political Life: The Organization of Affect and Cognition and Political Tolerance." In *Reconsidering the Democratic Public*, ed. George Marcus and Russell Hanson, 249–72. University Park: Pennsylvania State University Press.

Thibaut, John, and Laurens Walker. 1975. *Procedural Justice: A Psychological Analysis*. Hillsdale, NJ: Erlbaum.

Tierney, Kathleen. 2006. "Social Inequality, Hazards, and Disasters." In *On Risk and Disaster: Lessons from Hurricane Katrina*, ed. Ronald J. Daniels, Donald Kettl, and Howard Kunreuther, 109–28. Philadelphia: University of Pennsylvania Press.

Traugott, Michael. 1992. "The 'Deliberative Opinion Poll' Is a Well-Intended But Flawed Idea." *Public Perspective* 3:27–29.

Tulis, Jeffery. 1987. *The Rhetorical Presidency*. Princeton, NJ: Princeton University Press.

Turner, J. C. 1991. *Social Influence*. Pacific Grove, CA: Brooks/Cole.

Tyler, Tom R. 2001. "The Psychology of Public Dissatisfaction with Government." In *What Is It About Government That Americans Dislike?* ed. J. R. Hibbing and E. Theiss-Morse, 227–42. Cambridge: Cambridge University Press.

———. 1994. "Psychological Models of the Justice Motive: Antecedents of Distributive and Procedural Justice." *Journal of Personality and Social Psychology* 67:850–63.

Tyler, Tom R., and Steven Blader. 2000. *Cooperation in Groups: Procedural Justice, Social Identity, and Behavioral Engagement*. Philadelphia, PA: Psychology Press.

Verba, Sidney, and Norman Nie. 1972. *Participation in America*. New York: Harper & Row.

Verba, Sidney, Norman Nie, and Jae-on Kim. 1978. *Participation and Political Equality: A Seven-Nation Comparison*. Cambridge: Cambridge University Press.

Verba, Sidney, Kay Lehman Schlozman, and Henry Brady. 1995. *Voice and Equality: Civic Voluntarism in American Politics*. Cambridge, MA: Harvard University Press.

Vinokur, Amiram, and Eugene Burnstein. 1978. "Depolarization of Attitudes in Groups." *Journal of Personality and Social Psychology* 36:872–85.

Walsh, Katherine Cramer. 2007. *Talking About Race: Community Dialogues and the Politics of Difference*. Chicago: Chicago University Press.

———. 2004. *Talking About Politics: Informal Groups and Social Identity in American Life*. Chicago: University of Chicago Press.

———. 2003. "The Democratic Potential of Civic Dialogue on Race." Paper presented at the annual meeting of the Midwest Political Science Association, Chicago.

Walton, Douglas. 1992. *The Place of Emotion in Argument*. University Park: Pennsylvania State University Press.

Warren, Mark. 1996. "Deliberative Democracy and Authority." *American Political Science Review* 90 (March): 46–60.

———. 1992. "Democratic Theory and Self-transformation." *American Political Science Review* 86:8–23.

Wattenberg, Martin P. 2002. *Where Have All the Voters Gone?* Cambridge, MA: Harvard University Press.

West, Darrell, and Burdett A. Loomis. 1998. *The Sound of Money: How Political Interests Get What They Want*. New York: W. W. Norton.

Williams, Melissa. 2000. "The Uneasy Alliance of Group Representation and Deliberative Democracy." In *Citizenship in Diverse Societies*, ed. W. Kymlicka and W. Norman, 124–54. Oxford: Oxford University Press.

Wood, Wendy, Sharon Lundgren, Judith A. Ouellette, Shelly Busceme, and Tamela Blackstone. 1994. "Minority Influence: A Meta-Analytic Review of Social Influence Processes." *Psychological Bulletin* 115, no. 3: 323–45.

Wuthnow, Robert. 1994. *Sharing the Journey: Support Groups and America's New Quest for Community*. New York: Free Press.

Young, Iris Marion. 2000. *Inclusion and Democracy*. Oxford: Oxford University Press.

———. 1996. "Communication and the Other: Beyond Deliberative Democracy." In *Democracy and Difference: Contesting the Boundaries of the Political*, ed. S. Benhabib, 120–35. Princeton, NJ: Princeton University Press.

Zdaniuk, Bozena, and John M. Levine. 1996. "Anticipated Interaction and Thought Generation: The Role of Faction Size." *British Journal of Social Psychology* 35:201–18.

Zukin, Cliff, Scott Keeter, Molly Andolina, Krista Jenkins, and Michael X. Delli Carpini. 2006. *New Engagement? Political Participation, Civic Life and the Changing American Citizen*. New York: Oxford University Press.

INDEX